YOU MUST REMEMBER THIS

Books by Walter Wagner

YOU MUST REMEMBER THIS

SOLOMON IN ALL HIS GLORY
(Novel)

THE TRIP BEYOND
(with Brian Ruud)

TO GAMBLE, OR NOT TO GAMBLE

THE TROUBLE WITH WALL STREET
(with Lewis A. Bracker)

THE MAN FROM MIRACLE VALLEY
(with Don Stewart)

TURNED ON TO JESUS
(with Arthur Blessitt)

BORN TO LOSE, BOUND TO WIN
(with A. A. Allen)

THE CHAPLAIN OF BOURBON STREET
(with Bob Harrington)

THE GOLDEN FLEECERS

ST. JOSEPH'S UNIVERSITY   STX
PN1998.A2W24
You must remember this /

3 9353 00003 8123

Walter Wagner

YOU MUST
REMEMBER THIS

PN
1998
.A2
W24

G. P. PUTNAM'S SONS

NEW YORK

167861

For Ken Murray . . .
who was there when the paper was blank

COPYRIGHT © 1975 BY WALTER WAGNER

All rights reserved. This book, or parts thereof,
may not be reproduced without permission from the publisher.
Published simultaneously in Canada
by Longman Canada Limited, Toronto.

SBN: 399-11274-X
Library of Congress Cataloging in Publication Data
Wagner, Walter, 1927—
You must remember this.
1. Moving-pictures—United States—Biography.
I. Title.
PN1998.A2W24   791.43'092'2 [B]   75-12699

"YOU MUST REMEMBER THIS" ©1931 HARMS, INC.
Copyright Renewed. All Rights Reserved.
Used by Permission of Warner Bros. Music

PRINTED IN THE UNITED STATES OF AMERICA

CONTENTS

FADE-IN

Fade-in

NO ONE BOOK can capture the diversity that is Hollywood. I hoped that most of the high points of the Hollywood Iliad have been touched here. Each of the twenty-four interviewees, including the late John Ford and Claire Windsor, approaches Hollywood from a different perspective, and each, it seems to me, advances the narrative. Slim though it may be, there is a thread between Mary Pickford and Mike Medavoy.

The men and women whose oral memoirs follow found themselves, by accident or choice, playing in a tough league. A very tough league. The camera, they found, was savage. The camera, sometimes, was kind. It was also a narcotic. Whether Hollywood was compassionate or cruel, they became addicted to the singular rewards and disappointments of a medium that changed the world. They had the incredible opportunity of simultaneously living through Camelot and Pompeii. (At least it wasn't Omaha.) No matter how they fared, their recollections glitter and they have remained steadfast to Hollywood. Two of the interviews in these pages make the point most starkly and poignantly.

After her harsh, roiling confrontation with mass hysteria and the death of her husband's career, the wife of Fatty Arbuckle can still look back and say, convincingly, "I'm not bitter against anyone or anything because I've had it all . . . the sorrow and the hurt and the happiness. I did a command performance for the dowager empress of China. I met General Pershing and danced with the Prince of Wales."

Martin Rackin, when he was head of production at Paramount, was embroiled in vicious studio politics, a saga that has no parallel in fiction. "Marty," the studio's top lawyer said at the bitter end, "what the hell's happened? I've been with this company for twenty-eight years, and I've never heard anything like this. I'm here to tell you that you have two hours to get off the lot." Still Rackin can say, "The picture business has been my passport to the world."

If there is savagery in these pages, there is also kindness. If there is hate, so, too, is there love. If there are nightmares here, there are also dreams fulfilled.

Why this book is dedicated to my friend Ken Murray and the words used in the dedication require an explanation.

In the early 1950's Ken had a popular, hour-long television variety show on CBS. A conscientious craftsman, he involved himself in every facet of the show. To make it as perfect as possible, he would order a final run-through shortly before air time.

One particular show in the hot summer of August, 1951, had been unusually difficult to put together. But after long days of labor, Ken breathed easier. The sketches finally worked. The gags had been honed, and they were funny. The pace was right. Two guest stars who almost canceled were now locked in.

A network vice-president had observed the run-through. "I don't like the show, Ken. It's going to bomb."

Ken arched his eyebrows. "Do you have any suggestions about how I can improve it?"

"No, but you'll think of something."

"If I do, it had better be fast. We go on the air in an hour."

"Sweetheart," the vice-president said, "I know you can do it."

Ordinarily mild-mannered, Ken lost his temper. Archly, he asked, "Where were you when the paper was blank?"

Ken Murray was with me when my paper was blank, every step of the way, opening doors to many of the people I interviewed. Without Ken, this book would not have happened.

Others who were there when the paper was blank: Joe Bleeden of NBC who arranged my meetings with Keystone Kop Eddie LeVeque and Mrs. Minta Durfee Arbuckle; Jay Johnson, himself a silent film buff and gifted practitioner of the movie organ, suggested and paved the way for me to meet Gaylord Carter; Denver Pyle, a neighbor, a friend, and a gifted actor, best known perhaps for his role as Sheriff Frank Hamer in *Bonnie and Clyde*, introduced me to Ward Kimball; Bill Scholl, publicity director of United Artists, put me in touch with Frances Goldwyn and Mike Medavoy.

Beverly Hills literary agent Jane Browne called one Sunday morn to say that a client of hers, Jesse Lasky, Jr., was in town and would I care to interview him. I would and did, and Lasky was generous enough to supply me with material which does not appear in his own excellent book *Whatever Happened to Hollywood?*, published in 1975 by Funk and Wagnalls. I also wish to thank Lee Ray, Shel Stewart, Richard Carter and Victoria Brooks, who helped arrange my appointment with Jack Lemmon.

More than fifty Hollywood people were interviewed for this book. My gratitude to all those who gave me their time and shared their candid memories is boundless. To those who ended on my "cutting-room floor" my apologies. Space limitations and the attempt to develop, however loosely, a flow and a history of Hollywood forced the excisions.

Besides suffering with me the joys and travails of yet another book, my wife, Maxine, is due more than ordinary

gratitude. Her alertness resulted in the interview with Hollywood centenarian Walter "Cap" Field. Finally, my profound
thanks to Iona Darland for the long and arduous task of tire-
lessly transcribing the many miles of taped interviews.

—WALTER WAGNER

Toluca Lake, California
March 5, 1975

1

Mary Pickford

THE FIRST MOVIE STAR

1143 SUMMIT DRIVE—Pickfair—is still the most famous movie mansion in Beverly Hills. Miss Pickford, the dowager queen of Hollywood, has lived in the four-story castle since her marriage to Douglas Fairbanks in 1920. Ten of the original fifteen acres have been sold, a concession to vanished glamor, age, changing life-styles and accrued profit. The remains of Pickfair, valued at $2,500,000, suggest a well-preserved sarcophagus, a pyramid of celluloid and Chippendale.

In the small, cozy Rodin Room, adorned with sketches by the French sculptor of nude dancing girls who seem about to pirouette from their frames, Buddy Rogers, Miss Pickford's husband since 1937, is resplendent in purple slacks, white belt and flowered, open-neck shirt. It is 11:30 A.M., and he is drinking his fourth beer of the morning.

"We keep the house available to the public; tourists come up here all the time." The deeply tanned seventy-year-old Rogers adds, laughing, "They don't bother me, except I can't swim in the nude." Rogers glances at his watch. "Have a good talk, pet," he says, announcing he has a golf date.

At eighty-one, Miss Pickford has kept her hair blond. Her smile is winsome, the face remarkably unwrinkled. She is wearing a blue, shapeless frock. Behind her is a portrait painted by Enrique Median in 1961, displaying her with long, golden curls, the Mary Pickford of circa 1915. The timbre of her voice is alternately childlike and firm. She insists on speaking first about "the greatest misconception people have about me."

I'm not a recluse, although the press is constantly saying that. I'm not Garbo. I don't *vant to be alone.* I had a fall and hurt my leg about a year ago, so I don't go out much, except for a drive now and then with Buddy. I see Lillian Gish and Mildred Loew—she's Adolph Zukor's daughter—whenever they're in town. They're two of my oldest friends. I see my business manager and a few other people. But most of my friends have died, unfortunately.

I retired from the screen in 1933, feeling I'd earned my rest. I used to work from six in the morning until midnight— the actress by day, the producer by night. It was a struggle; I never had time for myself.

Please tell my public that my health is good and that I feel fine. I'm so concerned about my public—I owe everything to them. I still get, oh, seventy-five to one hundred fan letters a day, mostly from overseas where my old movies have been revived. Did you know I once got eighteen thousand letters a week and I had eighteen secretaries helping me answer them?

I try to keep up with things. I watch television, and some nights we screen films in the projection room. I read a great deal—the Bible, Shakespeare and detective stories. But I don't know anything about the New Hollywood. From what I've heard, it's just as well. It all sounds so dreadful . . . nudity, pornography, X-rated films. Hollywood has gone to pieces. There's no love, no love stories, and they don't love their work. They don't *care.* All they want is money.

I made my films for the family. The whole concept of realism has changed. We made pictures, you know, wholesome, good, clever, funny, amusing, charming, for entertainment. Right or wrong, our business was entertainment. I think we were right.

Hollywood was such a lovely place then. Everybody knew everybody, and it seemed to me that it was such a small place. It was so intimate. We had the Mayfair Club, what they called the Hollywood Four Hundred, and we'd meet once a month at the Biltmore Hotel for dinner and dancing. Everyone was there, Valentino, Chaplin, Gloria Swanson. In those days we were all one big happy family.

I miss my career, but I retired voluntarily after I made *Secrets*, my last picture. I wanted the public to remember me the way I was in *Pollyanna, Suds, Tess of the Storm Country* and *Little Annie Rooney*. I wanted the public to remember me as the little girl with the curls. I always said I'd retire when I couldn't play little girls anymore. I always thought of myself as an entertainer for my own generation.

I didn't want my films to be shown again. There was such an outcry when I said I wanted to destroy my films. I had gallons of letters telling me not to. Lillian Gish and I had the only argument we ever had because of that.

"Don't you dare destroy your films, Mary," Lillian said. "They don't belong to you. They belong to the public."

I said, "Well, time's passing, and people will compare me to modern actresses, and I just don't want that. The films have served their purpose. I'm going to burn them."

But I was talked out of it. So I spent about a quarter of a million dollars restoring them, new prints and new musical scores that reproduce the organ accompaniment theaters had in the silent days. The response has been very gratifying. I think we're going to release the films in the United States soon. Do you think my public in America will like that little girl on the screen?

I was born in Toronto. My father died when I was five, and Mother worked as a seamstress, trying to support my sister, brother and myself. But there was never enough money. We had an old two-story frame house, and Mother rented a room to a couple who produced stock plays. They asked to use us kids in them. That started my career. I played Eva in *Uncle Tom's Cabin*. I did little Willie in *East Lynne* and the baby in *Bootles' Baby*. Hal Reid, who was a producer and the father of Wallace Reid—who became a big star and died of drug addiction—was in Toronto with a play of his own. He saw us onstage and offered to take us to Broadway for a play called *The Little Red Schoolhouse*. I couldn't wait to go to New York. I knew I had to get out of Canada to make money. Besides, I'd heard the streets of Broadway were paved with gold.

The gold was brass. The play had a short run, and then I pounded pavements looking for work. I was finally hired for a road company production which opened in Pottsville, Pennsylvania. It was far from Broadway, but at least I was the star. The magenta handbills, I can see them still, read: "*The Fatal Wedding*. Baby Gladys Smith Is a Wonder." I played the role for nineteen weeks, one-night stands in dirty theaters all over the country.

We closed in Chicago, and I went back to New York. I was ten years old when I marched into David Belasco's office. He was Broadway's most famous producer. I said I wanted to work for him. To my astonishment, he offered me a role in his next play, *The Warrens of Virginia*. There was only one condition. Mr. Belasco insisted I change my name. He said "Gladys Smith" was too pedestrian. So I became Mary Pickford. The play was written by William DeMille, and his brother Cecil was in the cast. It ran about two years. When the play closed, I was out of work and desperate, though I'd saved two hundred dollars.

Mother shocked me when she suggested I apply for work to D. W. Griffith at the Biograph Studios. "They say the pay is good in movies," Mother said.

I went down there and met Mr. Griffith. He said, "You're too little and too fat, but I may give you a chance." He did.

I must have made fifty or sixty one-reelers for him, little

14

things that ran seven, ten, twelve minutes. We'd just go out in the morning and make a movie. At that time I was earning more as a writer than as an actress. Mr. Griffith would pay me twenty-five dollars for the story, but only five or ten for starring in it. I must say I cheated a little because I always wrote stories which showed me off to my best advantage.

Mr. Griffith took the company to Hollywood a few years later. I wasn't happy about it because my first love was the theater. I was constantly hoping for an opportunity to return to the stage. I didn't even want anyone to know I was in pictures. Making movies, so far as I was concerned, was slumming.

In Hollywood I made a whole batch of pictures in which I was billed as "The Biograph Girl" or "The Girl with the Golden Curls." The exhibitors didn't know my name, and of course, neither did the public. The theater owners would send in the money and say, "Give us more of those pictures with that girl who has the curls." After a year or two of that, I had to let people know my name. The public demanded it. The public realized I was a star before I did. That's why I always say I owe everything I have to the public.

I went to Mr. Griffith and told him he'd have to use my name in the advertising.

"If I do that, I'll have to pay you more money," he said.

He didn't want to advertise my name or pay me more money. But I made him. Then my career started going up, and all the other actors followed my example. They began selling their names. They call me "the first movie star," and in a way I guess I was. I suppose I started what we call the star system.

I left Biograph when Adolph Zukor offered me more money to work for him at Famous Players-Lasky, which is now Paramount. It turned out that Papa Zukor, which is what I always called him, didn't have much money. To pay me and the rest of the cast and finance *Tess of the Storm Coun-*

15

try, Papa Zukor pawned his wife's necklace and his own insurance policy. The picture became a tremendous hit, and it made the studio. Years later, when we were in New York together, Papa Zukor pointed to the Paramount Building. "Mary, darling," he said, "you built that building." I still love Papa Zukor deeply, though I haven't talked to him in years. He's one hundred and one years old.

I'd saved my money, and I was earning ten thousand dollars a week. Even so, I thought Douglas and I should have our own company. Forming United Artists in 1919 was my idea. I brought in Mr. Griffith and Chaplin. The latter was a mistake.

We rented offices at Sam Goldwyn's studio. I'm told that Mr. Goldwyn looked out of his office window one day and said, "My God, ten thousand dollars a week and she's walking to the set yet. She should be running!"

The reason I wanted my own film company is that I felt most people in the industry didn't know what they were doing. I didn't think that people who knew nothing about the business should try to run it. Mr. Griffith always said I was the only star who wouldn't take direction. They called me Retake Mary. I'd insist to Mr. Griffith that a scene be shot over and over again until I felt it was right. Film only cost two cents a foot in those days.

But the most important reason for organizing United Artists was that we could produce and finance and distribute and have control over our own work. And we did pretty well. They called us the Big Four. Throughout the twenties, the thirties and the early forties we made Chaplin's *City Lights*, *Modern Times* and *The Gold Rush*. I starred in *Pollyanna*. Douglas made *Robin Hood* and *The Three Musketeers*. Then a lot of important people began distributing their films through United Artists: Sam Goldwyn, David Selznick, Alexander Korda and Walt Disney.

I had such a lovely office at United Artists. I wonder what's become of it. I wonder who has it now.

16

I finally sold all my stock in United Artists in 1956 and made a lot of money. I sold because there were too many problems and nothing was the same. Mr. Griffith was dead. So was Douglas. Gloria Swanson was a stockholder for a while. She'd sold out at the right time and made a lot of money, too. I never wanted Chaplin in the company. That was Douglas' idea. He and Chaplin were very close. Chaplin used to be here three or four nights a week for dinner. It came down to the place where I was running the whole company. Chaplin was no businessman. In business matters, he was, to put it in Mr. Goldwyn's famous two words, "im-possible."

It would aggravate me terribly when Chaplin wouldn't come to business meetings where we had important problems to discuss, decisions to be made involving millions of dollars.

One time I drove to Chaplin's house and rang the bell. I was going to drag him to a very important meeting, by his hair if necessary. But he wouldn't even open the door. He peeked out from behind a curtain, threw open the window and said, "I paid one dollar a share for my stock, and that's all it's worth. Sell it for one dollar." Silly, stupid things like that.

When I was with Papa Zukor, Chaplin wanted me as his leading lady in a picture to be called *Bread*. Chaplin said he would see to it that I would get ten thousand dollars a week for four weeks to star with him. At the time I was earning about five thousand a week. Chaplin was very generous with Papa Zukor's money, too generous. The picture was never made.

I haven't seen Chaplin in years and years. What's happened to him is sad. To some extent, I recognize him as the artist he was. I don't agree that he's the same artist today. I think he cheapened himself by killing the Little Tramp . . . and the Tramp turned around and killed him. I never liked any of his pictures when he wasn't in tramp character. To tell

17

the truth, I never saw most of his pictures. A lot of people shared my opinion that he was a cheap, hamfat comedian, throwing pies and acting in a very undignified manner.

He wasn't grateful for his career. When he came back to get that special Academy Award a few years ago, he called me, but I wouldn't see him. I don't ever want to see him again . . . and you can print that! It's disgraceful that he never became a citizen of the United States.

I remember Douglas with great, great fondness. I must have a thousand pictures of him. But I think he loved me more than I.loved him. Douglas became restless as the years went along. He had a terrible fear of growing old. But it was his restlessness, his lack of contentment with all the blessings we had that led to our divorce.

The first time I saw Buddy I thought he was the handsomest man I'd ever seen. He had blue hair. A friend introduced us, and I insisted that Buddy be my leading man in my next picture. That was *My Best Girl,* and we did make it together.

Buddy often joshes me about the fact that while he was in college, his favorite leading lady in the movies was Norma Shearer, not me. But I've forgiven him for that. We've had a long and a good marriage.

I was talking to Gene Raymond the other day. Gene and Jeanette MacDonald were married a day or two before we were. The four of us sailed on the *Lurline* on our honeymoons to Honolulu.

"Gene," I said, "do you remember that the press gave your marriage to Jeanette one year? And they gave Buddy and me six months."

The press was betting on how long our marriages would last. Until Jeanette passed on, I figure the four of us had sixty or seventy wonderful years together.

People forget Buddy had quite a career of his own. He was known as America's Boyfriend when he was in films. I got the name of America's Sweetheart in World War I. I was an honorary Army colonel, and I was standing with Sid Grauman on Market Street in San Francisco during a parade of the Third Field Artillery. Thousands of people were cheering the troops . . . and me.

Mr. Grauman said, "America, it's a wonderful country, and you're America's Sweetheart." The name stuck.

Everywhere I went in those days there were cheers. I visited Russia after the Communist revolution. I was amazed that the Russian public knew me. Hundreds of thousands of people turned out to welcome me. I didn't meet Lenin or any of those Communist officials. But I met President Woodrow Wilson once. I was invited to the White House with Marie Dressler. I was very young, and he was the President, and if I would have had something to say to him, I couldn't say it. But Marie wasn't as shy as I was. She told the President a story that was on the naughty side. I was so embarrassed. So was President Wilson. He stood there straight-faced, no smile, no answer.

People said I was earning a million dollars a year. I never made that much, but one year I paid fifty thousand dollars in income tax.

I never had any difficulty making the transition from silents to talking pictures. My training was the stage. My love for the theater was a gift from my mother. No matter how little money she had she always went to the theater and sat in the third balcony, what was called Seventh Heaven.

All of us had heard that John Gilbert didn't have a voice. Someone said that God would give vocal cords to maybe one person out of a million. I was at Paramount the day they tested Wallace Beery's voice. They'd built a sound experiment studio over there. He went inside at about nine o'clock in the morning, and four hours later the doors opened and a young boy came running out and shouting, "Wally Beery has a voice! Wally Beery has a voice!"

I never doubted my voice for a moment because of my

stage experience. I won my Oscar in 1929 for *Coquette*, which was my first talkie.

We never planned that Pickfair would be a celebrated house. It just happened. The press called Pickfair the White House of Hollywood. The king of Siam was here. Name them . . . the Duke of Windsor, Lord Louis Mountbatten, Albert Einstein, Harold Lloyd . . . just everybody's been here. Of course, our parties were always decorous. Nothing wild. No Fatty Arbuckle kind of party.

Everything was gay and charming except for the occasion when the Beverly Hills police called me and said I was going to be kidnapped. I was told it was a dangerous situation. I hired a girl, a double, and she wore a wig with curls. She'd leave the house through the front door while I slipped out the back. They caught the two men. After that we had to hire guards, and for years we had watchdogs.

Looking back, there's nothing I would change in my life, except maybe I'd work harder. People no longer work hard. They do as little as possible for the most money. That includes everybody, servants and the people who are making movies today. It's just money, money, money. Grab all the money you can and run. My only regret is that I never made a film with Clark Gable. I loved him.

I'm afraid that I have to stop talking. I tire easily these days. I didn't think you'd have the patience to listen to me this long.

But I do want to confide one more thing to you. I dream often that I'm before the camera again. The other night I dreamed we were all making a film . . . Mr. Griffith, Douglas, Buddy, Valentino, Clark Gable, even Chaplin playing the Tramp. And there I was right in the center of it . . . Mary Pickford, the little girl with the golden curls.

2

Walter "Cap" Field

THE WORLD'S OLDEST EXTRA

HIS PICKFAIR IS located on the outer fringe of Sun Valley, an unfashionable suburb about half an hour's drive from Hollywood. Field's home is a $5,000 two-room shack he built himself in 1942 from scrap lumber. Dog-eared stills from many of the more than 2,000 films he says he's appeared in are nailed to the walls. They are autographed by everyone from William S. Hart (who made the first movie with a story line, The Great Train Robbery, *in 1903) to John Wayne.*

The year he was born Ulysses S. Grant was President of the United States. "The first President I voted for was Grover Cleveland. They came 'round to the saloon, that was the precinct in them days, and paid me five dollars for my vote."

On August 29, 1974, Cap—the nickname derives from his experience aboard ships as a seaman, officer and captain—celebrated his one hundredth birthday. He's the oldest active performer in motion pictures.

"I don't know why I've lived so long. Maybe drinking warm beer and chasing women helped. I've had five wives, but I ain't seen any of 'em in years and years. I'm right in there with a lot of them big stars who've been married lots of times. Maybe that goes with the business. I have three children that I know of. Sure, I'm still interested in women. But nowadays they just kinda look at me and smile."

He's a veteran of the Spanish-American War. "I guess you could

*say I knew Teddy Roosevelt. He liked horses, and so did I. We
talked about horses quite a bit down there in Cuba."*

*Balding and blue-eyed, he wears a neatly trimmed beard and a
flowing walrus mustache. "Before I got bit by that black widow spi-
der, I weighed one hundred sixty-five pounds. I'm down right now to
about one hundred thirty."*

I was born on the road, you might say. My folks was on a
paddle-wheeler going from New York to New Jersey. A
storm come up and the water was so rough and my mother
so scared that she had me ahead of time.

Never did finish school. Don't think anyone did in them
days. I ran away from home when I was fourteen or fifteen
and got me a berth on a square-rigger. Then I went into the
Spanish-American War. We sunk three gunboats off the
coast of Cuba. I guess I'm the only vet of that war never
charged up San Juan Hill with Teddy Roosevelt. Them fellas, they lie a lot. I saw a little bit of Teddy, but he was in the
Army and I was in the Navy, so our paths didn't cross too
much.

After that fracas I shipped out a lot, on all kinds of vessels.
I landed in San Diego around 1913 and went to work for the
city as a lifeguard. A man come up to me one day and said,
"How'd you like to be in the movies?"

"Sure, why not?" I said.

I'd seen them nickelodeons and liked the stories. Bill Hart
was my favorite. He was on the order of John Wayne, both of
them very particular and dedicated. I missed working with
Bill Hart in *The Great Train Robbery*—that was before my
time in Hollywood. I worked with him later, though, in *Wild
Bill Hickok* and *Tumbleweeds*. Bill, he always wore a white hat,
he was the good guy, and I played a heavy in a black hat. He
shot me dead in both them pictures. But I never held it
against him. I was already used to being killed in darn near
every picture I made.

From being a lifeguard I went to work at that old AMMEX

outfit in San Diego there. We made Mexican movies. All the stories was about Mexico, political stuff. I think they was having a revolution down there or maybe they was afraid they might have a revolution. Anyway the government was making all these pictures telling their people how great the government was and how rotten the rebels was. I was the only American at AMMEX, even wore a big Mexican hat. All that whole thing amounted to was a bunch of Spanish actors and writers and a lot of Mexican burros. Them pictures was primitive, raw, you might say. But they was all right for their time. I don't know, maybe they helped convince the Mexican people they had a pretty fair government.

The First World War came along, and I was sent to the San Pedro Naval Base as an instructor. I trained maybe ten thousand men, making sailors out of them, or trying to.

Hollywood didn't really get started until after the war. I went there in 1920 and hitched on at Stern Brothers, which was on Poverty Row. They had a passel of little old no-account studios there on the Row: Chesterfield, Tiffany, Mascot, Metropolitan, Screen Guild. The only one lasted was Columbia. Harry Cohn, he saw to that.

I made dozens of pictures at Stern Brothers, one-reelers, two-reelers. They was Westerns, most of 'em. Once in a while I had a characterization, a bit we'd call it, playing a rancher or a miner or a hillbilly. I'd have some lines to say, but in most of 'em I was a heavy with no lines. The ordinary extra got three dollars a day and lunch. Sometimes I'd make five if I did a little stunt work or when we put on a big fight scene and I had to take a punch or two. You got seven, eight dollars if you did a character part with a little dialogue. Back then if the weather was bad, they'd hand out rainchecks to us extras. You had one of them rainchecks, they'd be sure to hire you back. I began getting a little reputation there, and pretty soon I'd never need the rainchecks. They all knew Cap Field.

One of the cowboys who worked a good deal on the Row

was a young fella named John Wayne. He did a lot of pictures there. That was before John Ford made a star out of him when he put Duke in *Stagecoach*. I'd worked in many pictures with Duke. When Ford hired him, Duke said, "Cap, you're in this Ford picture with me." And I was, too. I played a cowboy, and Duke, he killed me just as dead as Bill Hart did.

John Ford was one of the most decent men there was in Hollywood. I did a mess of pictures with him. He was always good to me. Put me into every one of his pictures he could. And even if he wasn't on the pictures, I could call him and say I needed a job and he'd arrange it at the studio that I'd get put on in whatever they was shooting.

Another man I admired was Douglas Fairbanks 'cause he would do all his stunt work mostly himself. Once in a while they'd have a stunt man for him if there was a scene that was too almighty dangerous and he could get seriously hurt. That would ruin the picture. I worked quite a few of his pictures, *The Mark of Zorro, The Three Musketeers, Robin Hood* and I don't know how many others. Fairbanks, he had this one thing. He was a mite touchy about his height. He was about five foot seven, and he wouldn't hire anybody in a picture that was taller than he was or even as tall. I was okay, though, 'cause I'm five foot six.

The prettiest actress I ever did see was Dolores Del Rio. She was all woman. When she made *Evangeline* in 1929, I worked the whole picture with her, five months. Miss Del Rio, she'd make sure all of us was taken care of real good. Come down to see us after the day's shooting was over to ask if we was being treated all right. A fine lady. *Evangeline* was a sea and land picture. I directed the landing of the ships when we worked off the California coast. They used over five hundred extras in a scene that called for them to be brought out to the square-riggers in the harbor in small boats. Then all them extras had to climb aboard, and I didn't lose a man. I'd trained 'em good, made sure they was all good swimmers. Then we spent about eight weeks in Louisiana on location, and when we come back home, we had just a beautiful picture, a million-dollar picture, which was a big amount of money in them days. Then we come to find out the talkies had just come in. Hadn't heard a word about it while we was back in Louisiana. All they could do was add a bit of music, and it never turned out to be a very large picture because of the talkies.

The talkies didn't hurt me none. I like 'em better than silents. Talkies give you a chance to express yourself. In the silents half the time you didn't know what the picture was all about. The working conditions got better, too, when sound come along. They put benches out for us, and after so many hours you'd get a layoff, a little break. Pretty soon they made it so you had an eight-hour day and you was paid more if you worked overtime. In the silents we never bothered about the time as long as we had the daylight. We would get to the set when the sun was coming up and work till dark. Most days we'd be on the set before the old sun come up.

The only job I ever turned down was when they wanted me to work with Clark Gable in *Mutiny on the Bounty*. They wanted me to be the skipper of the schooner. But I was an old sea dog, and I knew that ship wasn't worth a darn and that it was dangerous. It was overloaded; they had too much stuff on it. It drew too much water, wasn't safe no matter how you looked at it, and you didn't know if it was going to stay up or down. I wouldn't take a chance on that thing. I warned 'em, but they went ahead anyway. The ship pretty near sunk two or three times while they was making the picture. Turned out all right, I guess. The ship served its purpose, no one got hurt, but everybody took a big gamble.

I got my chance to work in a picture with Gable out to MGM in *Too Hot to Handle*. Gable played a newsreel cameraman, and in one scene he was in an airplane photographing a

25

bunch of men jumping off a burning ship. My job was to pick 'em up in a boat that was off-camera. But a lot of them extras either couldn't swim or wasn't long swimmers. Six, seven of 'em nearly drowned. I think I saved a couple of lives there. Never would of happened if I'd of been director of that sequence like I was in *Evangeline*. I'd of made sure we had good swimmers.

I had a couple of parts in *Gone with the Wind*. I was a soldier in one scene and got bushwhacked and shot while I was riding along a road. Another time I was killed in battle. Once they carried me out to the train from the depot on a litter. I guess I was killed or wounded four, five times in that picture. The best scene I had was when I was a soldier leaning out the window of a train and I was kissing my girl good-bye. I sort of forgot myself, got carried away a mite. I leaned over so far kissing that girl that I fell plumb out the window. Hurt my head a little, but it was worth it. That girl was a pretty young thing, and I've always liked 'em young. I never had time to talk with Gable when I was doing that picture. I was too darn busy playing all my parts.

Stunt work pays the best, but I'm too old for it anymore. Stunt men earn their pay. You never know what might happen. In *Stagecoach* we was doing a scene, riding across the prairie, and there was a big deep hole in the ground, like a shell hole and the grass had grown over it. I didn't see the darn thing; you could hardly see it if you was on top of it. So I was tearing along on my horse, and that horse, he seen the hole and jumped it. But the three or four guys behind me, their horses didn't see the hole, and they went down, and all of them was in the hospital for a week.

I doubled for Jack Holt in a lot of his pictures. In *North of the Rio Grande* I was leading a gang of cowboys, and we was being shot at. Some of them bullets splattered on the rocks, and shrapnel from the rocks hit me in the arm and across the stomach. I didn't say nothing till the picture was over. When

26

I told the director I got hurt a few days before, he said, "Why didn't you say something?" I said the money was too good and I wasn't going to take a chance being taken off the picture. I made two, three hundred dollars out of that one.

Another time, when I was playing in *Gunga Din,* I was a British soldier, and they was taking my body into a compound on a horse. They had to dump me on the ground, but my foot got caught in the stirrup and I broke my toe. Didn't say nothing about that, either, till my part was finished.

I was in *Two Years Before the Mast* with Alan Ladd. I'd met him when things got slow and I had to take a job as a swimming coach at a pool in North Hollywood. I taught Ladd how to swim, and he was grateful. He put me in that picture. I showed some of them youngsters how to slide down the ropes so they wouldn't burn their hands, taught them to climb the rigging without fear. I was watching the big fight scene in the picture between Ladd and the stunt man who was playing the heavy. They was having at it on top of the mast. The stunt man was to fall into the water from the mast when Ladd hit him the last punch. Well, the ship rolled just the wrong way as he started to fall, and he didn't light feet first but stomach first, and it knocked him out. I took off my shoes and dived over the side into the water and brought the man in. The stunt man later became an assistant director, and he still calls me for jobs.

I never wanted to be a big star. Never had the itch, never needed that kind of money, never wanted that kind of money. I don't regret anything. I played in all types of pictures, with Rin Tin Tin, in Mack Sennett comedies, in *Captain Blood, Cardinal Richelieu, Les Miserables.* I even played an ice skater in the *Ice Follies of 1939* with Joan Crawford, Jimmy Stewart and Lew Ayres. I'd done a lot of ice skating back East. Till a few years ago I could still figure skate pretty good, could even figure skate my name.

Besides working sea pictures, the best type of picture is the

Westerns. If you've got a good director, he'll serve real beer
or liquor in the saloon scenes. They used to just give us colored water or sarsaparilla. But lately they don't serve much
of the real stuff 'cause a lot of them fellas overdo it. When
they get to drinking, they turn real rowdy and unruly, and
they don't do their parts right.

I been in television ever since the darn thing came in.
Played parts in *The Fugitive, The Don Knotts Show,* and back
there on my ninety-fifth birthday I was working with Mike
Landon in a *Bonanza.* They give me a little birthday party
with a cake and all, and every member of the cast autographed a copy of the script for me. In that picture, Mike
Landon was real nice to me. He added something extra in
one scene by slapping me on the back and saying, "Hiya,
Rocky." That was a bit . . . give me a little more money.

The last thing I played for television was in a six-parter
called *Prairie Lawyer* with this new fella, Hal Holbrook. The
story's about Abe Lincoln's early years. It was very interesting to me. Lincoln died only a few years before I was born. I
was one of the jury members, and we voted Abe's client not
guilty 'cause Abe was such a good lawyer.

The biggest year I had I made about ten thousand dollars.
I've made as little as a few hundred some years. But I make
out all right. I have my veteran's pension, one hundred and
one dollars a month, and Social Security. I can still drive my
car. I passed my last driving test when I was ninty-nine. The
state said I was the oldest fella ever to do it.

I sort of feel sorry for these younger men, what with the
little work that's around. Jobs are tougher to get; they're not
making enough pictures. They're still making too much stuff
in Europe. Even the television situation is bad. Too many reruns. I knew when the unions let the networks use so many
reruns, the jobs would dry up. That was my holler there for a
long time. Everybody laughed at me. But I said, "You let 'em
put in all these reruns and you'll be out of jobs." And that's

what happened. The pay is bigger nowadays for an extra. The minimum is one hundred and thirty-eight dollars a day. But eighty, ninety percent of the extras in this town work maybe a half dozen days a year. Seems like we had more money when we was making less but working more often.

I live alone, and I don't mind it. My daughter says, "Why don't you move into the Motion Picture Country Home?" And I tell her, "I don't want to be out there with all them old people."

I married my last wife when I was sixty-four. She was twenty-five. She died here about five years ago. My doctor tells me I got ten or fifteen more years to live, but I don't believe him. I never look ahead. I take things as they come. Funny thing, though, every time I get a call and show up on the set everybody is surprised. They're surprised that I'm still alive.

I got five, six scrapbooks in there I could show you filled with clippings and the names of all the pictures I been in. I'd go get 'em for you, but I'm feeling poorly today and don't think I can make it to the bedroom.

My daughter had a good old party for me on my hundredth birthday. There was lots of folks. My daughter thought my reaching the age of one hundred was a special occasion. "It only happens once in a lifetime," she said. So she invited all the stars I'd worked with through the years, Duke Wayne, Mike Landon, you know, people like that. None of them showed up. But we had a hell of a time anyway.

3

Minta Durfee Arbuckle

SHE NEVER CALLED HIM FATTY

IT IS JULY 4, and sweltering. Hilly Coronado Street north of Sunset Boulevard reverberates with the sound of exploding fire-crackers and blasting gusts of Latin music. Half-naked children dodge traffic like bullfighters, laughing as their sparklers perform ve-ronicas in the sky. The street in the last decade has become the prov-ince of Mexican-Americans. The homes are small and sturdy, the lawns a sick yellow. It is a street of losers, of poverty, of neglect.

Fatty Arbuckle, who was involved in the most celebrated of Holly-wood scandals, never lived in the modest wood frame home on Coro-nado Street now occupied by his first wife. But his memory is alive there. Living room and bedroom are strewn with pictures and paint-ings of him . . . Fatty at twenty-six with an English pit bull-dog . . . Fatty with Mack Sennett, with Chaplin, with Mabel Nor-mand, faded photographs of a long-ago wedding to the woman who has made the home a shrine to the screen's first important comedian.

On a tray in front of Minta Durfee Arbuckle are the remnants of a TV dinner and half a bottle of scotch. She is petite and hazel-eyed, an eighty-three-year-old firebrand who warms quickly to the subject of "a man I loved so much that I never remarried, a man who means so much to me that I'm still proud to bear his name."

I always called him Roscoe, never Fatty, and he called me Minty, the only man I ever permitted that intimacy. It was his secret love name for me.

30

I met Roscoe in 1908, on this old streetcar. We were just children then, darling. As I was getting off at my stop, I noticed a great big stout boy. He was heavy but handsome. Oh, God, he looked like he had been scrubbed to death. He had a complexion that any woman in the world would die to have. His hair was so blond. And he was dressed meticulously, white trousers, white shoes, blue coat and a straw hat.

He said, "Pardon me, miss, I would be very glad to carry your suitcase."

I said, "I don't like blonds, and I don't like fat people. And how dare you speak to me?"

I don't know what got into me. Actually I was attracted to him, but I couldn't let myself be picked up, could I?

The next thing I knew I received a bouquet of flowers with a note that said, "Dear Minty: Someday soon you and I are going to be married. Maybe then you'll let me carry your luggage. Your determined Blond Fat Boy."

He came 'round to my house, I don't know how he found out my name or where I lived, and began to court me. We were quite a contrast. He weighed more than two hundred and fifty and I was ninety-eight pounds then. I'm one hundred fifteen or one hundred sixteen now. And I had dark, lovely chestnut hair that hung pretty near to my knees. It was so long that I could sit on it. We were married five months later on the stage of the Byde-a-While theater in Long Beach, California. It was a vaudeville house and Roscoe was on the bill.

We didn't have time and we were too poor for a honeymoon. I was in vaudeville, too, working as an "end" girl in a chorus line of the Kolb and Dill circuit. I was between jobs, just back from San Francisco the day I met Roscoe.

Roscoe had more talent than people realize or remember. He wasn't only a comedian; he had one of the most gorgeous singing voices that God ever gave anybody in the world, so much so that when Caruso met him in New York City in

31

1915 he said, "Mr. Arbuckle, if you would give up the picture business, I'd make you one of the world's greatest singers."

After the run ended at the Byde-a-While, we went on tour. I'd gotten a job in the company's chorus line. The show also had a prima donna, a juggler and an animal act. Roscoe was the star and sang the accompaniment to what was called in those days illustrated slides. Just pictures of sunsets or desert scenes that were flashed up on a little screen. When the tour was over, we came back to California. Pretty soon Roscoe turned peevish because he wanted to work but couldn't find a job.

He was so desperate that one day he went out to Keystone, thinking he might get some work for a few days in movies.

He opened the gate at Keystone, and there was nothing but a big, empty, barnlike building with a wooden floor. He looked around and didn't see a thing in the world. There wasn't a soul in sight. For no reason Roscoe began to sing. All of a sudden a man with a great big shock of gray hair and a mouthful of tobacco juice appeared through a door and said, "You, big boy, be here tomorrow morning at eight." Then— bang! The door slammed shut. And that was the way Roscoe met Mack Sennett, that's how plebeian it was getting into movies in those days.

Roscoe was depressed when he came home. He'd changed his mind about the movies, and he didn't want to work for Mr. Sennett. "The dust in that place was so thick I thought it was going to hit me at the waistline," he said.

I played the gorgeous little mother and said, "Listen, son, you go back tomorrow." I talked him into it, and you know the rest of the story. He became a very famous comedian, a great comedian.

One night Mr. Sennett, Mabel Normand, Roscoe and I went to dinner. Mr. Sennett said to Roscoe, "Why don't we put Minta in the movies?" Just like that! Roscoe agreed, and the next day I was at Keystone, watching everything and trying to learn the motion-picture business.

A couple of nights later the four of us went out again, to a theater on Main Street in Los Angeles. Mr. Sennett said there was a vaudevillian playing the Sullivan and Considine circuit that he wanted to see. The man's act wasn't much. He was in a shabby silk hat, an old, worn-out coat and a frayed tux. He had a mustache and carried a cane. His gag was that he was intoxicated, drunk as Hooley's cat, as they would say, and he did a series of pratfalls. That was his whole act.

Mr. Sennett invited him to dinner with us. I never saw a man whose street clothes were so dirty. He wore a checked thing, I call them racetrack suits. Mr. Sennett asked him, "Will you come to the studio tomorrow?"

"No," he said, "I have another engagement in San Diego. I have a good job, and I don't want to leave it."

And that was our first meeting with Charlie Chaplin.

A few weeks later Chaplin did turn up at Keystone. Mr. Sennett had teamed Roscoe with Mabel Normand, and they were the most perfect combination the world ever knew. They were terrific working together as a comedy team, and the audiences loved them. Mr. Sennett decided he wanted another team, so he put Chaplin and me together. I was getting forty dollars a week and Chaplin fifty.

I never thought Chaplin would make it. "Minta," he said to me one day, "you get along with everybody. You love people. I'm too shy, and I feel uncomfortable around here. I feel lost, I'm in a foreign country, and I don't know anyone."

I reassured him as best I could, but the next thing that happened didn't help Charlie's confidence much. They had a custom at Keystone, like hazing in college. Everybody who was new went through it. Charlie and I were rehearsing this scene; it was his tryout, the first thing he ever did for the movies. Charlie was making love to me, and his line was, "Come sit on my lap." So I went and sat on his knee. He started to kiss me, and those devils in the studio had put water in a tarpaulin over our heads, and they let it go. Both of us were almost soaked to pieces. Charlie was so darn mad that he ran around like a wet hen. "I won't stay," he shouted, "I'm leaving." But he settled down after a while. I became Chaplin's leading lady and costarred with him in his first ten pictures. My salary went up to twenty-five hundred dollars a week.

I loved Keystone more than anything in the world. We were the most dedicated people that ever lived. That's why we were so successful and our pictures will never die. They're classics, and the world will never see their like again.

Roscoe and Mabel were coining money at the box office. Every picture they made was a hit. Mabel was a dainty, lovely woman, the most glorious darling girl you'd want to meet. She and my husband were supposed to be the greatest pie throwers in the history of movies. There's a lot to throwing pies. It's an art. If you just throw a pie, it isn't funny. You had to have the right comedic situation. The facial expression had to be perfect—that is, the person who was going to be hit in the face had to be unsuspecting, oblivious.

It was Mabel who accidentally invented pie throwing in the movies. There was a little bakeshop near the studio, and one day Mable was hungry and she said she was going across the street to get herself a pie. She came back with it, and one of our costume men started to tease her. Mabel threw that homemade pie smack into his face. Just as she did, Mr. Sennett came through the door. It was so funny that everybody began to laugh. So Mr. Sennett put pie throwing into his comedies from then on. They still throw pies in the movies, but today the pies are really nothing. It's that swish stuff that you put on top of some foods. We used real pies, soft, creamy blackberry and raspberry. They photographed best. Silly as it may sound, pie throwing is a lost art. I worked in a picture with Jack Lemmon a few years ago, and he told me, "You know, Minta, nobody could throw pies like Keystone people."

Roscoe and I stayed with Mr. Sennett for four years. Then Paramount offered Roscoe the first three-million-dollar-a-year contract in the history of movies because the exhibitors were making so much money on his films, far more money than they were taking in from the things Chaplin and I were doing.

Roscoe had been a poor boy, abandoned as a kid by his father, who was an alcoholic. So I guess he had to make up for his impoverished childhood. He spent money wildly. He was the first star to have the entourage. Roscoe bought me a Rolls-Royce, the first one in Hollywood with a genuine silver radiator. And jewels, my darling, like you've never seen. He was the most generous man on earth. I never knew a man as generous as he was, not only to me but to everybody. He couldn't say no to anyone. Roscoe used to give me all the money he didn't spend himself. My dear, I've sat with thousands and thousands of dollars in my purse. Roscoe always said, "I'll make it, darlin', and you spend it."

We toured the world, went to China and Europe, and for a cross-country trip to promote one of Roscoe's new pictures, Evalyn Walsh McLean, the woman who owned the Hope diamond, lent us her private train. We stopped in twenty-three cities, and every place we went the crowds came out to cheer and greet us.

In 1921 Roscoe and I had a disagreement, and we decided on a separation. There was no other woman involved—I want you to put that down. And I wasn't romantically involved with another man.

I went to Massachusetts, to the home of friends in Martha's Vineyard to think things over. When I arrived, I told my maid, "Ruth, don't unpack the suitcases."

I had a premonition. Somehow I didn't think I was going to stay there long.

The following morning I played golf, and when I got back to my suite, a call came in from my sister Marie in New York. She said, "Minta, can you imagine anything like this? Roscoe is being accused of raping and murdering Virginia Rappe."

I thought I hadn't heard right. "What did you say?"

"It's in all the papers. They say Roscoe raped and killed Virginia Rappe."

Well, my dear, I could have jumped out of my skin. I was in utter shock. Virginia Rappe, of all the people in the world for Roscoe to be involved with. She was a small-time actress at Keystone who was so promiscuous she'd spread syphilis all over the studio. I hate to say that word because it sounds like I'm a nasty old woman, but it's the truth. Mr. Sennett had to close the studio down for several days while he had everything repainted and fumigated. Mabel Normand and I were admonished by Mr. Sennett to stay away from Virginia Rappe, and certanly not to emulate her conduct. Yet Virginia was a girl that wouldn't have hurt anybody in the world. She was just a victim of her mother and her manager, both of them too ambitious for her, considering the little talent she had.

"Call the chauffeur," I told Ruth. "We're going right back to New York and catching a train for San Francisco. I want to be with my husband."

But I had to be sure I was doing the right thing. I visited my attorney in New York, and he said yes, it might help Roscoe if I went to San Francisco. So he bought tickets for my mother and myself.

There must have been a hundred reporters waiting for us when we arrived. They were there from all over the world, and they were horrible. I also hate to say this, but reporters can be the meanest people on the face of the earth. It was like they were out to massacre us. They asked everything about my personal life with Roscoe. How often we went to bed together. Why we'd separated. Did Roscoe have a temper? Had he ever been mean to me? But I never opened my big mouth. You wouldn't think it the way I'm running off now.

There wasn't a hotel in San Francisco that would take us. We had to stay at the Olympic Athletic Club, and that was on the QT. The hotels were afraid that the crowds would be too great, or maybe they just didn't want us.

Roscoe had been in jail for seventeen days when we went to see him. He looked like he'd lost weight. We weren't even permitted to see him alone. There was a screeen in the visitors' room, and the reporters were behind there, trying to .overhear our conversation. It was so bad that we had to whisper.

Roscoe took my mother and me in his arms and said, "I love you both."

I said, "'How are you, darling?" And we carried on like nothing had happened.

"On my way out the chief of police stopped me and said, "Mrs. Arbuckle, your husband has no more right being in a cell than I do. It's the most horrible, political, hateful thing I've ever seen in my life."

The headlines never let up. Front page every day. Most of it was whipped up by William Randolph Hearst. Imagine, he was publishing eight editions of his paper a day, all of them with these terrible stories about Roscoe. You'd think Roscoe's trouble was the only problem in the world. But Hearst wasn't out only to sell papers. There was more to it than that.

I'd meet Hearst's mother, Phoebe, a few years before at several social gatherings. She was one of the finest women California ever had. She was above reproach, but something went tilt with her son. Hearst resented Hollywood, and he resented Roscoe, who'd come from nothing and was a star and a millionaire. But Hearst with all his money and power couldn't make a star of his mistress, Marion Davies. Marion was a miserable failure in movies. She made a picture called *Cecilia of the Pink Roses,* and they still claim that it's the worst picture ever made in the history of the business. Hearst had built the whole Cosmopolitan Studio for her in New York. Poor Marion, God bless her soul, she was one of the greatest pawns who ever lived in the world. She'd had every handsome leading man in her pictures, but the exhibitors would come and tell you what they would pay. They'd pay two hundred fifty dollars a day for an Arbuckle picture, one hundred or seventy-five dollars a day for a Chaplin. But they wouldn't pay five dollars a day for a Marion Davies. So Hearst closed down Cosmopolitan, and Marion came to the Coast. But nobody would take Marion on. None of the studios wanted her until Hearst bludgeoned Louis B. Mayer into letting her work at MGM. But Hearst, not MGM, financed the pictures she made in Hollywood, none of which were any good either.

I don't blame Marion; she got sick and tired of that old man running around like the wild ass of the desert trying to make her a star. When she saw it wasn't going to happen, that her career was just skittering out, she went to live in that castle at San Simeon with that dreadful, dreadful old man.

There were other things working against Roscoe. In those days San Francisco people loathed Los Angeles and Hollywood people. Their noses were so far in the air you'd need a ladder to reach their nostrils. And the district attorney who was prosecuting Roscoe wanted to be governor.

It was Roscoe, not Virginia Rappe, who was the victim. I'd asked Roscoe straight out, "Did you have anything to do with Virginia's death?"

"No," Roscoe said. "As God is my judge, I'm innocent." That was good enough for me.

The only evidence, if you can call it evidence, that they had against Roscoe was what the newspapers said about him. And most of that came from Maude Delmont, who was the cause of the whole thing. But they never published in the papers that Maude Delmont had seventy-two affidavits out against her for being a professional correspondent, a woman that's found in bed with a husband when a photographer bursts into a room and takes a picture. That was when they had these setup divorces and the only grounds for divorce was adultery. Maude Delmont had gone to the well too often, she'd made it into a racket, and so the cops were down on her. When the cops found out Maude had been at the party at the St. Francis Hotel, she must have made a deal with the district attorney. They'd forget about the seventy-two affidavits if she'd frame Roscoe. I'm as certain of that as I'm certain of anything, because in all three trials they never put her on the stand once. She would have made a terrible witness, and her testimony would have been shredded by our lawyers. I think our lawyers made a great mistake by not calling Maude Delmont to the stand. I don't know why they didn't.

The first thing our lawyers tried to do was to get the charge against Roscoe reduced from murder to manslaughter.

Roscoe was in handcuffs when he was taken from his cell and walked through a hallway to the courtroom for that hearing. There were people milling around who'd seen this man on the screen. They knew him and started to applaud. But there was one woman in the crowd, the head of a vigilante women's group with thousands of members, who had a lot of her followers with her. As soon as she saw Roscoe, she said, "Women, do your duty." And they all spat at Roscoe. His face and clothes were covered with spit.

The charge was reduced to manslaughter, and his bail was set at fifty thousand dollars.

I suffered with Roscoe through every minute of that long ordeal of the three trials. The first one ended in a hung jury. So did the second. The prosecuting attorney carried on like he didn't care if Roscoe had killed Virginia or not. He was only interested in a conviction at any price, no matter how many lives he ruined.

The most damaging witnesses he had were Zey Prevon and Alice Blake. Zey was a pretty blond girl, on the voluptuous side, who'd come from a very fine family. She hadn't married well, and she'd had a child out of wedlock. Alice Blake, who seemed like a nice girl, had had a run-in or two with the law.

Both were chorus girls, and they'd been browbeaten by the district attorney into testifying that they'd heard Virginia say, "Roscoe, you're killing me," when they supposedly were having intercourse. A dying person's word is supposed to be the truth. But Roscoe said he hadn't had intercourse with Virginia. Our lawyers proved with medical records that Virginia died of cystitis, an inflammation of the bladder. She had such a severe case that she had to use a catheter to eliminate. Her sphincter muscle wouldn't work.

When Zey Prevon testified at the third trial, I prayed that at last God would give her the strength to tell the truth for her own sake because she was perjuring herself. All of a sudden, while she was on the stand, Zey screamed out, "I can't sit here and tell these lies. I never heard Virginia Rappe say, 'Roscoe, you're killing me.'" Zey started to cry and cry. Then Alice Blake came on the stand and confirmed Zey's story.

Court was adjourned, and to relieve the tension, Roscoe and I went for a ride, and this is a very humorous thing. We had this great big car, and we were going to San Jose. Outside town, Roscoe made some error or other in driving. A policeman stopped us. When he recognized Roscoe, he said, "Mr. Arbuckle, you're my favorite comedian. You're in enough trouble. I'm not going to give you a ticket. Good luck. I don't think you did it."

Not everyone felt that way. Some of the mail that came to us was unbelievable. There were threats against Roscoe's life and against mine. Some wrote and said that Roscoe had torn down the moral fiber of the country, that he was a monster, that he deserved to hang. But there were thousands of letters from people who supported Roscoe and said they believed in him.

The last trial finally ended. Now this is supposed to be one of the great things in legal history.

The judge said to the jury, "You have heard the evidence. You are excused to go into the jury room and consider your verdict."

The forelady, a great big heavy rustic woman, replied, "Your Honor, there's no need for us to go into the jury room. We find the defendant, Roscoe Conklin Arbuckle, not guilty!"

That didn't take a minute and a half after the thing had dragged out for more than a year.

My mother rejoiced. "Ye shall know the truth, and the truth shall make you free," she said after hearing the verdict. "Amen!" I said. We weren't churchgoing people but spiritual people, and we thought that God and that last jury had judged Roscoe fairly . . . had given him justice.

But after he was found not guilty, Hollywood was closed to him because the women's clubs and the Legion of Decency were still out for Roscoe's scalp. It didn't matter to them that he was found innocent.

Roscoe couldn't find a job in pictures, and that three-million-dollar contract was just a piece of paper.

This awful Will Hays, who was the censor in our business, instead of standing up like a man and declaring Roscoe absolutely guiltless, was absolutely ruthless.

I went to Mr. Hays to plead for Roscoe. I've never seen a man in all my lifetime that looked more like a rat dressed up in men's clothing than Will Hays.

I told him, "My husband has been freed. He should be allowed to work."

"I don't know if that's possible, Mrs. Arbuckle," Mr. Hays said.

"My husband is in the middle of his career. He's one of the world's most beloved men. He's the best comedian in the world. That's why they gave him a multimillion-dollar contract."

Then Mr. Hays said, "I'll see what can be done. But I think this is something that Mr. Arbuckle will have to live with."

I sat with Will Hays for an hour and a half, but I couldn't do anything with him.

The ban against Roscoe stuck. The only thing he could do

was to make a vaudeville tour all over the United States . . .
and the interesting thing is whenever he stepped out on the
stage he got the biggest applause you ever heard in your life.
He filled theaters in Chicago and Cleveland and everywhere
else he appeared. He'd come out, and before his act he'd talk
to the people.

Roscoe would say: "I'm a free man. I want to go back to
work. I want to do the same thing I've been doing for years. I
want to make people laugh. I want to make people happy.
That's all I've ever wanted to do in my life. I'm an innocent
man. Yet I can't come back. I'm still young, and I want to
work again. But they won't let me."

The audiences would give him an ovation. Roscoe was trying to turn public opinion back to himself.

He called me one night while he was on that tour. He said,
"Minty, I'm here in Cleveland, and I've been watching one of
the cleverest hoofers, he's remarkable, he not only dances
but he ad-libs jokes. He should be making movies. I'm going
to phone a couple of people out there and write a few letters
for him because he belongs in Hollywood."

And that's how Bob Hope got into the movies—thanks to
Roscoe. I've discussed it many times with Mr. Hope, and he'll
tell you the same thing. It's gospel truth. Once Mr. Hope
said, "Minta, I'll never forget your husband for helping me.
Without him, I might still be in Cleveland."

Roscoe had most of the people in the country with him,
but he couldn't get some of these women and the industry to
give him another chance. His career was over. About all that
happened was that Jack Warner let him direct three shorts,
and Roscoe couldn't even use his own name. The name he
did use was sad and heartbreaking: Will B. Good.

Roscoe and I were divorced, but we stayed good friends,
even after he remarried. He'd telephone often, and we'd
talk, and sometimes I'd see him. I don't know why we got divorced. The only thing about Roscoe was that he wasn't a

42

man who could say, "I'm sorry." And that hurt me in some of the disagreements we had before and after the trials. We'd have an argument, and the next day he'd make up for it by buying me a diamond ring or a necklace or just some little present. But all he ever had to do was say, "I'm sorry." He never did. Roscoe and I had a child, but the boy died the first year we were married. We never had another one. Maybe if we'd had a child, there wouldn't have been a divorce. Maybe he never would have gone to that crazy party that ruined everything. I don't know. . . .

Roscoe died in New York City in 1933. They say it was a heart attack. But he'd been dying for years. They killed him in San Francisco . . . right at the bloom of his rise. He was only forty-six years old.

Legal expenses for the trials had cost seven hundred and eighty-five thousand dollars. Roscoe didn't die broke, but he didn't leave much. And when the crash came in 1929, I lost more than a million dollars in the stock market and another fortune in a cosmetics business in which I'd invested.

I had to start all over again. I had to go back to work and do the best I could. I've done a lot of lecturing, I've been on the *Merv Griffin Show,* and I've done extra work. I was in *Hello, Dolly!* with Barbra Streisand and Walter Matthau. I was in *The Unsinkable Molly Brown* with Debbie Reynolds. I had two scenes in which I wore such lovely gowns. I worked only two days, but Debbie saw to it that I got a contract for three weeks. I didn't want to take it. I didn't want charity. But Debbie said, "Oh, Minta, for the love of beans, sign the contract. A gal that can go through as much as you did and not complain about anything deserves this much."

It's been difficult adjusting to a lower standard of living. I had four maids, a chauffeur, the Rolls-Royce, a nine-room apartment in New York, a big house out here, and the jewels, loads of jewels and diamonds. I'll give you an idea. Roscoe gave me one bracelet that had two hundred and seventy-four diamonds and emeralds. I had a pear-shaped diamond that cost something like eleven thousand dollars. The first ring Roscoe ever gave me was five karats worth five thousand dollars. And he gave me an emerald worth fourteen thousand dollars. That jewelry would be worth a king's ransom today, but I had to sell it all for next to nothing.

I want you to know that despite everything that's happened, I'm not bitter. I can't stand bitter people. I don't have an ounce of bitterness in the world. I'm not bitter against anyone or anything because I've had it all . . . the sorrow and the hurt and the happiness. I did a command performance for the dowager empress of China. I met General Pershing and danced with the Prince of Wales.

You'd be surprised, but I'm not forgotten. I still get more fan mail than any old dame that has been in the picture business. And last year the mayor of Los Angeles declared my birthday Minta Durfee Arbuckle Day. I want you to look at this scroll the city gave me. Isn't it the most beautiful thing you've ever seen?

4

Eddie LeVeque

THE LAST OF THE KEYSTONE KOPS

HIS PROUDEST POSSESSION, once a river of gold that produced some $50,000,000 at the box office, is now of minimal value . . . to everyone except Eddie LeVeque, who owns the world-wide rights to the Keystone Kops name.

Born on June 4, 1896, he lives in a small two-bedroom white bungalow in Hollywood. In memory and appearance, he is still the compleat Keystone Kop: bulbous-nosed; a winking smile; laughing, upturned, bushy eyebrows; a round arc of a face with blue eyes that glint merrily and mischievously, especially when he talks about the unforgotten, zany antics of the screen's wildest police force.

El Paso, Texas, was my birthplace. My father was a gentleman gambler from New Orleans and my mother was Mexican. She came from the state of Chihuahua.

I've been in show business practically all my life. I was first influenced by my maternal granduncle, Rito Armendariz, who was the black sheep of the family. He was supposed to become a priest. Instead, he became an impresario, a pantomimist, a puppeteer who made his own marionettes, an actor, clown, writer and musician. He also spent a great deal of his time drinking. But the bottle didn't seem to hurt him. He died pushing ninety.

By the time I was four years old I was acting in some of his plays. I did a few boy parts, but more often I played girls,

45

just like in the days of the Shakespearean theater. When I was seven, my parents allowed me to go on the road with Uncle Rito and his troupe. At first my mother was against it. But my father said, "Well, it will make a man out of him. He loves show business. Let him be what he wants to be."

We traveled and did shows in big and little towns throughout Mexico, Texas and Arizona. Uncle Rito was one of the first movie fans. About 1904 he bought an Edison projector, and he was one of the first impresarios to combine live shows with movies. He'd rent French and American pictures. In some of the small towns we played electricity wasn't always available. The theaters would be lit by gaslight, and I'd crank the projector by hand.

I spent three years traveling with Uncle Rito and returned home only after his death. Until I was fifteen, I stayed in El Paso and went to the movies every chance I got. My favorite pictures were the Keystone comedies made by Mack Sennett.

One day at the YMCA I met a cameraman from Pathé named Lewis. I can't remember if that was his first or last name. He said he was going into Mexico to film the Madero revolution.* Lewis needed an interpreter and someone to help him carry the camera. I was so anxious to get the job I told him I was an orphan and was starving to death. He hired me at a dollar a day—American money.

In Mexico we took pictures of battles wherever we could find them. When we couldn't find a battle, we faked it. Lewis would have me round up a bunch of soldiers and stage a battle scene. "Tell them to move around," he ordered. "Tell them to do something. Tell them to pretend they are killing the enemy. These are moving pictures! Tell them to play it big."

*Francisco I. Madero was a wealthy, liberal landowner who wanted greater political freedom for Mexican peons. He led a successful revolt against dictator Porfirio Díaz and became President of Mexico in 1911. Two years later Madero was assassinated.

In the course of our travels I saw Pancho Villa several times but didn't meet him until later.

I spent a year with Lewis. He was called back by Pathé for another job. Before we parted, he gave me a letter to Colonel Selig, who owned the Selig Film Studio in Chicago.

I beat my way (hopped a freight train) to Chicago. The trip took three weeks. When I got to Selig, I was told that the studio was temporarily closed. I was hungry and needed a job. So I went to the American Film Company, another studio there, and I showed one of the executives the letter from Lewis which described me as a projectionist, cameraman, actor, assistant director and director. In those days anyone who had the slightest bit of experience with a camera could usually get work at a studio. The industry was in its infancy. I was hired at ten dollars a week and played bits in half- and one-reelers, mostly messenger boys, office boys and college boys.

The directors at American had all come from the stage, and they directed movies like they were plays. They understood nothing of the fluidity of the camera. The actors, four or five of us, would move toward the camera. That was the close-up. The camera never moved toward the actors. Incidentally, it's wrong to think that D. W. Griffith invented the close-up. I'd seen it often in the French pictures that Uncle Rito used to run.

After a year American moved to California, and I wasn't invited to go along. So I went home again. When I got to El Paso, Pancho Villa was in town. By now he was a general, and he controlled parts of Texas and all of northern Mexico. He was a short man with wide gaps in his teeth who wore a long mustache. A friend of mine was Villa's chauffeur. He introduced me to Villa, who promptly made me his interpreter. It was exciting for a while, but after a short time I got bored. And it began to dawn on me that I was working for a man who took pleasure in robbing, terror and rape. He was exploiting the same peons he was supposed to be helping, although I never saw any of that personally. All we'd do was visit one city after another in his big seven-seat open black touring car. The only break in the routine with Villa was when news photographers from the United States turned up. Villa loved to pose for them, and they were fascinated by his colorful reputation. Villa was the biggest publicity hound I ever saw, worse than any movie star. He'd let them shoot pictures of him as long as they liked. I was frequently in the snapshots. Once I borrowed a gun from a member of his gang and posed alone with Villa. It was something to do.

Traveling with Villa was really monotonous, so one night I slipped out of his camp and walked sixty miles to El Paso. I'd decided by now that I was going to Hollywood. To get there, I got a job on a passenger train as a news butcher, selling papers, magazines, books, postcards and Indian beadwork. The minute we arrived in Los Angeles I jumped the train and headed straight for Keystone. My wildest dream was to work there. I never even thought of trying another studio.

It was eight thirty in the morning when I got to the office of Harry Atkinson, who was the casting director. There were already fifteen or twenty poeple waiting, most of them just trying to get extra work.

I showed Atkinson some stills from the parts I'd played at American. He wasn't impressed until he saw a couple of snapshots of me with Pancho Villa. Somehow they'd gotten mixed up in the batch of pictures I'd brought along. Atkinson wanted to hear all about Villa. Charley Avery, who was an actor and a director at Keystone, wandered into the office at that moment, and Atkinson told him with awe in his voice, "Hey, Charley, here's a kid who's done some things at American and he's also worked for Pancho Villa."

Avery said, "I can use a prop boy." So I became part of Keystone. I could thank Pancho Villa for that much. I started at three dollars a day, which was a great deal of money then. I never had a contract, but I'd work four, five, sometimes six days a week. Room with breakfast, lunch, dinner and your clothes washed was costing me only five dollars a week. Carfare and ice-cream sodas were a nickel. Excellent Italian, French or Mexican restaurants served meals for twenty-five cents. You could have a glorious evening with a girlfriend, including a visit to Solomon's Penny Dance Arcade, for a dollar and fifty cents.

From prop boy I graduated into doubling for girls. When one of the female stars on the lot couldn't do a stunt or a fall, I'd put on a dress and do it for her, things like jumping from a speeding automobile or trolley car. I'd take the pratfall. I was agile and it came easy for me.

Then I started doing bits, and pretty soon Mack Sennett made a picture called *The Bangville Police*, which was all about these crazy cops. It turned out to be the first Keystone Kops picture, and I played one of the Kops. Everyone at the studio played a Kop, even big stars like Fatty Arbuckle and Chester Conklin. Mack Sennett himself occasionally played a Kop. So did Bobby Vernon, who became Gloria Swanson's leading man. Another comic, Ford Sterling, usually played the chief.

We must have made forty or fifty pictures starring the Keystone Kops. And the Kops were in a lot of the other comedy pictures shot at the studio. Whenever a picture got bogged down and they needed more laughs, they'd throw the Kops in for as many sequences as possible. It didn't matter much if the Kops fit the plot of the picture.

Over the years the Keystone Kops pictures were released dozens of times. Sennett would change the name of the pictures and lure the public in that way. They thought they were seeing a new Kops picture, but they never seemed to mind. That was one reason the Kops made so much money for Sennett.

Sennett, who'd started as an actor at Biograph, tried to call us the Mack Sennett Kops, but the public gave us our name.

The Keystone name was very famous then, and people just started calling us the Keystone Kops. Despite Sennett's displeasure, the name stuck. All the other studios tried to copy the Keystone Kops. There were the Universal Cops, the Stern Brothers Cops, the Christy Cops and the Sunshine Cops. But they never had the popularity of the Keystone Kops.

Actually Sennett didn't originate the Keystone Kops. When I was a kid, I'd seen crazy cops in those little French pictures that Uncle Rito showed. They were made in France by Pathé Frères, Gaumont and Éclair. Those French gendarmes would chase a crook on foot up and down hilly, narrow streeets. Pushcarts would be overturned. The crooks and the gendarmes would run into people and upset tables at outdoor cafés. The chase would go on until the crooks were eventually caught. Those short gendarme chases were the forerunners of the Keystone Kops. What Sennett added was putting the Kops in automobiles.

When we started shooting a Kops picture, we never had much of a script, just a story line that more or less gave us the beginning, the middle and the end of what the picture was supposed to be about. Before a Kops sequence, the director would say, "All right, boys, do what you want, do what's funny, only don't hurt yourselves." That was the only "direction" we received.

But is was strange, once we were in the car and the chase began, there was an exhilaration that came over you. You forgot yourself, and you just took chances. I took many a fall that was unnecessary, but everyone was trying to outdo everyone else. There was always that spirit of good-natured competition. The only thing that mattered was to make it funny. On the screen it looked like we were traveling zooosh, one hundred miles an hour. Actually we were going about forty, which was still dangerous when you leaped from a moving car. The fast chases were trick photography. The film would be speeded up mechanically. For the collisions we used what was called a moving panorama. It was a painting with trees and telephone poles and city buildings and trolley cars. A couple of carpenters or propmen would turn it, and the panorama moved, giving the impression that when our cars just bumped into each other lightly, actually we were in a head-on crash. Then, of course, we'd fall out of the cars and do flops, and it all looked real on the screen.

The pictures gradually became more sophisticated when we started using stories where the plots were laid in the city. But in the first ones everything was rural, countrified. There was the farmer, his daughter, the stupid boy who wanted to marry the farmer's daughter, the tramp in the haystack and the villain with the high hat and long coat who held the mortgage and had an eye on the girl. He was always promising to take her to New York. When she resisted his advances, the trouble started, and the father called the Kops.

The chase was the heart and soul of all the Kops' pictures. But there were sight gags interspersed with the chases. And close calls. Once they put me in a small shack, and two piano movers left a piano in front of the door. Then the shack was set on fire. The gag was supposed to be my trying to get out. But I couldn't get out. I really couldn't get out. The other Kops started throwing water on the shack. The piano was a breakaway, but for some reason it didn't break. When the other Kops realized my screams for help were for real, they rescued me by smashing the piano with axes. None of this, of course, was in the script. But the camera kept on cranking. It turned out to be one of the funniest parts of the picture.

The Keystone Kops pictures had a sparkle to them, a spontaneity that pictures today seem to lack. And they were genuinely funny, and that also seems to be lacking today. Doesn't anyone like to laugh anymore?

Sound killed the Kops. Nobody thought we'd be funny in talkies, and maybe the audiences by that time were getting a little tired of the pictures because they had all been shown and reshown and reshown.

After the Kops ended, I went to Paramount, then Metro. I've worked at all the studios. Never as an extra. Always doing bits. I've been in more than one hundred pictures, and I had my own small studio for a few years, and I worked on a Spanish-language radio station as a disc jockey for a long time.

But the memory of the Kops always stayed with me. So did the memory of the Keystone Studio. Mack Sennett was a brooding man. He walked around with a perpetual grouchy look on his face. But he was a genius. Think of the stars he made. Carole Lombard started there. So did Bing Crosby. Chaplin, Gloria Swanson, Mabel Normand, Fatty Arbuckle, Minta Durfee, Chester Conklin and Buster Keaton. There was also Mack Sennett's famous Bathing Beauties. I guess the only mistake Sennett made in those days was turning down a shy little man from Nebraska who wanted to be a comedian. Sennett didn't think he'd make it. The shy little man turned out to be Harold Lloyd.

In its heyday the Keystone lot was called the Crazy Factory. Some actors thought it beneath their dignity to work slapstick for Sennett. When I would say I worked at Keystone, other actors would say, "You have to be crazy to work at Keystone. That's a nut palace, a crazy factory."

Sennett was as crazy as John D. Rockefeller. He made a fortune with his nut palace. Unfortunately, he sold the studio and then lost all his money in the stock market. He ended up at the Motion Picture Country Home, and I used to go out there and visit him. He wouldn't talk much. He sat there with this faraway look in his eyes, like he was remembering, I don't know, maybe he was remembering the Keystone Kops or all the other things he'd done at the Crazy Factory. He used to curse out the directors and actors, always shouting and demanding more gags, always trying to squeeze more gags into picture. He knew what the world wanted. The world wanted to laugh.

Sennett died in 1960. I was one of the pallbearers. Only Keystone Kops were pallbearers. I know Sennett would have liked that. The Keystone Kops were his monument.

Sennett had made no provision in his will for the ownership of the Kops' name. So after his death I acquired the name from his estate. It didn't cost much, a little money for lawyers and the fee for the copyright. I never kept track of the amount . . . maybe it was a hundred or two hundred dollars. Now nobody can use the Keystone Kops name without my permission.

I'm the only original Keystone Kop that isn't retired. A few of the others are still alive. Eddie Sutherland lives in Palm Springs. Bill Campbell is at the Motion Picture Home. And Bill Williams is still around, though I haven't seen him in years.

I make a lot of personal appearances and bill myself as the Last of the Keystone Kops. I work parades, nightclubs, theaters, fairs and benefits.

The original Keystone Kops are as much a lovable historical curiosity today as Buffalo Bill was in the early 1900's, when he had his Wild West show. People just wanted to shake hands with him. People wanted to be able to tell their grandchildren, "I shook Buffalo Bill's hand." It's the same with me. When I appear in public, people shake my hand. They have their kids photographed with me. They ask for autographs. Men pump my arm off. Women hug and kiss me. But they aren't hugging and kissing me. They are hugging and kissing history. The Kops still have that impact. Even Charlie Chaplin, when he came back here a few years ago, remembered the Kops with great, great affection. He had two bungalows at the Beverly Hills Hotel, and he was seeing very few people. But when I called his secretary and said I was a Keystone Kop, she said, "Come on down. I'm sure Mr. Chaplin will see *you*." When I got to the hotel, there were dozens of reporters and photographers from all over the world trying to get to Chaplin. He wouldn't see any of them. But I was ushered in. I showed him stills of the old Keystone Kops, and tears welled in his eyes. He told me, "I'm sorry that I never played in even one scene as a Keystone Kop. You boys were funnier than I ever was."

I was raised a Catholic and taught to believe that if you lived a good life, you would go to heaven. You would go to heaven and rest in peace. You would sit on a cloud and play a harp. But *that* heaven sounds like a very tiresome place. In that sort of heaven I'd be eternally bored. My goodness, I would rather, well, not exactly go to hell, but I'd like to be somewhere more active than that.

I'll tell you one thing for sure. If Mack Sennett or some of the original Kops who are up there haven't already done it, the first thing I'm going to do if and when I make it to heaven is to start the Keystone Kops again. Never mind those harps. What a great time we'll have chasing each other around from cloud to cloud.

5

John Ford

ONE MORE HURRAH

ORSON WELLES WAS once asked to name the three best directors in the history of Hollywood. "I like the old masters," he said, "by which I mean John Ford, John Ford . . . and John Ford."

Frank Capra said of Ford: "Jack is half-tyrant, half-revolutionary; half-saint; half-Satan; half-possible, half-impossible; half-genius, half-Irish—but all director and all-American."

Born Sean Aloysius O'Feeny in 1895, he was the son of an Irish saloonkeeper. "There were thirteen children, far as I can count." In his long Hollywood career, Ford won an unmatched six Academy Awards—for The Informer *(1935),* The Grapes of Wrath *(1940),* How Green Was My Valley *(1941),* The Quiet Man *(1952) and two World War II documentaries,* The Battle of Midway *(1942) and* December 7th *(1943).*

In the bedroom on Copa de Ora Road in Bel Air, Ford, in green pajamas, looked like a pixyish pirate. The famous black patch over his left eye was in place (to protect it from daylight). He'd been home from the hospital for only three days following surgery for the cancer that would soon kill him. This was the last interview of his life.

Because of his visitor's last name, Ford assumed he was German. Herr Wagner, wie geht es Ihnen? *he rattled off in excellent German. Luckily, his visitor did speak German. After several other amenities and polite small talk in German, the conversation switched to English.*

"I should offer you a drink. This is gin and stout."

"No, thank you. I don't drink."

"Well, neither do I. But the doctor ordered this to put on weight. It tastes and smells horrible, but I have to drink two before dinner."

"It looks like root beer."

"Oh, God, now you've killed it for me."

"Sorry."

I've never written a book about my life because it's been too complicated. I have written articles. I have even written short stories. I will confess they are children's stories, but the idea of sitting down and writing a book is rather beyond me. My grandson contemplates doing it. I wouldn't have the patience, though on second thought if I told the truth it probably would be very exciting. But the truth about my life is nobody's damn business but my own. Perhaps I should amplify. I've done so many things, been so many places, that I'm afraid an autobiography would be too episodic. And there are certain things in my life that I would like to forget. I didn't murder anybody or rob anybody but I got mixed up in a couple of revolutions and that sort of thing. . . .

My father came to this country to fight. *You* can call it the Civil War, but my wife is from South Carolina, so we call it the War Between the States in this house. My father had two brothers and a brother-in-law. One was in the Confederate Army, and two were in the Union Army. When he arrived, the war was over. I asked him once, "Which side were you going to fight for?" And he answered, "Either side."

My wife's father was a Confederate, and both her grandfathers were Confederate colonels. Sherman burned her house down. She wasn't alive at the time, of course. But she was brought up on those stories. I had two uncles in the Union Army and one in the Confederate Army. In deference to my wife, I keep quiet about the ones in the Union Army. If you go down to the library, you will see a regimental flag that was made about the time of Appomattox. It came down to my wife. It's a very faint, very old Confederate flag. Ask my daughter Barbara to show it to you. She is a student of history, but it's all Louis XIV, XV and XVI. Right now she's on a Henry VIII kick.

As a kid I was fascinated by the nickelodeons of that period. Any time I got a nickel or a dime I would go to the movies.

How did I get to Hollywood? By train. Oh, you mean *why* did I come to Hollywood. I had a brother who was quite a considerable star in the film world, Francis Ford. I decided to follow him out here because I was at the University of Maine on an athletic scholarship and I didn't make it. I think I was there about eight or twelve days, I forget which. Incidentally, about an hour ago I received a letter from them asking if they could name their School of Dramatic Arts after me. I'm going to tell them to go ahead. It's a great honor.

I remember the last night on the train. I was coming tourist, and I had to go without dinner because I had no money in my pocket. So I arrived penniless, as the expression goes.

I started my career as a ditchdigger. In other words, I got a job on the labor gang at Universal when Carl Laemmle, Sr., was running the studio. Then my brother made me an assistant propman. I then became an assistant director.

How I became a director is a long story, but if you have the time, I'll tell it to you.

There was a big party one night for Carl Laemmle at the studio. There were seventy-five to one hundred guests, all very important, most of them from the East. They had never seen a studio before. The assistant directors, of which I was one, and the propmen acted as bartenders. We worked all night and managed to get an hour's sleep, or a half hour's sleep, under the bar. We still had to show up for work at eight thirty in the morning. But none of the directors showed up. I was on my set on the back lot, and my director hadn't shown up either. They were all sleeping it off.

Isadore Bernstein, the general manager of the studio, was

a very fine man, a very dear friend of mine. As a matter of fact, he was the best man at my wedding. He came riding up on his little pinto horse and said, "For God's sake, Jack, do something. Mr. Laemmle and all his guests are coming down here, and they want to see some action. I can't find any of our directors. You'll have to direct something. This is the only set with riders, extras and so forth."

I asked him what I should do.

He was frantic, and he said, "Do anything! Show them some action!"

I thought, What the hell can I do? By the time Laemmle and his guests showed up I had an idea. I told the cowboys—I think I had about twelve of them—to come riding through the street, whooping and yelling, and to shoot at the buildings, then to pull up at a hitching post, turn around and ride back again. They did it all great.

Mr. Bernstein came up and said, "That's fine. Do something else."

"What the hell more can I do?"

He said, "Mr. Laemmle's guests are all thrilled and fascinated. They have never seen horsemen, cowboys before."

I told him I'd try to think of something. I went up to the cowboys and said, "When I fire a shot, I want two of you fellows to fall." In those days they got two dollars for a fall. Now it would be about two hundred and fifty. So they came whooping down the street again, and I fired a shot. And all twelve of them fell off their horses. I thought that was a little incongruous, a little stupid, one shot felling twelve men.

Mr. Bernstein came riding up again, and I told him, "I didn't want that. I only wanted two or three to fall."

He said, "Oh, that's great. They don't know the difference. That's fine. Keep it in. Is it in the can?"

I said yes.

Then he said, "Now do something else."

I told him I had run out of ideas.

"Oh, you'll think of something. I'll go back and talk to Mr. Laemmle and his guests and keep them busy. You go ahead and think of something spectacular for the cowboys to do."

I was stumped. What could I do on that street? It was just a makeshift street, with wooden buildings and false fronts. Then I had a brilliant idea, or at least at that time I thought it was brilliant. In the natural course of the story we were shooting—I forget the name of the film now—the saloon was supposed to catch fire and burn down. It was a cheap street, and I thought why not burn the whole goddamn street down.

I had all the buildings set afire, and I told the cowboys that this time I wasn't going to pay them all for falling unless I specified it. So they rode down the street again, shooting and yelling while it burned.

Mr. Bernstein said, "Gosh, that was great."

I said, "You asked for something spectacular." Then I told him I was really out of ideas.

Mr. Bernstein said, "Well, I'll get Mr. Laemmle's guests away and we'll try to find another set whose director isn't drunk so we can show them something else."

"Thank God," I said.

I gave orders to put the fire out and stop the cameras. When Laemmle and his guests left, I was exhausted.

The aftermath of this was that it looked so good on the screen that they enlarged that little two-reel picture into a five-reeler. It turned out to be a very exciting picture. About four months later Harry Carey, who was an important silent star, needed a director for one of his Westerns.

Mr. Laemmle said, "Let Jack Ford direct it. He yells good."

So I became a director, and I was scared to death. But Harry was a very dear and very close friend and remained so until his death. Harry helped me immeasurably. Then I directed another picture from a story I had written, and I do remember the name of this one. It was called *The Sky Pilot*.

I don't know how many films I've made. Peter Bog-danovich, who did an article about me, the son of a bitch, I think he added them up and there were a hundred and thir-ty-two. I call Bogdanovich a son of a bitch because his article was inaccurate in many ways. He had me talking out of the side of my mouth in very bad vernacular. After all, I did ma-jor in English, and I'm from New England, and I am proud of my accent and very particular about my grammar. He had me practically speaking argot. He wrote the article with my permission, and he was going to expand it into a book. But he did not get my permission for that.

Frankly, I remember none of my silent pictures with any warmth. They were all hard work. My first silent hit, if I may use that expression, was *The Iron Horse*. It was a great epic of its time. I think it grossed seven million three hundred thou-sand some odd dollars. That was an astounding figure for those days.

I had no difficulty whatever making the transition from si-lents to talkies. By the way, neither did John Gilbert. John ac-tually had a very good, resonant voice. He'd been an actor on the stage, and he knew his business. He did a talkie, *Queen Christina*, with Greta Garbo. Then he stayed off the screen for a while and died. But that thing about him having a weak voice is untrue. He had a good voice.

That story about Victor McLaglen being drunk when he starred in *The Informer* is an ill-founded rumor. It is actually a libelous statement. There is an axiom in the picture busi-ness that nobody under the influence of alcohol can play a drunk. And I believe that. All the famous drunks that we have in the picture business and the people who play drunks are teetotalers when they work. You can't play a drunk while you are under the influence. Victor had to run too many gamuts of emotion, bravado, nervousness, fear, sometimes all in one scene, and go back to bravado again and resume the whole thing. He had too much to do to take a drink. He had some very tough lines. After all, he was not an Irishman, and he was playing an Irishman in this. He had to assume an Irish accent, which he did splendidly. It is untrue, absolutely untrue, that he was drunk while we were shooting.

I was surprised when *The Informer* won an Academy Award. You don't just pick up a story, do a picture of it, and say this is an Academy Award picture. I chose it because it was a very good, very sound and substantial story, a good character story.

Stagecoach was a typical Western, lots of emotion, lots of action, although at that time it was slightly out of line. I mean, the girl who played the lead was a prostitute. The boy, John Wayne, was an escaped convict. In those days you didn't do that sort of thing. But it had a happy ending, and that's probably why I liked it.

As it turned out, I received no criticism because I broke new ground with *Stagecoach*. But I got a lot of followers, copiers.

I had no special approach to *The Grapes of Wrath*. Darryl Zanuck called me in and just told me to go out and make it. He was the boss. And I was under contract to Fox at the time.

It had a good story, too. It was a story I was in sympathy with. I was born on a farm. We weren't rich or really comfortable or well-to-do. Because I was pinching poverty while I was growing up, I had complete sympathy with these people.

It was just another job to be done to the best of my ability. I didn't wave any magic wand or look into a crystal ball. I just went out and did it. It was a lot of fun because I was back working again with Henry Fonda, really one of my favorite actors, really my favorite actor. Why is he my favorite actor? That's a stupid question, isn't it? I will answer the best I can without being rude. Because he is a great and immensely talented performer.

I finished *Grapes of Wrath* under budget and turned it in.

With Darryl I didn't have to worry about how it would be cut because he was a great cutter. The night I finished I got on my boat and started to sail to Honolulu. Before I left, I had a meeting with Darryl, and I said, "I think it's a good picture. It's meaty and down-to-earth. But I think it needs a happier ending. I hate to see the picture end with Fonda walking across the dance hall and disappearing into the darkness. I think it should end with the mother."

He said, "That's a good idea. Let's think it over."

I sailed on the midnight tide. I was three days out and had a good forwarding breeze and I was at the wheel when a phone call came from Darryl.

"Listen to this," he said. "Listen to this scene I've written. I've looked at the picture twice since you left, and I agree with you that it needs a happier ending. It needs an ending of hope for the future. Listen to this carefully. Can you hear me?"

I told him we had a very good connection.

He read me the scene and asked if I wanted it rewritten.

I told him no, that it was great.

Then he said, "Who's going to direct it?"

I said, "Darryl, it's only a two-shot. I'd appreciate it if you went out and directed it yourself."

"Okay," he said, "I'd like to."

So he did it himself in one take. And they put it in as the end of the picture.

To use a familiar expression, Darryl is the last of the great tycoons. The last of the great operators, the last of the great executive producers. The man is really a genius. We've remained very close, very dear friends. As a matter of fact, I speak to Darryl more often than to many of my so-called friends out here. He calls from New York, and I haven't asked him what he's doing since he left Fox. I'm afraid to. It might break my heart.

I was at sea again when I heard that *The Grapes of Wrath* had won the Academy Award. Henry Fonda was with me, and he heard it on the radio. We were fishing. Henry is a great fisherman. As a matter of fact he's hooked on it. He's mad for fishing even though he never catches any fish.

I never went to an Academy Award ceremony. Why should I? I don't like those things.

If I do have a favorite picture, it goes back before *The Grapes of Wrath.* The picture I like to look at occasionally, even on television, is *Young Mr. Lincoln.* That I think is my favorite because it was a good picture and I liked Lincoln and I like a simple story.

I've always used a great deal of music in my pictures, although I don't have a good ear. I like country music, Western music. I go from the sublime to the ridiculous. I like classical music at times. I like your namesake, Herr Wagner.

I don't approve of some of the changes I've seen in Hollywood. I don't like pornography. I hate to go to a theater and look at pornography. I don't think it has any place on our screen. I think we made pictures better years ago than we are making them today.

The Quiet Man was made in my mother's and father's country, Connemara, Ireland. It was a lot of fun doing the picture. We got breaks on the weather, and when the weather wasn't particularly good, we still went out and took advantage of the bad weather. When the picture was shown in Ireland, all the critics were angry. They didn't like it. Every one of them came up with the same statement—that Mr. Ford had used a green filter on his camera to make the hills and the fields green. I really blew my top at them, and I had to laugh. I'd never heard of a green filter, and you can't use a filter on a Technicolor camera anyway. So I wrote each one of the critics a nice letter saying, If you would get out of that goddamn apartment and take a bus ride into the country, you would see that the hills of northern Ireland are green. But these stupid guys, these city dwellers living in Dublin, saying that I used a green filter—that really got my goat.

I have no idea why I have survived in this business. Luck, I guess. But I do believe in the American Dream. Definitely. Definitely. I think if you work hard enough, you will succeed.

To be quite blunt, I make pictures for money, to pay the rent. I do think that there is an art to the making of a motion picture. There are some great artists in the business. I am not one of them. I think Frank Capra is an artist. George Cukor is a great artist. So are George Stevens, George Sidney and William Wellman. No, Wellman isn't an artist. He's just a goddamn good director.

A director can either make a film or can break it. He must be conversant with the subject. He must hypnotize himself to be sympathetic toward the subject matter. Sometimes we are not. Being under contract you make pictures that you don't want to make, but you try to steel yourself, to get enthused over them. You get on the set, and you forget everything else. You say these actors are doing the best they can. They also have to make a living. As a director I must help them as much as I can. I think a director can help an actor or an actress, and he can also help the cameraman, the electricians and everybody else. I think he brings a great deal to a film.

I want to thank you very much. People call and make appointments and ask if they can drop by. They are all friends. But if they're supposed to be here at three, they usually show up at five fifteen—so your entire day is helter-skelter. And so now I am not receiving any visitors. None of them are punctual, but you were punctual.

Walter, you asked me why I didn't write my autobiography, and I told you that I've led sort of a peculiar life. And I also told you that I was never arrested for anything. I haven't committed arson or petty larceny or anything of that sort, but during World War Two, for example, I was in the OSS. I've had a checkered career. I've alternated my life between motion pictures and the Navy. I retired as an admiral of the Navy. I think you know that.

64

During my spare time I've been mixed up in a lot of things. I've made tours of colleges and universities and spoke, not very well, but in a colloquial manner and tried to get some humor in it, tried not to make my talk dry as dust.

Maybe I've given you the wrong idea—that I'm wanted for murder in Minnesota—but I've done so many things and been so many places. There are no warrants out for me. I am just telling you that everybody thinks of a motion-picture director living in Bel Air or Beverly Hills in a big house with a lot of servants and driving a Rolls-Royce. But we do have other things to do while we're waiting for our next picture. I like to get out and travel.

I remember coming back from a trip once during the war, and I talked before this audience, and I was telling them about some of the strange places I'd visited for the OSS.

This very supercilious and sarcastic man came up to me and said, "Tell me, Commander Ford, when was the last time you were in Tibet?"

I said, "Exactly ten days ago, sir." He looked so sort of flabbergasted. Then he said, "I don't believe it." And I replied, "Screw you. It happens to be true."

I hope I haven't been abrupt with you. I hope I haven't been rude. You see, people have been asking me these questions for more than fifty years, and no one's yet come up with an original question.

You say someone's called me the greatest poet of the Western saga. I am not a poet, and I don't know what a Western saga is. I would say that is horseshit. I'm just a hard-nosed, hardworking, run-of-the-mill director.

6
Gaylord Carter

SILENTS WERE NEVER SILENT

BEFORE PICTURES BEGAN to talk, his name and billing on a marquee—"Gaylord Carter at the Great Wurlitzer Organ"— was a formidable attraction. (Surprisingly, he is still a formidable attraction; the sound of the theater organ has not yet vanished from the musicscape of America.)

With a glissando down the keyboard, his instrument was sensitive enough to indicate a tear in Harold Lloyd's jacket; it was so power- ful that its thunderstop could cave in a theater!

The surviving star organist of the silent era is a youthful, natty, sixty-nine-year-old man in a brown Italian shirt and slacks. Five feet six, blue eyes punching holes in a sparkling, square-featured face, he lives in a charming beach house in the harbor town of San Pedro, a forty-minute freeway drive from Hollywood.

I grew up in Wichita, Kansas. My dad was a professor of music at Fairmont College. He didn't want me to be a musi- cian. "In this business," he said, "there's a lot of prestige but no money." Because he didn't believe I should be involved with music, that I should try another career, he never en- couraged me. I learned to play the organ and piano, I guess you could say, by absorption. I never had a formal lesson—if it's in you, it will come out.

I saw my first movie in Wichita's Palace Theater when I was twelve years old. The bill featured a kiddie cartoon and a movie called *Ondine*, which was a story about a girl swimmer who turned into a mermaid. I remember she was standing on a cliff wearing a gown that was blowing in the breeze. All of a sudden her gown disappeared. I thought, Oh, my goodness, she hasn't got any clothes on. It made quite an impression. I was hooked on movies from then on.

We moved to Los Angeles in 1922, and my dad opened a real estate office. One day a woman came in who had a theater for sale. "By the way," she mentioned in passing, "if you know a piano player, we sure could use one."

"My son plays the piano," Dad said. I'd turned into something of a musician by then, and Dad was reconciled to it.

The woman said she'd give me a try. I was sixteen years old and going to high school. Though I was an avid movie fan, I couldn't afford even the modest admission prices in those days. Naturally, I jumped at the chance and rode the streetcar for an hour and a half to the Sunshine Theater.

At that time every theater, down to the scruffiest neighborhood dump, had some type of musical accompaniment for the pictures. There were an amazing number of full orchestras at the major houses. In the pit of the Sunshine, they had a thing called a photo player. That was a piano keyboard with a couple of small sets of organ pipes, and you could pull a stop and these little flutes would tootle along with the piano. The photo player also had drums and thumps and foghorns and cowbells. You would pull these ropes, and the thing would clank and bang. When you had everything going at once, the sound was pow, boom! Like the roar of an engine in a boiler room.

I'd play the supper show, which began at seven P.M. My baptism under fire was accompanying Marion Davies in *When Knighthood Was in Flower*, not exactly one of the all-time greats.

The owner seemed to like what I was doing, so she bought an organ with all the traps, xylophones, bells, siren, tuba, flugelhorn, the whole bit.

I was earning a stupendous fifteen dollars a week, and my hero was Jessie Crawford, probably the most famous theater organist who ever lived. He played all the great theaters in Los Angeles and Chicago and finally went to the Paramount in New York, where he earned twenty-five hundred a week, more than most movie stars—then and now.

What the organ did was punctuate, underscore, bridge, follow the action musically in order to add a dimension to the picture that wouldn't be there otherwise. Believe me, without the organ accompaniment in silents most of the pictures would have been as dull as succotash.

People forget that silent pictures were never silent. Even when they were shooting these emotional scenes at the studio, say, John Barrymore making love to Mary Astor in *Don Juan*, there would be a violinist or a string quartet on the set. The music put the actors in the right mood. So in presenting organ music in the theater you were just amplifying what they were working to when the picture was being photographed.

There was a different movie every night at the Sunshine. I never saw the picture till I got there. They would have what they called thematic cue sheets which would give the title of the picture and the musical cues all the way through. That was supplied by the studio. Each picture had a cue sheet which was delivered to the theater with the print of the film. Sometimes the cue sheets didn't help. I could always tell when the projectionist had a heavy date—he'd speed up the tempo of the film, and I had to do some very fast improvising.

After playing at the Sunshine, this little neighborhood house, for about two years, I got a job at the Seville Theater in Inglewood. Now this was a little better house. I had a nice pipe organ, a little larger than the one I'd been playing.

I'd played for Arbuckle, Chaplin, Mary Pickford and Douglas Fairbanks pictures, but the biggest attraction was

Harold Lloyd. Instead of charging a flat rental fee, as was customary, he was on percentage. He knew his value, and he could make that arrangement because he owned his own studio and films. At the Seville, Lloyd would always have a representative from his office come to the theater to jot down the number of the first ticket sold and the last ticket sold, so in that way he had an accurate check.

The manager at the Seville would scream at Lloyd's price, but he knew if he didn't take the Lloyd picture, he wouldn't do any business. Still and all, the theater always made a profit on a Lloyd picture because Harold without question was the biggest business we would ever do there.

Harold and I got to be very, very dear friends. He was responsible for the biggest leap in my career. One day his representative apparently went to Lloyd and said something like, "There's a kid in that theater, and he's just kicking the heck out of the score. He's really making the picture do something." That particular picture, I recall, was *The Freshman*. Then Lloyd himself came down to see what I was doing. I guess he was satisfied. Years later, during one of my visits to his estate in Beverly Hills, he told me that he had mentioned me to the manager of the Million Dollar Theater in downtown Los Angeles. "There's a kid out in the sticks you ought to get in your theater."

Let me tell you about my first show at the Million Dollar. Here I was, really a kid from the sticks, flung into a *crème de la crème* atmosphere. The picture was *The Temptress*, with Greta Garbo and Antonio Moreno. The pit orchestra had thirty-five pieces. On the stage there was an atmospheric prologue with live performers *and* Paul Whiteman and his concert orchestra. That night Whiteman played George Gershwin's *Rhapsody in Blue*. It was the first time I'd heard it.

The Million Dollar was a presentation house, where many of the pictures would run six months. A presentation house was something. The program would open with me playing a solo. Then the pit orchestra would appear to play the overture, and I accompanied them. This was followed by a newsreel and a comedy short, which I played. After that came the atmospheric prologue preceding the picture. The orchestra would play the first four or five minutes of the picture, and I'd be at the console for the rest of it. Then an attraction like Paul Whiteman. All this for thirty-five cents if you got in before four o'clock in the afternoon. Incredible!

Our biggest premiere at the Million Dollar was the original *Ben Hur* in 1927, which played six months and could have played six years. In those days a premiere was as big an event as a Broadway opening. Outside there were klieg lights and limousines and crowds, a bubble of excitement, of enchantment. Everybody would dress for the occasion, the men in black ties and tails, the women in stunning gowns. The stars of *Ben Hur*, Ramon Navarro and Francis X. Bushman, were there for the first night. So was the director, Fred Niblo. And Mary Pickford and Douglas Fairbanks.

When the doors opened, I was playing. Before I went on, Frank Newman, the general manager, who was such a fine guy, came to me and said, "Gaylord, the people have to listen to you for a long time so just perfume the air with music."

In 1928 we had the premiere of *The Devil Dancer*, starring Gilda Gray. The picture was produced by Sam Goldwyn. Gilda Gray was a dancer from Poland whose real name was Marianna Michalska. She was credited with inventing the shimmy and was considered pretty hot stuff. She was appearing in the prologue, doing something called a fire dance. She finished her act with it.

That woman raised Cain with everybody. I remember the first thing that happened. When she saw her dressing room, she said, "Do you call this a dressing room! It's a pigpen! I'm not going to open in a place like this. Get it fixed up." So they put satin on the walls and made it look like a cushy boudoir. I never saw such a thing. I thought, Why are they fixing all this up for this tramp? She had a horrible reputation for promiscuity around town. She was a bum. Worse, she was an untalented bum. I can't imagine what Mr. Goldwyn, whose taste was usually impeccable, ever saw in her.

She'd watch her damn picture every night, sitting near me in a sloppy old dressing gown. She'd poke her finger into my ribs and say things like, "Why don't you wake up?," "You're playing too fast," "You're playing too slow," "You're spoiling the picture." Hell, I was killing myself, and here she was complaining constantly. Her picture, thank God, only lasted three weeks.

I was at the Million Dollar for three years, and then I went to the Paramount. It was a tremendously large theater, one of the largest ever built, seating about fifty-five hundred people. The pit orchestra was led by Raymond Page, who later became the musical director of the Radio City Music Hall in New York. It had an organ that cost a hundred thousand dollars. The Paramount is now a parking lot, and that magnificent organ is in a pizza joint in Burlingame, a little town near San Francisco.

When Hope Jones designed the theater organ, he called it a unit orchestra, which meant, of course, that you had a complete orchestra in one instrument. And it could do almost anything, create a sob or a din like you never heard in all your life. It had only one flaw.

Those great Wurlitzers had what was called a thunderstop. A thunderstop consisted of a huge pipe thirty-two feet long, maybe five feet square at the top with a big reed at the bottom. The vibration it gave off was so powerful you can only compare it to an earthquake.

A friend of mine was the organist when *The Ten Commandments* opened at the Egyptian in 1923. He used the thunderstop for the scene when Moses receives the tablets from God. The theater literally shook and rumbled. The sound almost cracked the pillars. Hundreds, maybe thou-

71

sands, of people might have been killed. Sid Grauman, who owned the theater, was so afraid of the thunderstop that he had it disconnected. In building the theater, the architect hadn't allowed for the thunderstop. I've never used it for obvious reasons; it was too dangerous.

While I was at the Paramount, the screen found its voice. The turnover from silents to sound was a wrenching experience for everyone in the industry—it just burst on us like a bomb. As soon as they could, the theaters let the orchestras go. And the organists fared little better. The Los Angeles *Times* ran a headline that read: SOUND PICTURES DRIVE ORGANISTS FROM THEATERS; MANAGERS REJOICE.

Pretty soon there were only two organists working in Los Angeles. Luckily, I was one of them. *The Jazz Singer* exploded in 1927, and there was a transition period which lasted until about 1933 for me. I played solos and specialty numbers and accompanied the newsreels, which were silent for a long time. And then I was looking for a job, too.

I went into radio and played for various programs. I did a show for a Los Angeles station from midnight till one A.M. called *The Phantom of the Opera*. I played spooky music, and it was quite popular. I got one fan letter that was addressed "Dear Fanny of the Opera." Then Amos and Andy moved out here from Chicago, and I was with them for seven years. I went into the Navy during World War II, and after that I alternated my time between jobs in radio and real estate investments.

About 1959 there was a revival of silent movies and a new interest in organ music. Suddenly I was in demand again, and I put together several shows, which I play in concerts all over the country. I've built up quite a circuit that I make once a year: San Diego, San Francisco, Portland, Seattle, Chicago, Kansas City, Denver, Phoenix, Dallas, Columbus, Akron and Cincinnati. In 1974 I was invited to Wichita and gave a show on the site of the old Palace Theater where I'd seen my first movie. There's a new theater there, the Century Two. I played organ accompaniment for two pictures, *Teddy at the Throttle*, which is about a dog that rescues Gloria Swanson from being tied to a railroad track, and *The Winning of Barbara Worth*, with Vilma Banky, Ronald Colman and Gary Cooper. That was Cooper's first picture, made in 1926.

I work with about twelve different movies. I've acquired prints of Buster Keaton's *The Navigator* and *The General*; Mary Pickford in *Rebecca of Sunnybrook Farm* and *My Best Girl*; Douglas Fairbanks' *The Mark of Zorro* and *The Thief of Baghdad*; *Ella Cinders* with Colleen Moore and a thing called *The Lost World* with Lewis Stone. Good silents are hard to come by. So many were destroyed or lost or buried somewhere in caves and forgotten.

Contrary to popular notion, silents aren't dead. Not for me and not for audiences. At some of my shows as many as three thousand people turn out at three dollars a head with a student rate of one dollar. My cut is twenty-five percent of the gross.

I'm astounded that half the audience is composed of young people. I did shows at the universities of Michigan and Cincinnati, which were enthusiastic sellouts. Many of these young people are taking film courses; some want to be filmmakers. Or they've read about silents or heard about them from their parents or grandparents. So they come out to see for themselves what silents are all about.

I'm not just saying this for the sake of nostalgia, but there was much about the silent days of moviegoing that was superior to what we have today. There was a certain feeling when you went into the big presentation houses that you don't get when you go to a movie theater today. For instance, you go to see *The Exorcist*. You wait around for a long time, you finally get in, you look at the movie, and then you go home. You don't get the feeling of grandeur you got when you used to go in and there was a great orchestra in the pit and a stage show.

The silents were good; they were good entertainment.

They stand on their own. The folks who come to my concerts say, "Gee, I forgot they were so good," "I didn't remember they were so funny," "I didn't know there were so many laughs."

Some of the pictures are dated, of course, especially the dramas and the melodramas. But a lot of the comedy routines, those gags are just as funny now as they were then. The material holds up.

Buster Keaton trying to open a can of ham with a meat cleaver is still one of the funniest things I've ever seen.

Safety Last with Harold Lloyd is the famous one where he climbed up the side of a building and hangs onto a clock. I've shown that to modern audiences who stand up and cheer after it's over.

Do you recall that sequence with Charlie Chaplin and Mack Swain in *The Gold Rush*? They're in a cabin that's teetering on the edge of a cliff. They roll down and then up. Then the cabin sways down and up again and again and again. They worked that gag so that you are absolutely on the edge of your seat. They finally manage to get out of the cabin at the last second as it goes over the cliff. That was an ingenious routine. Chaplin made it in 1924, and he never topped it. That picture he did in 1966, *A Countess from Hong Kong* with Brando and Sophia Loren, was just dreadful, probably the worst movie ever made. I don't know why Chaplin just didn't give up at his peak and enjoy his glory because nobody could touch many of the things he did.

If I had a magic wand or could play God, I wouldn't get rid of talkies and bring silents back. Talkies as well as silents have their place. I don't say that all talkies are better than all silents. I would say that silents had a tremendous amount of vitality. There was no dialogue to get in the way of the action. Now we've gone back to that to some extent, haven't we? Look at the chase scenes in *Bullitt* and *The French Connection* and *What's Up, Doc?* There are long sequences where there

74

isn't a word spoken. In *2001: A Space Odyssey,* the picture was silent for the first twenty minutes.

I do one show which is all for fun, for entertainment. It gets a wonderful reception. I start that particular show with a salute to Hollywood. I play "Hurray for Hollywood," "You Ought to Be in Pictures," the Laurel and Hardy theme, and the walking theme, *thump de dum, thump de dum,* that Gershwin wrote for *An American in Paris.* Then I play a series of love songs. There is one thing the theater organ does; it plays a love song real good. I salute four ladies of the screen. I play the love songs that are identified with them: "Dream Lover" for Jeanette MacDonald; "One Night of Love" for Grace Moore; "Love, Your Magic Spell Is Everywhere" for Gloria Swanson; then "Mary Is a Grand Old Name" for Mary Pickford. The show simply brings the house down. People adore it.

I could be out on the road every day of the year if I wanted. But fortunately my real estate investments have made me financially independent.

But I still enjoy doing the circuit four months a year. I still enjoy perfuming the air with music.

7
Claire Windsor

WAMPAS BABY

SHE WAS BORN Clara Viola Cronk in Cawker City, Kansas, in 1897. On and off the screen she was early Marilyn Monroe, the personification of the beautiful sexpot, an attractive, cloche-hatted, bob-haired star who made forty-five silents and sputtered out in seven talkies. Once she earned $3,500 a week, had a chauffeur, maid and a butler.

Those accouterments are gone from the pleasant stucco home on South Orange Street in Hollywood, where she has lived since 1927. "But lucky investments have made me quite comfortable."

In the midst of the following discussion the phone rang. "That was my date for tonight. We're going dancing," says the lively grandmother of two. She also has four great-grandchildren.

I was a wild kid. Maybe it was rebellion because I grew up in a very religious home. My father was a deacon and an elder in the Presbyterian church. My mother sang in the choir.

When I was sixteen, while I was still in high school, I married a college student, William Bowes. I'd only known him two days when he dared me to marry him. It wasn't only his dare, but I wanted my freedom so badly that I thought I should get married to have it.

The marriage lasted a year and a half. We had a son, Bill. I was divorced after I arrived in Hollywood in 1919 with my mother and baby.

76

We came to Hollywood to live with my older sister. I didn't even know pictures were made here. Even now, I can honestly say I wasn't very interested in movies or in being a star. Isn't that awful? It sounds ungrateful. But everything came so easy. . . .

The lady who managed the apartment building where we were living had a daughter who was an extra. She talked to me about doing extra work. The only reason I tried it was to earn money to support my son.

I went out to the Lasky studio, between Sunset and Hollywood boulevards, and the casting director, Mr. Godstadt, hired me right away at five dollars a day. I did a couple of walk-ons; once I played a bridesmaid, nothing important. But I found extra work and the movie atmosphere rollicking fun, which is why I stayed with it.

I'd played extra in two or three pictures directed by Allan Dwan. He called me one day and said, "I've just seen the rushes of *Luck of the Irish*, and you stand out like a sunset on a rainy day."

Allan Dwan gave me recognition. He noticed me and took me out of extra work. I became a bit player at fifteen dollars a day. I did several things for him, and I was perfectly content. Becoming a star was the last thing on my mind. It never occurred to me.

I was sitting at lunch in the commissary one afternoon when a woman came over and said, "I'm Lois Weber. If you have the courage, I'll have the patience. You're just what I need for a leading lady in my next picture." I was overwhelmed.

Lois Weber had been an actress for a time, and now she was very successful as a producer, director, writer and, I was to find out, a woman who knew how to publicize her stars, ethically or otherwise.

She was as good as her word. Sne starred me in a picture called *What Do Men Want?* It wasn't released for about a year,

I think because of the suggestive nature of the title. But there wasn't anything objectionable in the picture. It was a story in which I started out as a young girl who gets married. My husband and I have two children. Then there was something about a vampire, my husband fell into the clutches of a vampire, which was followed by all sorts of complications till the happy ending.

I was making three hundred and fifty dollars a week by now, and Lois had changed my name. "I can't see Clara Viola Cronk in lights," she said. She'd consulted a numerologist, whom I met years later at a party at Pickfair. The woman said, "I named you Claire because you were so fair and Windsor because you were so patrician."

While I was waiting for my picture to be released, I was invited to a big party at the Alexandria, which was *the* hotel then. I was introduced to Valentino, and we danced in the Palm Court. He danced me all over the floor, giving me that glance with his eyes that got everybody crazy afterward. He was just starting, he was about to make *The Four Horsemen of the Apocalypse*, the part that made him a superstar. He never took his eyes off me, and he asked me if I would have dinner with him some night and go dancing. I was thrilled to death because he was a wonderful dancer and so handsome.

He called for me a few nights later, and we took the streetcar and went back to the Alexandria, had dinner and danced for hours. Afterward he said, "Let's walk home." I thought that was odd, but then I figured maybe he'd spent all his money. Maybe the poor guy didn't have the fare for the streetcar.

Perhaps I shouldn't tell this about Rudy because he still has so many loyal fans who worship him. I didn't worship him. I was intrigued by his dancing and those glancing eyes.

When we were a few blocks from the hotel, Rudy said, "I live here. Let's stop off a minute and rest. I want to show you some of my pictures from Italy." I wasn't used to that "come up and see my etchings" routine, corny as it was even at that time. I was still a green punk kid from Kansas, and I didn't think it would be wrong to stop off and see his pictures.

His apartment was one dinky room. All it had in it was a couch with a lot of pillows, which must have been his bed. The minute the door closed he began chasing me around the room, tearing at my clothes. I pleaded with him, "Please, don't! Please take me home!" That went on for something like fifteen or twenty minutes. Finally, he was smart enough to see that he wasn't getting anyplace with me, so he did take me home. But he never asked me out again.

Several months later I was in a restaurant on Hollywood Boulevard, having lunch with my mother. My son was in a high chair between us, and all of a sudden I saw Billy laughing and giggling. I looked around, and two or three tables away there was Charlie Chaplin making funny faces at my baby. The man sitting with him came to my table and said, "Mr. Chaplin is giving a dinner party Thursday night, and he would like to know if you would attend. He'll send his car." I was delighted to think that this great comedian wanted to entertain me at dinner.

Chaplin sent Kono, his Japanese chauffeur, and I went to his home in Beverly Hills. There were a lot of other people there: Edna Purviance, who starred with Chaplin in many of his pictures, including *The Kid* and *Limelight;* Aileen Pringle, who was in *Jane Eyre* and *Nothing Sacred* with Carole Lombard and Freddie March. There was also a great opera diva who sang divinely, but I forget her name.

After dinner Chaplin fell asleep, and Kono drove me home. In the next few months I saw Charlie three or four times. While we were dating, *What Do Men Want?* was finally released, and Lois Weber decided not to take any chances. She said, "I want your name on every front page in the country." And it happened.

She cooked up a hoax, and I'm sorry to say that I went

along with it. It was a terrible thing to do. Lois hid me up in the mountains in an old cabin and then called the papers and said I'd disappeared. The headlines blazed: CLAIRE WINDSOR VANISHES; CHARLIE CHAPLIN OFFERS REWARD.

Lois had talked Chaplin into offering the reward, which was all part of the stunt. But she didn't tell Charlie it was a stunt. He believed I really had been murdered or kidnapped or raped or God knows what and that I might never be seen alive again.

I stayed in the cabin for three days. Then Lois sent an ambulance, and I was carried out, supposedly overcome by exhaustion, and checked into a hospital, which brought a great deal of additional publicity. None of the newspapers questioned the authenticity of my disapperance. As Lois suggested, I told them I'd been a victim of temporary amnesia and that I had somehow wandered up to that mountain cabin and that I had telephoned for help the minute I realized who I was.

When the thing died down, I went to see Charlie at Catalina. He met me at the boat. It was supposed to be a normal date, and Charlie was overjoyed when he saw me. He said he'd been ready to pay the reward. I felt guilty, and so I told him the whole story, that it was all a publicity hoax. Charlie was crushed and hurt, and that ended our short romance.

What Do Men Want? turned out to be a hit . . . and I was on my way. In 1921 I made five pictures and was named Wampas Baby of the Year. I didn't know exactly what it means; it sounded wild and crazy. But I was told it was important.*

*Wampas (Western Association of Motion Picture Advertisers) was actually a group of studio publicity men who gave an annual award of merit to the most promising leading woman. The "Wampas Baby Star" tag was worth reams of newspaper and magazine space. Each of the Wampas winners did well. Bessie Love received the accolade in 1922; Laura La Plante, 1923; Clara Bow, 1924; Mary Astor, 1925; Dolores Del Rio, 1926; Joan

One night early in 1922 Tony Moreno invited me to attend a dinner party at the Coconut Grove. Maurice and Hughes, a dance team, was the attraction and everybody was there, stars, studio executives, newspaper people. By that time I was pretty well known myself.

Tony invited another couple to our table. The girl was lovely and blond. I can't remember her name, either. The man was William Desmond Taylor, who was the leading director at the Lasky studio. We had a very enjoyable evening, just the four of us. Mr. Taylor was extremely good-looking. During dinner he told us that he had just returned from Europe and found that his valet-chauffeur, who had the right to sign checks in his name, was gone. Mr. Taylor said the man had stolen at least seventy-five thousand dollars from him. "If I ever find him, I'll kill him," Mr. Taylor said. He didn't mean that, I'm sure. People just say those things without meaning them.

Two nights after that William Desmond Taylor was murdered. The headlines were huge. The story said, "As soon as a certain star is found, the murder would be solved." My picture and those of Mary Miles Minter and Mabel Normand were on the front page.

The next day the stories were worse. They said that I had been with Mr. Taylor the night he was shot and found cold and stiff in his luxurious apartment. That was real bad. I was still very naïve. If it was now, I'd sue the newspapers for printing such lies. The stories also said that everyone connected with the case was going to be barred from the screen and that the district attorney had investigators out looking for me.

If police were looking for me, the only reason I couldn't be

Crawford, 1927; Lupe Velez, 1928; Jean Arthur, 1929; Loretta Young, 1930. The award was abandoned in 1931. Its last recipient was Joan Blondell.

found was that I'd been out of town for a week, shooting location scenes for *Fools First* with Richard Dix. I'd left town the morning after I'd met Mr. Taylor.

I called the district attorney in Los Angeles and said, "I understand you want to question me in regard to the death of Mr. William Desmond Taylor."

"No," he said. "I have no intention of questioning you. But do you know anything about Taylor that could help us?"

"There's nothing I can tell you except that he made a remark about killing his valet, who he said had stolen a lot of money from him. I only saw Mr. Taylor once, that night at the Coconut Grove in the presence of hundreds of other people."

"You never saw him alone?"

"Never! I only met him the one time that night."

The district atorney called me back a couple of days later and said I wouldn't be questioned anymore. He also said, "We know who killed Mr. Taylor." That's always stayed in my mind because no one was ever charged with the murder. To this day it's unsolved. Either the district attorney was lying or he didn't have enough evidence to prove his case in court.

A lot of people became suspects besides Mary, Mabel and me. Perhaps Mr. Taylor had met with his valet and they'd had a fight and the valet killed him. A lot people thought dope peddlers did it because Mr. Taylor was trying to keep Mabel from buying dope. She lived in the same court as Mr. Taylor and was supposed to be spending a fortune on dope. I knew Mabel quite well, and she didn't appear to me to be on dope. The only thing I ever saw her do was stuff something up her nose. She said she had a cold. I don't know if it was dope or not. I think cocaine is taken that way.

A nightgown was found in Mr. Taylor's apartment with the initials MMM. And that pointed to Mary. They also suspected Mary's mother. She was supposedly seen leaving Mr.

Taylor's apartment dressed in men's clothing and wearing high heels.

It's been more than fifty years since it happened, and my friends still ask me about it. If I had to guess who the killer was, I'd say it was Mary Miles Minter's mother. I heard on good authority she was having an affair with Mr. Taylor, too, and when Mr. Taylor seemed to prefer Mary, her mother shot him.

Mary Miles Minter never made another picture because of the scandal. Neither did Mabel Normand. I was lucky. I had an ironclad alibi, and I was never, after the first week or so, drawn into it as deeply as Mary and Mabel. I was very, very lucky in that I didn't know Mr. Taylor better than I did. He was a very attractive man. It would have been very easy to have known him better . . . if I'd had the chance.

I kept making picture after picture, and I was farmed out a lot. I did *Rich Men's Wives,* the best picture I ever made, at Metro. It was a wonderful part, a real tearjerker with me playing a wife cast out by my husband and my crying at the window begging to regain his love, which I finally did, of course, at the end. At the premiere everybody cried out loud. I did, too.

I went to Africa in 1923 to make *Son of the Sahara.* My leading man was Bert Lytell, who was a very big star. Well, the desert nights were long, and there wasn't much to do. Bert and I fell in love. It was a very romantic atmosphere for falling in love. We'd go out into the desert on camels to watch the sunset, and we'd listen to the Muslims calling prayers from their minarets.

One thing about Bert—he loved to swear. His favorite expression was "son of a bitch." After we finished shooting *Son of the Sahara,* I was interviewed by a newspaperman in Paris, where we'd stopped on our way back to Hollywood. When the reporter asked me the name of the picture Bert and I had made, I said, "Son of a bitch." It slipped out because that's what Bert called it and because that was what he was always saying. I could have died, I was so embarrassed. Even today when I mention the name of that picture, I have to be careful not to use that term.

Bert and I weren't married for a year. He told me he'd have to get in touch with his wife, from whom he was estranged. They'd promised each other they wouldn't get a divorce unless they found someone else they wanted to marry.

Bert came to an arrangement with his wife and got the divorce. We were married in Mexico City. It lasted two years. We never really got along. There were no camel rides and minarets in Hollywood. I've never remarried.

In 1925 I received the first of many invitations from Marion Davies and Mr. Hearst to visit San Simeon.

Marion was a great comic, and she loved to play charades. W.R.—which is what everyone called Mr. Hearst—would sit there and just laugh. He was so amused by Marion and the people that were invited to the castle from Hollywood.

I think Marion was very much in love with him. One night after dinner we went to a powder room with Bénédictines that a butler smuggled to us. W.R. didn't want Marion to drink.

Marion said that W.R., who was then in his sixties, was having trouble with his heart, that he'd had a heart attack and wasn't playing tennis anymore or riding horses.

I said, "Marion, if anything happens to W.R., would you marry?"

"No," she said. "My life would be finished."

Those are the words she used, and at the time I think she meant them.*

I said, "A lot of people wonder why W.R. never divorced his wife to marry you."

*Hearst died on August 14, 1951. Ten weeks later, on October 31, 1951, Miss Davies married Captain Horace Brown, who had a strong physical resemblance to Hearst.

"Why should he? He'd have to pay millions. Besides, my life with him is wonderful. I can entertain anybody in the world that I want. When they get an invitation they run up in a minute.* A lot of people think I've had two children by W.R. Claire, if I was the mother of his children, I would have them here with me. The two youngsters that are here at the ranch occasionally belong to one of my sisters. I don't have a thing in the world to hide."

W.R. and Marion usually would have forty-five for sit-down dinners. One weekend I came up on the train with Gloria Swanson. You had to be at dinner exactly on time. Although W.R. disapproved of drinking, cocktails were served in the reception room outside the dining room. W.R. never permitted drinking at the table. If anyone got drunk, they were not invited back. Errol Flynn committed the unpardonable sin of getting drunk, and he was banned.

Those were the golden years of my life. So many wonderful things happened to me. A lot of people wonder why I don't return to the screen. I never retired, you know; I just stopped paying my dues to the Screen Actors Guild.

I'm still stopped and asked for autographs, but I don't enjoy it anymore. I don't think I would enjoy making pictures again. I don't think I'd want all that again. I loved it when I had it. My life, you know, would make quite an exciting book. Would you like to write it? I've donated all my memorabilia to the University of Southern California. It came to twenty-six scrapbooks.

I made my final film in 1952. It had, I must say, an appropriate title, *The Last Act.*

---

*Not quite. Albert Einstein refused his invitation to San Simeon, but accepted one to Pickfair. Prominent non-Hollywoodites who visited San Simeon included Winston Churchill and George Bernard Shaw. "This is the way God would have built it, if He'd had the money," Shaw said of the castle.

To tell the truth, I knew I was finished when sound came in. The new stars were from the Broadway stage. They were coming out to take our place. I was never frightened of the motion-picture camera, but the microphone scared me to death. The talkies I did weren't very good.

In 1972 the Alexandria Hotel gave a party in my honor and invited two hundred old-time movie people. Allan Dwan was there. And Minta Durfee Arbuckle. And Edmund Burns, who costarred with me in *To Please One Woman.*

They showed home movies made at San Simeon—and they were all alive and zestful and youthful again, Marion, W. R., Mary and Buddy and Charlie.

The Alexandria named Suite 1219 in my honor. I took a few moments and slipped out to the Palm Court and saw myself dancing there with Valentino.

They gave me red roses, and I was dressed in one of my 1926 outfits—gold bows on my shoes and a gown of peach silk and lace.

I met a lovely young silken-haired girl. I'm not sure who she was except she said she was a friend of somebody and was trying to get into the movies. I told her, "Tomorrow is for you. Do good things with it. Bring back laughter. Movies today are too much like life, and life is too hard to keep being reminded of it."

A funny thing happened the other day. The phone rang and the voice sounded feminine and childish.

"Are you a little girl?" I asked.

"No, I'm a little boy, but my voice hasn't changed yet."

He said he'd like to come over and have me autograph a picture of myself.

"Dear child," I said, "how could you possibly know me?"

"I saw your star on Hollywood Boulevard."

That's the Walk of Fame, you know. There are sixteen hundred of us who have stars embedded in the sidewalk, all the people who made Hollywood great. My star is between Mae Busch and Vilma Banky.

8

George Jessel

THE JAZZ SINGER . . .
ALMOST

"AS YOU CAN see for yourself, you are interviewing me in a museum. There are six hundred pictures here, one hundred eighty plays, and maybe two hundred medals."

There is also a special Academy Award statuette saluting him as *"The Hero of the Foxholes"*—recognition of his numerous visits to entertain American troops in Vietnam.

Among the signed pictures: Anna Held, the French actress who died in 1918; vaudevillians Weber and Fields; George M. Cohan *("the greatest talent I ever met, greater than Jolson")*; Will Rogers; Wrong-Way Corrigan; the jazz age Mayor of New York Jimmy Walker; Norma Talmadge; Lana Turner and every President since Woodrow Wilson with the exception of Dwight Eisenhower.

He smokes forty cigars a day, flies 400,000 miles a year lecturing. *"I also work bar mitzvahs and funerals."* His fees range from nothing at benefits to $2,500 a night. *"I get that sometimes but not too often these days."*

The beachfront home in Santa Monica and the Beverly Hills mansion are memories. He lives in a modest brown ranch-style house in modest, smoggy Van Nuys, a Los Angeles suburb. Next door is a take-out restaurant that advertises *"home delivery of shrimps, ribs and chicken."*

He has come into his museum of a living room from the pool, wearing a beret and red trunks. Jessel is tan, well preserved, energetic, a bittersweet man who lost his chance to become a pivotal figure *in motion-picture history when Al Jolson replaced him in the 1927 pioneer sound film* The Jazz Singer.

My father was a playwright who failed in the theater. He went broke and didn't want me to have anything to do with the entertainment business, even though that's what I wanted to do from the outset. He died when I was nine, and soon after I was singing at the Imperial Theater in Harlem, where my mother was a ticket seller.

The theater advertised: "It's worth five cents to hear little George Jessel sing." "It still is," Darryl Zanuck cracked years later.

I formed a trio with Jack Wiener, who is now the sexton of the Israel synagogue in Hollywood, and Walter Winchell. Winchell and I went to public school together. He went about nine months, and I was there for six months. That's all the schooling I ever had.

Winchell and I were pals until he printed an item in his column connecting me with Isidore Fisch, who'd been accused of aiding Hauptmann in the kidnapping of the Lindbergh baby.* Winchell may have meant it to be funny, but it had a very bad reaction. I ran into him in the cellar of the Versailles nightclub, and I had him by the throat. They pulled me off while I shouted, "Let me finish this guy. I'll get the Congressional Medal of Honor."

Winchell and I got together in the last years of his life. Nobody else would speak to him. He'd lost most of his papers and influence, and he had mellowed considerably. You always mellow when you are failing.

After the Imperial, I went to work for Gus Edwards, who

---

*During his trial, Bruno Richard Hauptmann attempted to lay the entire blame for the kidnapping on Fisch, a friend of his who had conveniently died a year earlier. It didn't wash. Hauptmann was found guilty and electrocuted on April 3, 1936.

wrote songs like "School Days" that live to this day. Edwards had a vaudeville revue of kids, and I toured with him until I was sixteen. A lot of successful people came out of the Gus Edwards revue: Groucho Marx, the Duncan Sisters, Ray Bolger, Hildegard, ever so many.

When I left Edwards, I went out on my own as a single. I had my first big hit in 1919 in a play called *George Jessel's Troubles.* A critic said it was the best one-act musical comedy that Broadway ever had.

Several years later I went with Albert Lewis, who was my collaborator and producer. He found a short story in *Everybody's* magazine called "The Day of Atonement." We bought it and turned it into a three-act play. I changed the title to *The Jazz Singer.* It became a huge hit and ran for three years. Warner Brothers, which was a small outfit then, made an agreement with me to bring it to the screen. But they were paying me on the installment plan, and a lot of their checks bounced.

I took a few weeks off in 1926 and came to Los Angeles to discuss the deal with Harry Warner. I shared a suite at the Biltmore Hotel with Jolson, who was out here appearing in a play of his own.

Harry Warner and I quarreled about money. Warner Brothers hadn't been doing so good, and making a talking picture was a gimmick they hoped would rescue them. Harry Warner offered me twenty-five thousand in cash and seventy-five thousand in stock to do the picture. But he wouldn't even put the deal on paper. I asked for the hundred thousand in cash. Warner wouldn't do it because he and his brothers didn't have any money. Nobody said, "This first sound film is going to make history." Nobody said it because nobody, including me, was smart enough to anticipate what was going to happen.

One morning Jolson got up early and he said, "You go back to sleep, kid. I'm going out to play golf."

Instead, he went straight to the studio and signed the contract to do *The Jazz Singer*. He never mentioned it to me. I didn't even know that he'd been approached. I didn't know that he'd been signed for it until I read it in the paper.

When we talked about it, I said, "How did you get the picture?"

"I put up about a million dollars of my own money."

And that's how *The Jazz Singer* got made.

The picture grossed an amazing amount for those days, six, eight, ten million, something like that. Jolson made two or three million on it.

Sure, the picture changed the world, and Jolson is in the history books as the star of the first talkie. Sure, it could have been me. In one way I regret it and not in another. I did what I thought was the right thing to do at the time. Not only did I have very little faith in the Warner Brothers, but I didn't think *The Jazz Singer* would make a good talking picture. Jolson had only one line of dialogue, his famous theater speech, "You ain't heard nothin' yet!" Also a few songs.

I had no idea sound and the picture itself would become such a smash. I just wanted some more dough. A broker told me if I'd taken the seventy-five thousand in stock, it would have been worth about fifteen million twenty years later.

In 1929 I wrote a picture called *Lucky Boy* for Tiffany, a Poverty Row studio. It was a musical, but they changed the whole concept, the whole story and approach and turned it into a cheap, very corny thing. They were only interested in milking my name. George Jessel starring in *Lucky Boy*. Original story by George Jessel. Original dialogue by George Jessel. Original songs by George Jessel. Only Jerry Lewis has an ego like that. In his pictures the credits read: Carpets by Jerry Lewis, Doorknobs by Jerry Lewis. So I took my name off it. I still get royalties from the picture, though. They play it on television every Mother's Day. *Lucky Boy* is the film in which I sang my most famous song, "My Mother's Eyes."

90

I was producing and starring in the stage show at the Oriental Theater in Chicago in 1934. I did five shows a day, and I had several other acts on the bill. One was a singing group called the Gumm Sisters, a mother and three daughters. The act wasn't great, and since the show was running long, I decided to let them go. I told the manager, "Pay them off, but keep the youngest one. She's only twelve, but she sings like a woman carrying a torch for Valentino."

The family agreed to let her go on as a single, but every time I introduced her as Frances Gumm the audience would laugh. They expected some kid with a funny face in pigtails.

I told her mother, "I don't like your daughter's name."

"Call her anything you want," she said.

I had a Filipino valet, and one day before the matinee he told me, "Miss Judith Anderson is opening in a new play in New York. You ought to send her a telegram."

"Take this down," I said. " 'Dear Judith. May tonight add another rose to the garland of success that fits your great talent. Love, George Jessel.' "

When I went out on the stage, instead of introducing the girl as Frances Gumm, I ad-libbed, "Ladies and gentlemen . . . Judy Garland." Everything comes to me like that.

I produced more than twenty pictures at Fox, working with Zanuck. *The Dolly Sisters* was one of the best musical pictures ever made. *I Wonder Who's Kissing Her Now* was also a fine picture. So was *Wait Till the Sun Shines, Nellie.*

Brother, those pictures were entertainment. You still couldn't use the word "hell" or "damn" in a picture . . . except for Gable in *Gone with the Wind.* And there was a huge flap over that line of his, "Frankly, Scarlett, I don't give a damn."

Now on the stage we've had things like *Hair* and *Oh! Calcutta!* I went to see *I Am Curious Yellow, The Boys in the Band, Deep Throat* and *The Exorcist.* The first time I saw those pictures I was embarrassed. The third time I was even more embarrassed. But to be serious, Hollywood has gone to hell. It's like talking about Lincoln. He ain't here anymore, and neither is Hollywood.

I'd say the golden age of films lasted from the twenties to about 1952, when I left Fox. Everything was fine with Zanuck until business got lousy. Then he got real mixed up. With failure, everybody fights. Now movies have changed to the point where there aren't movies anymore. Only garbage. Now America sits home with the box. With few exceptions people don't go out. They don't even read the newspapers. They just get the news from Cronkite.

How different everything used to be. Norma Talmadge wouldn't have been caught dead in blue jeans. She was an elegant, elegant woman, who was once the most famous star in movies. I met her when she came to see me ten nights in a row while I was starring in *The Jazz Singer* in New York. Any woman who would do that I figured would be nice to have around the house. Our marriage lasted ten years. Thank God, I never had to pay alimony to Norma. I've never made a great deal of money, never, and most of what I've made I lost in the stock market, not to alimony.

Norma was the big love affair of my life, and it was a shame for both of us that it didn't last.

When I married Lois Andrews, she was the most beautiful girl in America—in one year her picture was on the cover of twenty-five magazines. She was only sixteen when we were married. That started all the jokes. Bob Hope said, "Jessel is a sentimentalist. When Truman made a speech about the draft, George cried like a baby. He thought they were taking girls from eighteen to twenty-five."

Lois and I weren't exactly compatible, and we'd been divorced for many years when she died. She was the mother of my daughter, and one of my biggest regrets is that I didn't do her eulogy. I was in Malta making a picture with Anthony Newley.

It's a strange thing. I'm here, I would say, nearly every night alone. But every young starlet who comes out here, the press agent tells her, "I know how to get your name in the paper. We'll say you were out with George Jessel."

I had lunch the other day with a wonderful lady , Greer Garson. Her husband, Buddy Fogelson, joined us. The next day one paper said that Jessel was necking in public with a redheaded starlet.

If I had it to do over again, I'd get a better education, study law and run for public office. Entertaining people is a great, great art. I think it's a gift of the gods, but many times it is very transient, insecure and lonely. At my age I find myself confronted with loneliness . . . and futility. For kids who are ambitious to get into motion pictures, unless they have some extraordinary talent, I would advise them that they have the same chance as they would selling Uneeda biscuits, women's corsets, white spats or razor straps. There are a thousand people for every job that's left in the movie business.

They say I'm the most patriotic entertainer in show business. Unlike Bob Hope, I never made a dime out of going to Vietnam. I didn't film *my* show and sell it for a fortune on NBC.

Now I have very little to do outside of a small public relations business that I own. One of my clients is the Republic of South Korea. I also do some writing, but what I enjoy most is public speaking.

During the regimes of FDR and Harry Truman I was called upon to toastmaster many dinners at the White House. It was Harry Truman who first called me the Toastmaster General of the United States.

My White House appearances stopped when General Eisenhower came in. I was no longer invited because the general listened a great deal to John Foster Dulles. Dulles didn't like me. He didn't like anybody who looks like me. He didn't like Jews, period. To my knowledge, Dulles did nothing for the sacred nation of Israel. He bought General Naguib, the one who came before Nasser, a large silver revolver as a token of the esteem of the American people. I don't remember chipping in for that one.

I made a speech in Washington, saying I believe Secretary of State Dulles wishes to change the content of the pledge of allegiance to our flag and have it end with liberty and justice for *oil!*

Harry Truman was the nicest, most thoughtful President I've known. I brought my daughter to the White House to meet him when she was eight years old. A month later she received a gift from Mr. Truman. He'd obviously had it made up especially for her. It was a pen and the engraving said: "Jerilyn Jessel swiped this from my desk. Harry S. Truman."

I've buried a lot of greats, Jolson, Fanny Brice, Jimmy Walker, Sophie Tucker. And I'm kidded about that, too, of course. Jack Benny said, "The nicest eulogy I ever heard Jessel deliver was about one of James Mason's cats. I never knew that cat had done so much for Israel."

I've sold more than seventy million dollars' worth of bonds for Israel, and they are naming a village outside Jerusalem in my honor.

I am trying to get buried in either Israel or Arlington National Cemetery, not soon, I hope.

I don't know who'll deliver my eulogy, but I've written the line for my tombstone:

"I tell you from the shades of darkness that it is all worthwhile."

I'd rather be remembered that way than as the guy who almost played *The Jazz Singer* on the screen.

9
Douglas Fairbanks, Jr.

RELUCTANT DRAGON

"DEAR MR. WAGNER: Thank you for your letter and for wanting to interview me for your book. I am working on a rigid schedule, eight performances a week [he was in town for a short run in the Samuel Taylor-Cornelia Otis Skinner play The Pleasure of His Company] *and various other business activities. . . . I will let you know next week when I will have some available time for a chat."*

The response wasn't a gentleman's way of saying no; it was a gentleman's way of saying yes. The appointment was duly arranged by phone without the roadblock of a secretary, agent, publicist, public relations representative or hangers-on. Though he can well afford the entourage, Fairbanks travels light. His luggage is style and courtesy.

Technically, it is Sir Douglas Fairbanks, Jr. *"I was knighted by King George the Sixth. People use the title sometimes in addressing me. There is nothing incorrect or illegal about it. I never use it myself. I'm also a captain in the Navy, but I don't go round introducing myself as Captain Fairbanks."*

He is, thank God, an aficionado of the Chateau Marmont, an unhurried hideaway off the Sunset Strip built in 1925. The lobby has a marble floor, a grand piano and weathered tapestries, a just right patina of fading elegance. The Chateau is preferred by the movie cognoscenti—Paul Newman, London, however—hence the English manners, accent and charm.

I have no idea when I first became aware that my father was a motion-picture star. I do recall that in 1915, when I was six years old, I visited him on the set and he had me photographed with a group of actors dressed as cowboys and Indians. I vaguely remember big sets behind me as I left the studio. Of course, I didn't realize the full significance of my father's position at that age. I was sort of more interested in the cowboys and Indians.

My mother, Beth Sully, divorced my father in 1918. [Shortly thereafter, Fairbanks, Sr., married Mary Pickford.] Mother's family, which had been quite well off, had fallen on what they called evil days. Even the divorce settlement from my father went down the drain rather quickly. So it became an economic necessity for me to go to work. When I was in my early teens, I became the sole support of, I believe, thirteen people: my mother, who was what journalists would describe as a society belle, my once-rich grandfather and grandmother, uncle, aunt, all that end of the family that had once been terribly well off. Bad business and stock-market investments destroyed the family fortune, which had been built through several generations.

I progressed, I suppose, rather rapidly and quite luckily. I was a prop job, an extra; then I graduated to small bits. Whenever I was on location, I tried to do as much production and camera work as the director would allow. At sixteen I landed a role in *Stella Dallas,* the silent version produced by Sam Goldwyn. The stars were Ronald Colman, Alice Joyce, Joan Bennett and Jean Hersholt. I was sort of the young juvenile. The film became quite a hit and gave me a little flurry that quickly petered out.

Early in the game I realized that I wasn't about to match my father's enormous success, a success he richly deserved. In the first place, he had a very great natural talent and a thorough knowledge of his job. It was sort of a family tradition that he became a lawyer and he went to Harvard Law for a while. He claimed he quit, but Harvard kicked him out, and I am more inclined to believe Harvard.

He'd always had a hankering for the theater. So he went to drama school in Denver and then in New York. Almost from the very beginning there was something about his personality that got over and projected itself along. He made his mark quickly because he had a vivid imagination, creative talent, enormous vitality and the intelligence to go along with it. And the timing was right. He happened along at a particular time when there was a demand or requirement for his particular kind of acting. He was known for his action roles, which was a natural thing for him. He was always very active and athletic.

He took grave exception to my becoming an actor. He objected for perfectly legitimate reasons. He wanted me to continue with school and lead a normal life. In fairness, I must say that my father wasn't aware of our financial situation, and my mother and the rest of her family were at pains not to tell him. He didn't understand the economic necessity behind my career, not for some years. When he did find out that we were down on our financial luck, he was very disturbed that he hadn't been told. It was, I suppose, a form of false pride on our part not to have told him.

My father and I were quite shy with one another. We were both embarrassed at display of any emotion or affection. Still, I was devoted to him. Because I was in films, I don't think he was devoted to me when I was young. However, he didn't let his anger show very much. Later, when he found out that I was in acting for the money, he was very much more understanding and much nicer about it. I don't mean to suggest he was ever not nice, but he became more tolerant and understanding.

Eventually, when my luck changed and I was able to stand on my own feet and achieve a certain modest success, he was the first one to tell everybody in the most generous terms I had done it on my own, without any help from him, and that any money I had earned was all my own doing and that any success that I had was done on my own.

It has never been possible since those days for any film stars to reach that degree of international popularity that he and Mary enjoyed. In their day, they were probably the best-known people in the world because of the wide distribution of silent films. Their silents had a global audience far greater than sound films because there was no language barrier and they could be seen for a price that everybody could afford. So when they traveled abroad, they received receptions that exceeded that of any head of state or any other film stars in the history of the business. It would be inconceivable today to achieve that kind of interest and success and adulation.

Mary and my father formed United Artists because they resented the amount that the big studios charged to distribute and advertise their pictures. They felt that as artists they should be able to control their own world, which they managed to do. They distributed their own pictures through United Artists at cost, and that eliminated the profit motive from that phase of the business.

Far from retiring reluctantly, contrary to rumor, my father was anxious to quit the moment sound came in. Not that he didn't like the sound films other people made, but he didn't see it as his medium, like an artist who has always worked in watercolors suddenly given oils. He said sound was fine, but it wasn't his thing. He saw films as a pictorial medium essentially. Everything else was icing on the cake as far as he was concerned. For him, films were the telling of stories by movement. The key ingredient was the visual effect of the whole drama. He felt that the intrusion of sound was not his form of storytelling.

He lost interest in picturemaking and would have preferred to quit with the onset of sound. But being a pro and one of the founders of United Artists, he kept on. He and

Mary and Chaplin had contractual commitments to each other to produce so many films a year. Chaplin would be a year and a half behind himself, so my father had to continue. I think he made about three talkies, but very reluctantly. He didn't have his heart in them. He didn't want to do them.

Too, when silent movies ended, the peak of his popularity also ended. But he had enough of a residual echo to get away with it. Whatever he did would have a certain market, but the medium was changing, and he didn't want to try to adjust himself to the new thing. Since silents were going out, he preferred to go out with them.

I saw my father for the last time a few hours before he died. We didn't expect his death. I knew that he was very ill. He'd been to my birthday party, and two days later he had his heart attack. He thought it was indigestion at first. He'd been warned periodically to slow down, but he didn't pay much attention to his doctors.

Nowadays he probably would have survived, what with the new drugs and new sorts of treatment. They might have been able to preserve him. But I don't think he would have wanted to be preserved, if it meant being bedridden. He enjoyed the business of living so intensely that when they told him that he would be an invalid for six months, that he would have to rest his heart and let it mend as if it were a broken leg, I think he lost the will to live. He told me on his deathbed that he would rather have died at the height of his vitality, in a plane crash or something, instead of ending up an old man dependent on other people. I think a lot of the fight went out of him after his attack, and he just gave in. He died at the relatively early age of fifty-six.

After *Stella Dallas*, no other part came along for me. Fortunately, I had a success on the stage in a play called *Young Woodley*, and that generated more things for me in films. I then had a series of reasonably good, solid but not spectacular jobs under contract as a leading man at the old First National, which became Warner Brothers. I did a number of films with Loretta Young, but the big break was *Dawn Patrol*, directed by Howard Hawks. That was such a big breakthrough that as a result of that film I was officially made a star and given a new contract with my name above the title, approval of story, cast, director, and so forth. Two or three years later I formed my own company and began to produce my own films, although I would loan myself out from time to time. I made a lot of flops and several hits. My entire film career has been sort of an up-and-down thing.

I married Joan Crawford, and if there were any conflicts because we both pursuing film careers, I was too young to notice it or worry about it much. Joan was extremely ambitious and hardworking, very quick to recognize and even imagine flaws in her work. She tried constantly to improve herself as an actress in every possible way. I think that was one of the outstanding characteristics about her that even superficial friends noticed.

Looking back, I suppose there were some career conflicts between us. There's bound to be that sort of thing, particularly with the kind of spotlight that was centered on everybody out here. It was a largely artificial spotlight ignited by the big studios, who would build things up out of all proportion or even invent interviews. I have looked recently at interviews I allegedly gave. I know perfectly well those interviews never took place. I didn't even know who the writers were, and they quoted me as saying things I never would have dreamed of saying. They were simply churned out by the publicity department of the studio.

So Joan and I couldn't have had a conventionally normal life with all the nonsense that was written about us, with two careers and two spotlights going. Our marriage lasted, I believe, about four years. A woman asked me the other day how old Joan was now. I said, "I really don't know, and if I did know, I wouldn't tell you." Somebody said there are no indiscreet questions, only indiscreet answers.*

I was up to Pickfair yesterday for a visit with Mary. She's always been absolutely wonderful to me, ever since I was a little boy. She would always intercede with my father. She was the one who saw to it that I would be invited up to the house from time to time for a swim or dinner whenever she felt I was sort of being left out of things. Mary took great care to see to it that I was never embittered or had any dark thoughts toward my father or her.

I've made more than seventy-five films, and there are a few that I enjoyed doing. *Dawn Patrol, Catherine the Great, Prisoner of Zenda* and *Gunga Din* come to mind. As for the rest, well, a job's a job, isn't it?

I remain active in my various businesses. So far as the screen and stage are concerned, I usually end up turning down scripts, unless one captivates me for some reason and the circumstances are right. I have done only two plays in the last twelve years, and those only on condition that I do not take on a long run. I haven't done a film in years. The last thing I remember was *Mister Drake's Duck*, a 1951 opus that, to put it kindly, was abominable.

I was at a party with a lot of film people the other evening and heard a great deal of grumbling and dissatisfaction about how Hollywood has changed, that the good old days were better. But I don't recall a time out here when people weren't talking about the good old days. There was always change and dissatisfaction. Silents into sound was quite a change, wasn't it? People in the industry complained that

*For the indiscreet record, Joan Crawford was born on March 23, 1904. Less discreet than Fairbanks, she has said of him, "He was trying to prove something, that he was as good a man as his father. I was his best audience, but that wasn't enough." They were divorced on grounds of incompatibility in 1933.

sound was going to ruin the business. People in Hollywood or anyplace else are generally afraid of change.

It is just that those good old days seem golden when you look back on them. I think it was Mark Twain who said, "These are the good old days, if we only knew what to do with them."

The most obvious change right now is that so few films are being made. The most interesting change I find is the lessened power of the studios. They got too big and too oppressive, and there was a sort of gradual rebellion against the machinations of some of the movie moguls. It was too bad that so many people had to suffer along with them.

I should add, on good authority, that the size of the fortunes supposedly amassed by many of the moguls and stars has been exaggerated, although there was a comparatively small group of people who did earn quite a lot, but very few have managed to retain it.

I never knew Hollywood as being particularly gay. There were only three good restaurants, really—Chasen's, Romanoff's and Perino's.

Parties were always in private homes from Beverly Hills to Pasadena. Santa Barbara was social headquarters for people from all over. And San Francisco was more socially conscious than Hollywood.

Here on the whole people tended to gather together in cliques. In San Francisco groups were more mixed up. At a dinner party there you'd find a scientist next to a politician. Here you'd have that only in certain households, usually when an international visitor was being entertained.

In retrospect, I don't know how spectacular or exciting the social life was here. The community was too, too small, and people worked too hard. They were up at six A.M. and home at eight P.M. There were a few who painted the town red. But they were in the minority.

These days I wag my tail through life, and though I'm not

one to harbor grudges, I must say that I never had much satisfaction out of Hollywood, except for the friendship and help I received from a few individuals.

Whatever I achieved was by sheer drive and necessity. Though I've had to work very hard most of my life, I'm quite lazy by nature. I would rather have been something else than a film star. For instance, I would have been the damnedest beach bum you ever knew.

10

Frances Goldwyn

ABOUT SAM—YOU MUST REMEMBER THIS

THE UNLIKELY PAIR met at a Manhattan dinner party in 1925.

She was Frances Howard, an aspiring actress, Catholic, the twenty-two-year-old, well-educated daughter of a wealthy Omaha, Nebraska, merchant.

At forty-one, Sam Goldwyn, the sparsely lettered scion of a Jewish ghetto in Warsaw, Poland, already had a career and then some behind him. In 1913 it had been his idea to flee from New York to the tag end of the continent. An infant filmmaker, he and his partners, ex-vaudevillian Jesse Lasky and an unsuccessful playwright named Cecil B. DeMille, headed west to avoid an infringement of patents suit filed by Thomas Edison. Goldwyn, using a lemon grove and a battered old barn as location sites, produced The Squaw Man, *the first full-length motion picture to be shot in Hollywood, then an ultraconservative, churchgoing community of four thousand. Besides the ideal climate, the local geography was ideal. The suit was settled years later, but Hollywood had been chosen by travelin' Sam in large part because it was less than two hours from the Mexican border, if Goldwyn and his cohorts had to skip to avoid Edison's process servers. Inadvertently, Sam Goldwyn had created Hollywood as the film mecca of the world, a not inconsequential monument for a man who once worked for three dollars a week in a glove factory, sleeping on the floor to save money.*

The eyes of Frances Howard Goldwyn are cerulean blue, the hair silver white, the features delicate, the words saucy and frank as she chain-smokes in the large den-projection room of the five-acre Colonial in Beverly Hills. The furniture is comfortable rather than ostentatious; many of the pieces have been there since the Goldwyns moved into the house in 1929.

The dinner party was in the apartment of the publisher Condé Nast. Gloria Swanson, looking her usual stunning self, was one of the guests. I was introduced to Sam, who was dapper and elegant in a pale-gray suit. He had a diamond-in-the-rough charm. He was there with an actress he'd just imported from Budapest. Her real name was Vilma Lonchit, which was changed to Vilma Banky for the screen. Do you remember Vilma Banky? Poor dear, she made a number of silent pictures, but that Hungarian accent killed her when sound came in.

Immediately after dinner, Sam asked if he could see me again. I said I'd be delighted.

The next evening he took me to a nightclub, the Golden Eagle.

"I don't believe in beating around the bush," he said. "You and I must be married."

"That's ridiculous," I told him. "I don't know you at all. We've only met once, and briefly. Besides, I'm going to Hollywood to be in the movies."

"Good. But first we should get married because if we're not married, anyone as young and beautiful as you running around Hollywood with me, well, people will take it for granted that you're my . . . girl."

What he meant was people would think I was his mistress. Sam was being discreet.

"You don't know what evil minds people in Hollywood have," he said, then proposed again.

"I'll have to think about it."

"You don't have to think about it because that is what you are going to do. You are going to marry me."

105

I'm afraid that scenario wouldn't make a very good picture. No suspense. Right off the bat, I thought to myself, Why not? There was an undeniable style to Sam, and I must have been in love with him because our marriage lasted forty-nine years, a very happy marriage I might add. Sam was ambitious, engaging and forthright. He told me his first marriage to Jesse Lasky's daughter had ended in divorce. "When a picture is over, it's over. The same with a marriage." He said he was lonesome and needed a wife, someone he could trust and confide in.

Ten days after I first set eyes on him, we were married quietly. There were no movie stars at our wedding, as there would be none at Sam's funeral. He had nothing against movie stars, except he felt that their presence destroyed the solemnity of an important occasion.

Our honeymoon was spent on the train. At that time it took five days to make the trip to California.

"There's one thing I want you to know," Sam told me as we were crossing the Arizona desert. "I've had two failures in business, and I haven't got any money. But with you at my side, I'll make some."

The company Sam had formed with Jesse Lasky and De-Mille had been compelled to merge with Adolph Zukor's Famous Players. Sam received nine hundred thousand dollars for his interest but lost it in several films that did not do well.

In 1917 he'd joined forces with Edgar and Arch Selwyn and formed Goldwyn Pictures Corporation. Incidentally, that's when he changed his name. Goldfish was the nearest to his Polish name that immigration officials could think of when he came to this country. Sam took his legal name from the "Gold" in Goldfish and the "wyn" in Selwyn.

In a couple of years, that company went bankrupt. Sam said, "I was on the brink of an abscess."* So Sam merged with

*Mrs. Goldwyn confirms that "about half" the famous Goldwynisms

106

Metro Pictures and Louis B. Mayer. Out of that, of course, grew Metro-Goldwyn-Mayer. But Sam and Louis quarreled terribly, and Sam left to go out on his own as an independent producer in 1924. His first few pictures were financed with money from the Du Pont family. After he had a series of hits, he financed all his films with his own money.

In the first few years after I arrived in Hollywood, Sam and I would sometimes meet Mr. and Mrs. Mayer at a social or industry occasion. Sam and Louis would ignore each other, but Louis would talk to me. Once he said, "Frances, Sam will have nothing to do with me. But I'd like to know you better. Why don't you come to the studio and have lunch with me?"

"Well, ring me up tomorrow. I'll ask my husband's permission."

Sam agreed to let me go because he wanted my opinion of Louis.

When I walked into the MGM dining room, everyone stared. They couldn't believe I was there because the whole town knew about the feud between my husband and Louis.

All during lunch Louis complained about Hollywood. Mostly, he complained that it was too chilly at night. I suggested he wear an overcoat. When I got home and told Sam

---

were actually uttered by her husband. The others were the product of his publicity department or Hollywood wags. From her own knowledge, she recalls the following as bona fide:

"I don't care if my pictures don't make a dime, so long as everyone comes to see them."

When a director complained that the script of a pending film was too caustic, Sam replied: "Never mind about the cost. If it's a good picture, we'll make it."

"I had a monumental idea this morning, but I didn't like it."

"In this business it's dog eat dog, and nobody's going to eat me."

At an Elsa Maxwell party when guests were asked to write their own epitaphs, Sam scribbled the immortal "Include me out."

that my conversation with Louis had been superficial and nonsensical and that Louis' prime worry was the weather, Sam laughed and shook his head. He said, "Now I realize more than ever the secret of becoming a success in this business. No partners!"

Sam never again had a partner, a banker or a board of directors to contend with, and it seemed to work out all right, didn't it? He made more than seventy films on his own, he made a great deal of money, and he won twenty-seven Oscars.

I never thought one way or another about Sam's success. I took it for granted. Even though I gave up my aspirations of becoming a movie star, I was a woman's libber a generation before that term became popular. I had an office next to Sam's at the studio and was, I suppose, his closest adviser as well as his wife.

Sam was a great admirer of talent, of quality, and he had taste.* I haven't the vaguest idea of how he acquired those attributes unless you buy the Freudian interpretation that he was compensating for his own lack of education and background.

He realized early that the story was the essence of any picture. You could load a picture with stars and production values, but that wasn't enough. "In the beginning," he always said, "is the script."

He employed every celebrated writer who'd work for him. Maurice Maeterlinck. Rupert Hughes. Mary Roberts Rinehart. Rex Beach. Ben Hecht. Charles MacArthur. Robert Nathan. Sinclair Lewis. Moss Hart. MacKinlay Kantor. By no means did they all become topflight screenwriters, but that wasn't Sam's fault, was it? He gave them the opportunity. Sinclair Lewis was particularly dreadful as a scenarist. But

---

*Through a haze of blue smoke, she laughs, adding, "He married me, didn't he?"

there were others who did well with Sam. Robert Sherwood—he was the only American playwright to win *four* Pulitzer prizes—wrote the screenplays for two of Sam's pictures, *The Best Years of Our Lives* and *The Bishop's Wife.* Dorothy Parker worked on *The Little Foxes.* Lillian Hellman did the script for *Dead End.*

Sam always went first cabin with writers. He wasn't bad as a star maker either. Will Rogers, Eddie Cantor, Ronald Colman, Gary Cooper, David Niven, Dana Andrews, Teresa Wright and Danny Kaye are a few of the stars who did their first or best work with Sam. Betty Grable, Paulette Goddard and Lucille Ball started as Goldwyn Girls.

Of all the fine pictures, *Stella Dallas, Arrowsmith, Dodsworth, Wuthering Heights, The Pride of the Yankees, Hans Christian Andersen,* his favorite and mine was *The Best Years of Our Lives.* It almost didn't get made.

During World War II I was reading a story in *Time* magazine about the plight of our returning veterans. There were photographs of our boys, some of them on stretchers, some on crutches, disembarking from a troopship. I was very moved, and I thought, What's going to happen to these boys when they get back to their hometowns? I told Sam he should make a picture treating the readjustment problems of veterans.

Sam didn't take to the idea for several months. Once he told me flat out he'd never do it. But I kept reminding him every few days. He finally saw the drama that was inherent in the situation of veterans returning home, and he became quite excited about the idea. He began working on it, and he made the picture. He called it "the finest picture my wife ever produced."

The industry, the world, has put Sam on a pedestal. He deserves that pedestal, but too few people know his human side.

From the moment he bought a story, he was a man obsessed. He would scream and holler, bellow and yell his way through the entire production. Everyone understood that was just Sam's way, and he rarely fired anyone. Many of his department heads and technicians were with him for thirty or thirty-five years. Their wives learned that during the making of a picture they wouldn't see much of their husbands. Sam demanded long hours and total involvement from everyone. There was so much to do, and one of Sam's greatest fears was that he wouldn't live long enough to do all he wished to do. If it had been possible, Sam would have made pictures for nothing. Money wasn't his primary motivation; he just loved the business. During the shooting of *Guys and Dolls,* his team was so deep into the day-to-day problems of the film that the publicity man only found out his wife was going to have a baby when, to his astonishment, he read the news in *Variety.* His wife said, "It was the only way I could inform my husband. When he got home late at night, he was too tired to listen to anything about our family. But I knew he read *Variety* religiously. It also gave me a great deal of pleasure to scoop my husband on a story."

Sam must have been born with a telephone in his hand. Thank God, he never put a phone in his car. But it irked him that he would be out of touch for even the fifteen-minute trip between the studio and our home. When we took occasional holidays at Palm Springs or Pebble Beach, he was apoplectic by the time he arrived. The first thing he'd do was phone the studio, phone New York, phone anywhere in the world he thought was necessary. One year his phone bill ran more than forty thousand dollars. God help the operator, during a transoceanic call, when the connection was bad. He'd vent his anger on the phone company in a stream of expletives that I wouldn't care to repeat. To him it was only logical that if Alexander Graham Bell had gone to all the trouble to invent the telephone, it should always work when he wanted it to work . . . which was most of the time.

Many times he'd buzz his secretary, Peggy Yeoman, on the intercom and ask her to get "what's-his-name" on the line. Peggy was expected to know exactly who Sam wanted to talk to.

Remembering names wasn't one of Sam's strong points. Once he asked Peggy to connect him with the wrong director. He wanted Billy Wilder, but asked for Willy Wyler. For some fifteen minutes Sam assumed he was talking with Wilder rather than Wyler. Then he chewed out poor Peggy for getting him the wrong director.

Despite his Goldwynisms and lapses of grammar, Sam would start the day by reading the New York *Times*, all the Los Angeles papers plus *Variety* and the *Hollywood Reporter*. Then, of course, there would be at least half a dozen phone calls. He once called Queen Elizabeth in London. He wanted to talk to her about doing a film concerning the British royal family. He couldn't understand when he failed to get her on the line. "After all," he pointed out, "I wasn't calling collect."

We'd drive to the office, and since Sam was a physical fitness and exercise fanatic, the chauffeur would drop us off several blocks from the studio. Rain or shine, every day we'd walk for half an hour, arriving at ten A.M. on the dot. Then the first thing Sam would do was clear his desk. He detested clutter. He'd hand letters and his other paperwork to Peggy or me or any bemused individual who happened to be in the office. A few minutes later he'd scream at Peggy to retrieve an important letter. "Why are *you* sabotaging my mail?" Peggy got so she'd check Sam's wastebasket every night to be certain he hadn't thrown out something that belonged in the files. It didn't help much. Goldwyn Studios probably had the worst filing system in Hollywood.

Sam loathed shopping, which he considered a waste of time. It would take a virtual act of Congress to get him to a tailor for a fitting, yet he was very fussy about his wardrobe. Fred Astaire would send him a couple of pair of sports shoes each Christmas, which Sam was especially grateful for because he wouldn't have to take the time out and go to a store to buy them.

One day Gary Cooper dropped in wearing a Windsor knot in his tie. That fascinated Sam. They spent an hour together, Coop trying to teach Sam how to tie a Windsor. But the intricacies of that knot remained a mystery to Sam all his life. Whenever he tried it himself, it looked like a piece of crumpled string.

Sam had no hobbies. To provide him with some diversion, I had a croquet court, complete with special grass and landscaping installed on the lawn. I also saw to it that all the proper equipment was there. Sam liked the game and organized the Goldwyn Croquet Club. The Sunday games became something of a Hollywood tradition. His membership list was a who's who of show business. Sam had three rules, which he chalked on a blackboard in the summerhouse alongside the court: Don't get excited, correctly remember balls you are dead on, and have patience with fellow members who are not as good as you are.

For years there was an annual tournament. A large silver engraved trophy went to the winner. It was one of Sam's great regrets that he never won the trophy.

Sam never carried anything in his pockets, not even the keys to the house or money.

He never entered the house through the front door, but walked in the delivery entrance near the kitchen. The reason for this was that he'd sent too many sets of keys to the cleaners with his suits or just lost them.

Shirley MacLaine was making a picture on the lot and asked Sam if she could see *Stella Dallas*. Sam ran the picture for her in a projection room. After the showing they decided to stop on the way home for an ice-cream soda. When it came time to pay the check, Sam had no money, and neither did Shirley. The waitress didn't recognize either of them, and she was quite nasty. In a loud voice she called them "a couple

ABOUT SAM—YOU MUST REMEMBER THIS

of deadbeats." Everyone in the place was looking at them. They were saved by the manager who came out to see what all the fuss was about. The manager knew Sam and apologized. Sam could pay the next time he dropped in. "If it's so easy not to pay," Sam said to Shirley, "let's have another soda." They did.

Those small eccentricities only proved how human he was. When it came to the business of making pictures, he was the thorough professional. If money could buy perfection, he spent the money.

He despised yes-men, and about the only reason he'd fire anyone was for agreeing with him all the time. He didn't want people to tell him anything unless they were sure of what they were talking about and could answer all his questions. It was better to admit ignorance of the subject under discussion than to fake it or tell a white lie to cover your lack of knowledge. If you did that, he always found out.

Sam not only had an innate ability to judge stories, but had an uncanny capacity for sizing up people. From the door of his office to his desk was a distance of twelve feet. By the time a stranger reached his desk he had him pegged. He was seldom wrong.

Life rolled along pleasantly enough. As Sam got older, he developed a fear of aging. He saw so many of his contemporaries pass on that he became touchy on the subject of age. When someone at the studio jokingly called him a senior citizen, he was depressed for days.

He had his stroke in 1969 and that caused him to retire, reluctantly.

He went into seclusion and emerged only once publicly when President Nixon came to the house to give him that medal. There were scores of people on the lawn, Secret Servicemen and I don't know who all.*

*Nixon awarded the nation's highest civilian honor, the Medal of Freedom, to Goldwyn on March 27, 1971. Although Goldwyn more than

113

We had a party for Sam on his eighty-ninth birthday. It was a fiasco. It was simply too upsetting and exhausting for Sam, and he was weeks getting over it. When he reached ninety, I kept mum. Fortunately, Sam forgot the birthday. There was no party. He still had the heart and blood pressure of a young man—but nothing else seemed to work. Except his appetite.

Shortly before his death Sam looked at Hollywood and didn't much care for how the industry had changed. He said that he always made films for the whole family. The censor never turned one of his pictures down because he was his own censor. He didn't have to undress his actresses to sell his pictures. He said he'd been more successful making clean films than those producers who were making dirty pictures.

At two o'clock in the morning on January 31, 1974, Sam died in his sleep, of old age. He was ninety-one.

My husband had been to enough Hollywood funerals and realized what circuses they could be.* Sam left specific instructions that his funeral was to be quiet and private. Only members of the family were present at Forest Lawn. The gates of the cemetery were closed and guarded while he was buried.

Sam went out in the same style with which he lived and made pictures. For him a quiet funeral was a matter of taste. A matter of dignity. A matter of respect. God, you might say, finally decided to include him in.

---

merited the award, its presentation was not without Presidential cynicism. Goldwyn had been ailing for two years, was eighty-seven years old, and not expected to live long. The medal was late in coming, as the same medal was late in being presented to John Ford by Nixon in March, 1973, when all Hollywood knew the director was dying of cancer.

*The most blatant was the memorial service for Columbia Studios president Harry Cohn in 1958. Two sound stages were set aside, and thousands of mourners viewed the casket. Goldwyn's final judgment of Cohn: "He never learned how to live." The harshest, now legendary, comment came from Red Skelton: "Well, it only proves what they always say—give the public something they want to see, and they'll come out for it."

11

Jimmy Fidler

THE MAN WHO INVENTED HOLLYWOOD
GOSSIP

*LANKY AND KINETIC, he lives in "Little Beverly Hills,"
the San Fernando Valley community of Toluca Lake bounded by
Warner Brothers and Universal studios. His rambling hacienda is
a ticket stub away from the homes of Bob Hope, Dorothy Lamour,
Ann Blyth and the Disney family.*

*Born in St. Louis, Missouri, in 1898, Fidler is presently married
to his sixth wife.*

My father was a traveling salesman for a snuff company.
They used horses and buggies in those days. He would drive
from town to town and come home and say, "I just saw the
most beautiful place in the world, and we're going to move
there." We generally did.

We lived in Memphis, Tennessee, for a couple of years
when I was young. I became a nickelodeon man. By the time
I was in my teens I was a solid movie buff. I especially enjoyed the comedians. Charlie Chaplin was going big by then.
So was Ben Turpin, a cross-eyed comic who played slapstick.
I liked a lot of the dramatic pictures, too, and to this day I
haven't gotten over the impact of silents.

It seemed natural for me to want to become an actor. I
thought I was a handsome dog, and that if I could get to Hollywood, I would make it as an actor.

I arrived out here when I was nineteen. I had an uncle

who was the editor of the Los Angeles *Herald-Express,* and he helped me get registered with Central Casting and two or three studio casting offices. I nearly starved to death. So I got out of it quickly. I discovered I didn't have the temperament to be an actor. Even if I were an actor today or had become a successful actor, I think I would have hated it because I don't like to be idle. I couldn't stand the thing of waiting at home for a call to do a picture.

My uncle got me a job with Sid Grauman at his big Million Dollar Theater, where Lawrence Tibbett, the great opera who made a couple of movies in the thirties, got his start. My job was to publicize the theater, that brand of the Grauman enterprises. I met a lot of people in the industry and was offered a job as a press agent at Paramount.

Those were the days of Wallace Reid and Valentino. Theda Bara was around, but not working much. The Vamp character she played had pretty well crested. Gloria Swanson and Pola Negri were there, too. So was Mary Miles Minter, who'd replaced Mary Pickford when Mary decided to go out on her own.

The queen of the lot, without question, was Gloria Swanson. The king, if there was one, was Wally Reid. Valentino came later. But Wally was too much of a playboy to be taken seriously as a king. The cloak didn't fit.

I knew about Wally's drug problem. His wife, Dorothy Davenport, and I both wanted to break the news to the public that he was on dope. The idea was that releasing the story of Wally's addiction would bring sympathy to him. Here was a man fighting for his life, and we wanted America to wish him well, write him letters of encouragement and hope. But the studio wouldn't go for it. If you went against the will of the studio, it meant your job. So I couldn't do anything. I still think a campaign like that might have saved his life.

The studio sent him off to a cabin in the hills with Ted Hayes, who used to be Jack Dempsey's trainer. Wally was under studio and doctor's orders to break his habit. But the

mistake they made was to try and have him break it overnight. He couldn't do it.

As I said, Wally was a playboy. He liked good times. He
was a nice guy. He couldn't say no to an invitation, to do anything. He played scores of benefits, many for the American
Legion. He was on the go so many hours that he broke his
health down, and in order to keep going and do his job well
in pictures, he went the Judy Garland routine, pills to keep
him up and then on to stronger stuff. He was only thirty-
three years old when he died.

There was also trouble with Valentino. When he went to
New York in 1926, it was to sue the studio. He wanted to
break his contract. Among the arguments he used as a weapon was the supposed fact that he'd had poor publicity. I was
the guy he blamed. Valentino wasn't really a bad person. He
sent me a confidential wire apologizing for his statement in
the press that he'd had rotten publicity. He said he hoped I
understood that this was a legal thing and he was using every
argument he could find. I could have taken the wire to
Adolph Zukor and wrecked that part of his case. When I first
got the wire, I was indignant because he'd had a hell of a lot
of publicity. I'd done great campaigns on him, although I
think he would have gotten publicity anyway. Certain people
are naturals for a big play in the press. The upshot was that
the suit was settled. But before Valentino could get back to
Hollywood, he died in New York. Peritonitis set in after an
operation. He was younger than Wally Reid, thirty-one.

My job at Paramount was a good one, but I was ambitious.
I wanted to do bigger things. So I quit and went out on my
own as a free-lance press agent. One of my clients was a man
named Walter Hiers. He was a jolly fat guy, very nice, who'd
been brought in to take Arbuckle's place. But he had nothing—he didn't click at all. Nobody remembers his name.

When the crash came in 1929, I lost all the money I'd
saved. I was shot down by the market, I dropped a bundle in
a building and loan outfit in which I'd invested, and my di-

vorce cost me a lot of money. The three things brought on what was right next to a nervous breakdown. I was in pretty bad shape, and my doctor said I should spend three months at the beach and not think about work or Hollywood or anything else.

I couldn't really afford to spend the three months at the beach, but I went anyway and holed up in an old shack. The thought of doing nothing was repugnant. I had to think about something. So I thought about my life, and my stomach just turned against press agentry. Being a press agent is not a pleasant job. A press agent is a hound dog, the last one to be paid, the first one to be blamed. I had people who owed me for three, four, five months, some of the biggest stars in town. I'd have to go in and beg for my fees. It was vile, and how I hated it.

I got of that business and started writing for fan magazines, and I became West Coast editor of the old *Screenland* magazine.

David Sarnoff, who then owned RKO as well as the Blue Network, the predecessor of NBC, decided that to publicize his stars, he would put them on radio. The show was to be called *Hollywood on the Air*. The actress who was picked for the first show was Dorothy Jordan, a lovely girl but not a big star. She was chosen because her husband was one of the head men at the studio.

Dorothy was a friend of mine, and she called and asked me if I would like to do the interviewing on the show. So I became the first guy on radio to trade gossip with a star. This was years before Louella Parsons and Hedda Hopper.

Dorothy and I did what I'm sure was the most horrible interview that was ever on the air. It was stilted. We stumbled along through the thing, both of us scared to death. It was really bad, but what happened was that in two or three days letters began pouring in. Dorothy got between twenty-five hundred and three thousand pieces of mail, and I got about four hundred. As I say, the interview was so awful it was surprising that anybody would listen to it much less write in. But they did—and they wanted more.

I realized that if a bad interview could bring me four hundred letters, good interviews with bigger stars, well done, with time taken, could become a big thing and make whoever was doing the show a big man in radio. He could become somebody.

I did *Hollywood on the Air* for about a year. I did it free. When it got so that I was averaging three thousand letters a week, they began paying me fifteen dollars a week. But that was for stamps to answer the letters, and the fifteen dollars didn't begin to pay for the postage.

I had everybody on that show, Jean Harlow, Bing Crosby, all the major stars. I had Garbo. I was the only man ever to interview Garbo on radio. Many of the letters asked why I didn't give news about Hollywood instead of just interviewing stars. So that's what I started doing. Hollywood gossip was born on that show. This was 1933, and the country was really movie-mad then, more so by far than it is today.

I wanted to make more money and put on a show called *Jimmy Fidler in Hollywood.* But nobody would buy it; I couldn't find a sponsor. Then a young guy by the name of Jack Warwick came out. His father was with a large advertising agency in New York, and they had a lot of big accounts. Jack was out here for endorsements and product tie-ups with stars.

He was a young, unmarried guy, and he wanted to meet attractive girls who were in the movies. I had a pretty good book, and I saw to it that he got his fill of dates. He had as many beautiful actresses as he could handle.

Jack and I were having breakfast one morning, and I told him, "I've been trying to sell this gossip show, and I think you should buy it. Here you are a college man, well educated, a sophisticated man in advertising, and look how much interest you have in these actresses. If you're that interested, what about all these shopgirls throughout America? Don't you think they'd be interested, too?"

That hit him, and he went back to New York and sold my show to the people who made Tangee lipstick. I went on the air with a fifteen-minute show and a twenty-week contract. The response was phenomenal, not because of me—I've never thought I had a particularly good radio voice. I think anybody who might have been doing gossip at that time would have had the same success.

I cut out the interviews and just gave them Hollywood. I'd start with an open letter to a star or one of the moguls, do an editorial, and then do my reports and gossip about the industry. I also did the bell reviews.

Tangee, which was a small company, was selling lipstick like mad. Sales were jumping. They renewed the show for another thirty-nine weeks. On the strength of the renewal and the prospect of having a job for a time I got married again. That gave the agency an idea. They wrote a commercial which said, "Our Jimmy is getting married, but instead of giving Jimmy a present, we're going to give it to his listeners." Tangee put together what they called a "miracle cosmetic kit." It was a darn good bargain. It only cost the listener ten cents to get it, and it cost the company about twelve cents to put it out. It was a kit with lipstick, eyebrow stuff, rouge and powder.

That giveaway gimmick cost me my job because so many women wrote in that Tangee didn't have the money to put out all these kits.

Variety ran a banner headline: FIDLER DRAWS 255,000 REPLIES. An agent at the William Morris office read the story and called me. I signed with them, and they got me sponsored by Luden's cough drops. Tangee had been paying me five hundred a week, but when I went with Luden's the contract was for fifteen hundred a week. That lasted for thirty-nine weeks.

The show was sold next to Procter and Gamble, and that was like working for the Lord. They were the big men. I sold their Drene shampoo, and soon I had letters from the man who ran the Drene operation, saying sales were the highest in their history.

I stayed with P and G for seven years. My salary went up every year. I also started writing my syndicated newspaper column, and I was earning about five thousand a week.

The head men of P and G were fine gentlemen, but they were of the old school. There were kicks coming in from the studio bosses and from the studio publicity men about me because I was pretty sassy and because I'd knock a lot of pictures. If I didn't think a picture was worth three or four bells, I'd give it just one bell. If a studio had spent three or four million on a picture and it got only one bell from me, all hell would break loose. In all the time I was on the air I had only one picture which I awarded no bells. It was called *Something of Mystery*. I said the only mystery about it was why they ever made it. Occasionally, there would be a five-bell picture like *Gone with the Wind*, but that was rare.

P and G canceled me because of the pressure. They didn't want controversy. I was off the air for a short spell. The Morris office was having difficulty selling me to another sponsor because the word was around that I was a troublemaker. But then they sold my show to the company that made Arrid, the underarm deodorant.

Compared to gossip these days, my stuff was tame through the thirties and forties. The big stories were which *married* female stars were expecting babies. Today it's been reversed. The big "baby" stories concern actresses who have children but aren't married. Another big story in those days concerned who was getting married. Now it's who is living with whom. Actually it didn't much matter what I said—the only important thing was to get the item first.

One of my biggest scoops was Errol Flynn's marriage in Mexico City to Nora Eddington. I had the story four days before I was to go on the air, and you can imagine me sitting on pins and needles expecting someone else to break it any minute. Flynn then was the biggest male star in the business; he was a hero and at the same time a playboy of the first water. He was just box office on anything. My luck held, and I broke the story first. Flynn called me a liar, said he wasn't married, but two weeks later he admitted it.

Louella Parsons was on the air by now with a show called *Hollywood Hotel*. She interviewed stars, and sometimes she'd do a little bit of gossip. The singing star of her program was Frances Langford, a lovely person. Frances was engaged to an actor, so called. He wasn't a good actor but a nice guy named Jon Hall, who played with Dorothy Lamour in all those island pictures.

I got a tip that Frances and Hall were going to Kingman, Arizona, to be married secretly. To confirm it, I called the general manager of the radio station in Kingman. I said, "I want to drop a hundred in your pocket if you can get the facts for me, find out if Frances Langford and Jon Hall are married."

Well, he got back to me on the phone and confirmed it. He said they had been married in Kingman. He gave me the facts. But I didn't have their marriage certificate in front of me, and I felt a little trapped. I had good evidence of their marriage, but I wasn't one hundred percent sure. They couldn't hurt me in a suit, but it would hurt me to say that they were married if they weren't.

This was on a Sunday, about ten minutes before my show was going on the air.

I called Frances at home and said, "I'm phoning you to confirm your marriage."

She said, "Jimmy, Louella had the whole thing on the front page of the *Examiner* this morning. We're going to be married on Christmas Eve."

This was November, and I'd read Louella's story, which

had been played big. They'd given her the whole damn front page of the amusement section.

"What I'm talking about," I told Frances, "is your marriage in Kingman, Arizona, last Thursday night."

She denied it. "Where did you get such a wild thing?"

"Frances, I've known you a long time, and I like you. Louella listens to my show. If she hears on *my* show that her own singer got married and didn't give it to her first, you write demise to your career so far as *Hollywood Hotel* is concerned, 'cause she'll have you fired in five minutes. She probably has enough influence to have you kicked out of Hollywood. I know the story is true, and I'm going on the air with it. I'm only calling you so you can call Lolly and tell her before she hears it from me."

I made it appear that I was one hundred percent sure, like I was a nice guy doing her a favor. I wasn't a nice guy at all. I was a reporter, and I had a story I wanted to use.

Frances sighed and said yes, she and Hall had been married in Arizona.

I had my scoop. I don't know how Frances ever explained it to Louella, but they patched things up between them okay. That particular beat gave me special satisfaction because I had the inside on a story involving one of Louella's own people and because Louella was a competitor.

I was on the air continuously until 1951, when television came in. Then everybody went off. TV cut through like a scythe. It cut everything, all the radio programs; even Jack Benny was out. An agency man came to me and said, "Jimmy, radio is dead. Long live TV. We're not renewing your contract."

I'd been on over five hundred stations, and I had huge ratings, thirteen to fifteen from Hooper. I was getting three thousand to four thousand letters a week. And here they cut me off even though the sales of Arrid had netted the biggest profit the company ever had. The product sold because I had a women's audience. They believed my gossip, and they bought what I sold.

The thing that radio and television have lost today is sponsor identification. I've been trying to tell advertising men to revise their thinking, to bring back sponsor identification. People would go into the stores and say, "I want that deodorant that Jimmy Fidler sells. I want that lotion that Winchell sells. I want that soap that Louella sells, the toothpaste Bob Hope is always talking about." *That* was identification, and that translated into sales. They might not remember the name of Arrid, but they would remember Jimmy Fiddler and ask for the product I was selling.

There isn't any of that now. If you went to a guy on the street, I bet you couldn't take one hundred products that are advertised on television and find five, if that many, that could be identified through a star's association with the product.

Anyway, the ad agency said they'd like to hold onto me under a one-hundred-and-fifty-dollar a week retainer. The idea was to put me on television, but they were unable to buy network time because in that period everything on television was coming from the East Coast.

After a year of trying to live on one hundred and fifty dollars a week and digging into my savings, I forgot about television. I decided to go in myself and sell my show to radio. I had to make a move—this house alone was costing me three hundred fifty a week.

Now I'm syndicated on about two hundred and ninety stations. Not for fifteen minutes. They use me in one-minute flashes that they run into their news—"Let's go to Jimmy Fidler in Hollywood." Sometimes they run two or three flashes together.

You hear a lot about the rivalry between the people who write and broadcast gossip. I never had that problem. I was always quite friendly with my competitors. Louella understood I was just being a good newsman when I beat her out on the Frances Langford-Jon Hall story. That's probably why she never held it against Frances.

I was on the air before Winchell with Hollywood gossip. Walter never devoted his program solely to movie gossip. He'd treat news from the entire world with occasional items about Hollywood.

Walter didn't like Parsons or Hopper, but we were good friends, so much so that when I was in the midst of a divorce from one of my wives, he called me and said, "Jimmy, I just got a wire from your wife, and it's a horrible thing. It's a great news story, but it's venomous." He read it to me, and it *was* terrible. She was a very vicious woman. Winchell said, "I'm not going to use it."

"Walter," I said, "you're a newspaperman. Use it."

"I can't do it."

Winchell went on the air and said, "The Jimmy Fidlers are getting a divorce." And that was it. I can imagine my ex-wife's chagrin when she listened. She was out to nail me, to get revenge for whatever her reasons were. But it didn't work.

Professionally, I've never been malicious, but I've never been a softy either. My family always came first. I'm a religious man, and that comes second. But right close to and next to my family and God is my livelihood and business, my success. So I've never cared if somebody didn't like me. Errol Flynn and George Jessel and a lot of other people didn't like me because I trespassed on their private lives or said things they didn't care for or wrote stories they didn't want written. So long as I was being paid five thousand a week, I was going to tell what I knew if it didn't irreparably hurt anyone.

I've never used stories that I thought would really hurt somebody. I don't mean hurt their feelings. If somebody was getting a divorce and nobody knew about it but myself, I didn't hide that for fear that I would hurt the feelings of the people involved.

There were times when I killed stories that would have hurt. I recall one instance of a female star who could have been enmeshed in a very bad scandal. She was a hell of a big star and was involved with a male star, not as big as she was, but big. The male star was married and had two children. Overtly, he was happy. I had the story cold that these two stars had been going every week for several months to a hideaway cabin, spending one, two, or three days at a time together there. I could have used it, but it would have broken up a home and ruined several lives. I've never told the story, and I never will. The people involved are still alive, and if I told it even today, it would rankle and hurt. It would be a crucifying story.

The big difference I see between Hollywood past and present can be summed up in one word: glamor. There was glamor attached to silent pictures, particularly. The minute the stars became talkers and started opening their mouths, glamor went out the window. There were no longer shadows up there to be imagined the way the audience wanted to imagine them. The stars became human beings, talking just like the people next door talked. You can't put your finger on one star today who comes close to approaching the glamor of Valentino, Pola Negri or Swanson. As I say, they were shadows. Glamor—it's gone.

There's no question that there will always be a huge public appetite for gossip. There's still an insatiable desire on the part of the public to know about the private lives of Hollywood people.

I don't question for one minute that if I were to say to you, "Guess what I've just heard about Sinatra or Raquel Welch," that you'd be on the edge of your chair, saying, "What is it?" That is just instinct. It's human nature to want to hear the inside, the gossipy thing about somebody you admire or know.

It is equally human instinct to pass on gossip. Much of my information over the years has come from some of the big-

gest stars and many of the most important people in the industry. Somebody would call and say, "Jimmy, did you hear
about so and so doing such and such?" I'd get a story that
way, and my informant was delighted to hear the story he
fed me on the air. Gossip is as much human instinct as
breathing.

There was gossip about Mark Antony and Cleopatra. And
hell, there must have been gossip in the Garden of Eden
about Adam and Eve.

12

Richard Arlen

PORTRAIT OF A HERO

*THE VETERAN OF more than 250 films is slightly out of
breath as he lumbers up the hill of his acreage in Sherman Oaks, a
wealthy residential community that rims Hollywood. Arlen has
spent several hours tending to his sprawling garden below the spacious modern house.*

*His figure is trim, the features are lingeringly handsome, and
though the hair is stark white it is disconcerting, almost impossible,
to believe that he was born in 1899. He is one of those men for
whom age is an irrelevancy.*

*"I never dreamed of becoming an actor," he says in the dying
light of a summer day as he flounces into a chair on his black slate
patio. A moment later he mixes and sips a scotch and water.*

I grew up in St. Paul, Minnesota, as a kid who wanted adventure. The men I most admired were the old seat-of-the-
pants barnstormers that I'd seen at the county fairs. I suppose that generated the desire in me to become a pilot.

Movies? My god, you used to glance up and down the
street, and if nobody was looking, you'd walk into the theater, and you'd leave through the alley so no one would see
you. Hollywood represented sin, sloth and sex. It was a den
of iniquity. Everybody in town knew that. Everybody in town
accepted that.

When the war came along in 1917, I went up to Winnipeg
and enlisted in Canada's Royal Flying Corps. I was trained

and sent to England, where the only action I saw was ferrying planes to the front lines in France.

After my discharge, I finished high school. I wasn't a scholar, and I think the main reason they gave me a diploma was to get me out of the school.

I went to Duluth and wrote sports for the *Tribune* until I got a letter from two pals of mine. They were in Breckenridge, Texas, working in the oilfields. They invited me down. It sounded more exciting than writing sports, which I wasn't very good at anyway.

I got a job as a tool dresser, tough work, long hours, short pay. I did that for about six months. Then they offered the three of us a chance to work in Colombia, South America. Adventure? That was it! We all agreed to go. They gave us a month off at full salary, and the three of us went to Los Angeles for a vacation. We didn't come to see Hollywood. That had no appeal for us; it never crossed our minds to look for movie stars or visit a studio.

While we were in L.A., war broke out between Ecuador and Bolivia. The company postponed its plans to drill for oil in Colombia. South America was deemed too dangerous just then.

My pals went back to Breckenridge. I didn't because it was fifty miles from the railroad, and I wasn't crazy about living way out in the toolies. Besides, I didn't see much of a future in the oil business.

I had a stake of a little less than twenty-five dollars, and I got to the place where I was living on fourteen cents a day. But you could almost get by on that in those days. Chili and beans, two pieces of toast and a cup of coffee cost ten cents. Carfare was a nickel. If you want the honest-to-God truth, the publicity department at Paramount later built up that story about my living on fourteen cents a day. It was never quite that bad. Put it this way: I was invited out to dinner often.

Still and all, I had to find some kind of work. I answered a

129

blind ad in the Los Angeles *Times.* The job turned out to be an assistant in a film lab on Sunset Boulevard, the old D. W. Griffith studio. It paid eighteen dollars a week. In a couple of days I was running a projector, printing, drying and processing film, breaking it up and putting it into cans. I also delivered the finished film to the studios on a motorcycle.

One of my stops was Paramount, which was at the end of a dirt road lined with pepper trees, almost open country. Across the street from the studio Valentino used to exercise his Arabian horses. You'd see him out there almost every morning with eight or ten of those beautiful animals.

The motorcycle the lab supplied me was in awful shape. When I arrived on the Paramount lot this particular day, I tried the brake and it didn't work. I slammed into a truck and broke my leg. They took me to the studio infirmary. The doctor there felt sorry for me, I guess, and he passed the word to the casting director that it would be a nice gesture if the studio gave me extra work until I could move around again. So it was a busted leg that really got me into the business. I was on crutches, but I would work crowd scenes. The job paid ten bucks a day, and it was a godsend.

I got to know Arthur Todd, who was one of the best cameramen in the business. In those days the cameramen owned their own cameras, and they were very careful about who they permitted to handle their equipment. Todd figured he could trust me, my little experience in the film lab impressed him, and he took me on as his assistant.

We were sent on location to Fort Huachuca in Cochise County, Arizona, to work on a picture called *Quicksand.* They'd forgotten to cast an actor back at the studio, and the director asked me if I could ride a horse and play a bit as a sergeant.

"For how much?" I'd heard about all these actors getting fifteen hundred, two thousand a week, some of them five thousand a week, and I thought that if I was going to play a part, I ought to get some of that big money, too. I talked it over with Todd, and he said, "Don't work for less than two hundred fifty a week." The director agreed to that, and I was on the picture ten or eleven weeks. It took forever to shoot a picture in that era. But nobody worried much about it, they spent all the time they thought they needed, even for a B picture like *Quicksand.*

When I got back to Paramount, I was offered the lead in *Vengeance of the Deep.* The only reason was the thing was going to be shot in Hawaii and it called for the hero to do several scenes swimming in shark-infested waters. No stunt man was assigned to the picture, and I grabbed the job because here right away I figured was my chance to become a star. There were sharks in the water all right, but I was a good and a lucky swimmer. There was a camera mounted on the beach and another one grinding away on a boat, ninety yards offshore. I always managed to hit the beach a few seconds before the sharks.

Vengeance was an awful picture. One critic said the water scenes were interesting, but when the actors got on dry land, they emitted an odor worse than the sharks that were killed in the picture. He intimated that the actors, not the sharks, should have been shot.

The thing played in St. Paul, and my father saw it. He was less impressed than the critic. He came running out to Hollywood to see me, and he said, "Is this going to be your vocation?"

Defensively, I asked, "What's wrong with Hollywood?"

"I think you can do better," he said. "I think you ought to go to law school. After all, your whole family are lawyers." Dad, of course, was a lawyer, one of the first graduates of the University of Minnesota. Both my grandfathers were lawyers, and it was a family tradition.

My confidence wavered. It wasn't too late to get out of the movie business. I wasn't going like a house afire in my so-called career anyway. So the next morning I went to the Hall of Justice in downtown Los Angeles and walked into one of the courtrooms. The judge was hearing a narcotics case. It droned on, and it all seemed duller than dishwater.

I told my father, "I've given it a shot. I know I can't make it as a lawyer. Since I'm not proficient in anything else, I may as well stay in the movies. This is a going business. It's young, and someday it's going to be very big."

He stayed in town for two weeks and met a lot of people. Much to my surprise, *he* changed *his* mind. "I agree with you," he said. "I think some of this has a tremendous future."

The studio cast me next as the lead in *Martinique* with Bebe Daniels. I wasn't ready for it. It was a costume picture, and I didn't understand anything about that sort of film. They had me all dolled up in a velvet coat with lace sleeves, with my hair curled and everything. I looked like a Harvard cheerleader with an American puss when I was supposed to be a sophisticated and suave French boy.

I went to Hector Turnbull, the director, and said, "I'm all wrong for this. I feel out of place. I'm completely miscast."

He told me, "Let's see how it works out. Let me be the judge."

We shot a couple of takes in the next few days, and it wasn't working out. They got Ricardo Cortez to play it, and he did a great job.

I went into a picture with Jack Holt called *Enchanted Hill,* and that led to another thing called *Behind the Front,* which starred Wally Beery and Raymond Hatton. It was one of the most successful pictures of 1925 because of Beery and Hatton, not me. Then I made *Old Ironsides,* playing Stephen Decatur.

After that, nothing happened. I was under contract, but I was afraid the studio was going to let me go.

One day, depressed as hell, I was walking up the main stem, and I ran into Charley Barton, who was an assistant director. He said, "Come on, I want you to test for *Wings.*"

I'd heard about *Wings* and knew it was going to be a very important picture. It seemed as though every leading man in

town except me had been tested, William Haines, Jack Pickford, and some people who weren't even under contract to
the studio.

I told Charley, "Naw, they don't want me."

"Let's try it anyway," he said.

The test was a very emotional scene in which I have a premonition of my death, and I had to cry. I kept squeezing an
onion, which I had in my hand out of camera range, and the
tears came like a waterfall.

William Wellman, who was going to direct *Wings*, saw the
test the next day and bellowed, "I want that guy. He isn't a
great actor, but he sure can cry."

For Wellman, the picture was a labor of love. He'd been a
pilot in the Lafayette Flying Corps, and he was going to tell
the story of the outfit dramatically but honestly and authenti-
cally. *Wings* had a big budget, and the studio wanted the pro-
tection of established stars. The brass wondered about Wellman's sanity when he cast me and Buddy Rogers as the male
leads. So far as audiences were concerned, we were nobodies.
Clara Bow was the only star in it. Wellman also gave Gary
Cooper, who was then an unknown, a bit in the picture.

I felt right from the beginning that *Wings* was going to be
successful. The whole project had an aura of magic about it,
of charisma, or whatever you want to call it.

We spent six and a half months shooting it in San Antonio,
Texas, using the entire United States Air Corps, which consisted of four pursuit planes. There was no trick photography. Buddy and I, who played young lieutenants, did our
own flying, and we did all the aerial dogfights ourselves.

I played David, who came from a very well-to-do family.
The plot was based on a true incident that Wellman heard
about while he was in France. David is shot down behind the
German lines. He manages to get hold of a German plane,
and he's flying back to his own lines. Buddy, who's been out
on patrol looking for me, sees the black plane with the German cross and he shoots me down. This is the end of the pic-

ture. He doesn't know it's me until he lands and goes into this little French church, where I'm dying. Then he realizes what he's done—killed his best pal. My death scene was an actor's dream.

I'll tell you how much impact the picture had. When Buddy is about to gun me out of the air, people in the audience all over the country would jump to their feet and scream, "Don't shoot him! Don't shoot him!" They fainted by the dozens.

In New York *Wings* opened at the Criterion Theater. They built the world's largest electric sign to advertise it. The admission price was three dollars! In 1927 nobody had ever heard of a picture playing for three dollars. It ran for two years in New York, and it's still being shown all over the world, still making money. It was made for about a million seven hundred thousand, and it's grossed at least ten times that amount.

Wings did wonders for everybody associated with it. I'd been at Paramount about three years at two fifty a week. They tore up my old contract and gave me a new one for three thousand five hundred a week, fifty-two weeks a year. Buddy Rogers and Wellman also got new contracts. The picture made Gary Cooper a star, although he was in it for only sixty seconds.

Wings also won the first Academy Award. But the impact of the Oscar didn't hit us as much as it would today. As a matter of fact, it didn't hit us at all. When I heard that we'd won, I thought, it's nice that the picture got an Academy Award, but what is an Academy Award? The ceremony, if you can call it that, was held outside Doug Fairbanks' dressing room, with a few people standing around. At the time, the Oscar had no significance whatever. Fairbanks had started the whole Academy thing. He thought people in the industry who did outstanding work should be rewarded at the end of the year with a statuette or something.

A few months before *Wings* was released I was sent over to see a fellow named Harry Cohn of Poverty Row. It was well named. The Columbia lot was full of termites; the termites were walking down the streets. I went into Cohn's office, and along the baseboard there were tops of tin cans to keep the rats from coming out. Cohn had a battered desk, a couple of crummy-looking chairs, and a script for a picture called *Blood Ship*.

Cohn said, "I know Paramount sent you over here out of courtesy, and they told you to say no to me. Is that right?"

"Mr. Cohn, that is exactly right."

"Well, goddamn it, at least you're not a liar."

He asked me to read the script, and he called that night to ask me how I liked it. I told him that I loved it; it was a wonderful story.

"Would you like to make the picture?"

"It's okay with me if it's okay with Paramount." Somehow Harry managed to get me loaned out, and I did the picture.

I'll tell you how smart Cohn was. He knew *Wings* was going to be a big hit; the grapevine was out on it. That's why he wanted me. I'll say this for Cohn—he tried to borrow me for every good thing he ever did. I think I was the only actor besides Gary Grant that got along with Harry. We never had any words. He treated me as well as I've been treated by anybody in the business.

Wings was the last of the silent spectaculars; it brought silent pictures to a close with a bang. I stepped into talkies with *Four Feathers*, which was David Selznick's first epic. I lucked in again, getting the chance to work with Selznick, a supercraftsman. He had the patience of Job with me. No matter what the hell he told me to do, I did it. It paid off because the picture was a smash.

Next I did another thing with Clara Bow, *Dangerous Curves*. People still remember her as the It Girl. She was a wonderful little actress who had great ability. Even now when you look at her in *Wings,* she's so vivacious and alive; she just lights up the screen. I guess that's what you call "it."

The Virginian came along in 1929. There were three big parts in it which were played by Gary Cooper, Walter Huston and myself. The reason they took Coop was that we were such close friends, and they figured that if he played with me in his first talkie he wouldn't be nervous.

Coop and I drove up to Sonora in central California, where the picture was going to be shot. It was only three hundred and twenty miles from Hollywood, but the roads were so dreadful that it took us three days to make the trip. We shared a room at the Sonora Inn that had an old bathtub on stilts.

It turned out that Coop *was* very, very nervous about the picture. "I just can't retain the dialogue," he said.

"Sure, you can," I told him. "It's just a matter of concentration."

I'd even practice his lines with him while he was in the bathtub.

We began shooting and at the end of three days, we only had about forty seconds of Coop on film. He just couldn't remember his lines, and he spoiled take after take. He was going with Lupe Velez at the time, and Lupe showed up on location and distracted Coop even more. But the worst part of it was that Lupe had been the girlfriend of Vic Fleming, who was the director on *The Virginian* and later on directed *Gone with the Wind.* Coop had won out, and that didn't sit very well with Fleming.

Vic called me into his room and said, "You tell your big stringbean friend that I'm going to replace him."

"Hell, Vic, you can't do that just because of Lupe."

"It's not that. He won't learn his dialogue, and I can't take twenty years to make this picture."

I called B. P. Schulberg in Hollywood. He was the general manager of Paramount. "Holy mackerel, Ben, you can't do this to Coop. You can't take him off the picture. He's just a little nervous because it's his first talkie. Sure we only have forty seconds of film on him so far, but it's the greatest *think-ing* performance I've ever seen."

"That's all I want to know," Schulberg said. "Coop stays."

I went to Coop and told him he wasn't canned. By this time, of course, he'd heard the rumor that he was going to be replaced. You never saw a happier guy. Almost losing the picture made something click in Coop. He had no more dialogue trouble after that.

The Virginian was a whale of a picture. Coming only two years after *Wings,* it solidified my status as a star. I was fortunate that those two pictures happened early in my career. They were milestones, and I never topped them, although there were some other good ones. I played the Cheshire Cat in *Alice in Wonderland.* That was in 1932. Then there was *Helldorado, The Devil's Pipeline, Minesweeper, Buffalo Bill Rides Again* and *Law of the Lawless.* I was able to play leading men till I was fifty-five years old. One I enjoyed doing later on was *The Best Man* with Henry Fonda.

In 1965 I was making a thing called *Apache Uprising* and rehearsing a benefit play at night for the Masquers [a theatrical club]. I wouldn't get home until three or four o'clock in the morning. I broke out with a fever one night of 104.5, and they called the doctor and sent me to the hospital.

When I woke up the next morning, I never had such a scare in my life. The TV set was on and the newscaster was saying that I was dead—"Richard Arlen died last night of pneumonia."

Then it struck me as humorous because by now I was feeling fine. The nurse came in, and I said, "I have some interesting news for you. It seems that I died last night."

She said, "Yes, they've been talking about it all up and down the floor."

"I'm hungry," I said. "I'd like a little breakfast—bacon,

137

ham, four eggs, hash browns, lots of toast and a gallon of coffee."

"Now I'm sure you're not dead."

I never found out how that story got around. Needless to say, I was happy to be in a position to deny it.

I'm still offered parts, but I don't particularly care about working anymore. The fun's gone out of it. There isn't a movie industry left as I knew it. The people have changed, the pictures have changed, everything's changed so much that it's all been destroyed to a large extent.

I'm thankful for the wonderful years I had in what we now refer to as the golden era of the motion-picture industry. It was awfully good to me. But the business has to start all over again. I'm not a square, but I don't think you can build a successful, ongoing industry with smut and filth and cheap sex.

I think before the industry can start over again we'll first have to go completely under.

When I came into pictures, there were heroic images on the screen and people believed what they were looking at. My head was magnified up on that screen sixteen times its size.

There were heroes created by pictures, and kids and their parents wanted to pattern themselves after the stars.

This is hard to believe, but there are four or five hundred kids named after me. Richard Arlen this and Richard Arlen that. Barry Goldwater's son-in-law is one of them. His name is Richard Arlen Holt. Arlen Specter is another. He was one of the key men who investigated the assassination of John F. Kennedy for the Warren Commission, and he was the district attorney of Philadelphia. He's from a Jewish family, and when he was born, his mother said, "All the children in the family have been named for people in the Old Testament. Why don't we give him a modern name?" His father said, "Well, who do you want to name him for?" And his mother

138

answered, "A movie star. Why not name him for Richard Arlen?"

See what I mean? The movies created heroes.

If parents these days are going to name their kids after Linda Lovelace, this country is in more trouble than we think.

13
Darla Hood

THAT OLD GANG OF MINE

THE MISCHIEVOUS MOPPETS *of the Our Gang comedies have had an astonishing longevity—on film. Producer Hal Roach first brought the slapstick antics of the Gang kids to the screen in the 1920's. Under the title of* The Little Rascals, *the fifteen-minute shorts are still seen on more than 100 television stations.*

The most popular, best remembered era of the Gang was the decade prior to World War II. The young stars were Carl "Alfalfa" Switzer, Billy "Buckwheat" Thomas, Spanky McFarland and the winsome Darla Hood.

Miss Hood is a hazel-eyed brunette, a petite bundle of energy who weighs eighty-nine pounds. "I'm living proof that dynamite comes in small packages," she says with a laugh. With her second husband and three children, she lives in a neat ranch-style home in North Hollywood, California.

When I was born in Liddy, Oklahoma, the population jumped to five hundred and one. My father was president of the bank, and Mother taught piano but was bored to death by small-town life.

"Darla," she used to say, "you're my ticket out of Liddy."

She'd made up her mind that I was going to be a movie star and talked Dad into letting me take singing and dancing lessons when I was three years old. I still remember the long drives to Oklahoma City, a three-hundred-mile round trip. Mother was a very determined woman.

140

My teacher was Kathryn Duffy, and she was marvelous. There was no one in Liddy, of course, who could compare to her. I'd been taking lessons for about six months when Mrs. Duffy decided to go to New York for a short brushup course in choreography. She asked my mother if I could go along. Mother agreed.

I've asked my mother why she let me go to New York with a virtual stranger when I was so young. I wouldn't let my children make a similar trip under similar circumstances.

"Honey," Mother said, "you had stardust in your eyes, and I knew you were going to be somebody."

We stayed at the Edison Hotel. One night we were having dinner, and the orchestra leader handed me the baton and asked me to lead the band. Everybody applauded afterward, so I sang a song and danced.

Joe Rivkin, a talent agent for Hal Roach, happened to be in the audience. He came over to our table and said to Mrs. Duffy, "Your daughter is adorable. We're looking for a little girl for the *Our Gang* comedies, and I wonder if we could give her a screen test."

"I'm not Darla's mother, but I think it will be all right." Mrs. Duffy didn't bother calling home to ask my mother's permission because she thought nothing would come of it.

I was tested at a studio in New York. I did a little scene they gave me from one of Shirley Temple's movies, danced, and sang a song called, "I'll Never Say Never Again."

Then Mrs. Duffy called Mother. "They've been looking all over the country for a little girl, and they want Darla." The rest of the Gang was set up, they had Alfalfa, Buckwheat and Spanky, and they needed a little girl before they could begin shooting. "They want her in Hollywood right away to make the *Our Gang Follies of 1936*. She can't come home first."

Mother was thrilled; this was exactly what she wanted for me, her dreams coming true. I came out, and Mother met me here. I went to work immediately, and Mother signed a nine-year contract with Hal Roach, which called for a starting salary of seventy-five dollars a week.

Dad didn't move out until a year later. He was a conservative banker and wanted to be sure my career wasn't a fly-by-night thing. When he did get to Hollywood, the only job he could find was as a teller at the Bank of America for twenty-five dollars a week. His little girl by then was making six or seven times that, and if it bothered him, he never let it show.

Gordon Douglas was one of the first directors I had. Later he did *Harlow,* the remake of *Stagecoach, Tony Rome* and *The Detective.* He's a very big director now, but he cut his eyeteeth on the Gang.

I made over one hundred fifty of the Gang shows. I was the telephone operator and the secretary in the Gang's clubhouse. A lot of the plots revolved around Spanky and his "women haters club." The complications came when Alfalfa would fall in love with me. That would get him into all kinds of trouble with the rest of the Gang because none of the boys were supposed to like girls.

Whenever they could, they involved Pete in the stories. Pete was the ugliest black-and-white short-haired dog I ever saw in my life. He had that black ring painted around one of his eyes, which made him look sad and funny at the same time. He was just an old mutt, but I guess he worked cheap. In one show we went around trying to raise money to rescue Pete from the dogcatcher. I was sort of sorry we succeeded. It would have been more fun to work with a cute dog like Daisy in the *Blondie* series.

I was in the Gang from 1936 to 1945, and there were only three or four of the shows that I wasn't in. And that was only because those stories involved the boys going off on an adventure someplace where it wouldn't look right for me to go with them. So they'd write me out occasionally, but otherwise I did every one of them. I lasted the longest of any kid who ever played in the Gang. I think that was because I stayed small for a long time. I'm only five feet two now.

142

Alfalfa was the tall one with the freckles and a little sprig of hair stuck on top of his head which they greased in place. Buckwheat was the black youngster, and Spanky was the fat boy.

I think the Gang has remained popular with audiences to this day because we all seemed so natural. We don't appear to be child actors, like the *Brady Bunch* or *The Partridge Family*. We had scripts, but half the dialogue we made up as we went along, just like any bunch of kids doing things together. And that is the appeal of the Gang, the naturalness of it.

I'd been in the Gang for about a year when we went on the road to make personal appearances in theaters around the country. I didn't think anything of it at the time, but Buckwheat and his mother couldn't sit in the same car on the train with the rest of us. Our teacher was along and she'd give us our lessons for three hours in the morning, and then she'd have to go back to the other section and teach Buckwheat. And he could never stay in the same hotels we did, and mind you, this wasn't in the South; this happened in Minneapolis Chicago and Detroit. Buckwheat was my favorite of all the kids. One day on the set he tripped over a cable and banged his head so badly that there was a big egg on it. I felt so sorry for him because he was so sweet and his mother was so darling. I went up and hugged and kissed him. Later, backstage, my mother said, "Don't you ever kiss him again. Don't you ever touch him." I couldn't understand why because I thought he was such a nice kid.

It was so cold in Detroit, and I always wore this tiny short skirt so my underpants showed. I guess I was the original mini-skirter. I almost froze to death, and the only thing that saved me was when Spanky got the measles. We were quarantined, but Alfalfa and I came down with them anyway. I don't know which was worse, the measles or touring on the road, which I didn't enjoy. Anyway, our getting the measles put an end to the tour, and we came home.

Except for Alfalfa, I got along well with all the kids. The

troublemakers were the fathers of Alfalfa and Spanky, They were the real stage mothers. I mean it was just constant bickering about who got the best part and who got the most lines or close-ups. They'd complain to Mr. Roach or whoever the director was. They finally had to count lines so that each kid would get the same amount. It got to be ridiculous. After a while it got to be disgusting. Being the only girl, I didn't fare badly because I had no competition.

The worst kid in the Gang was Alfalfa. His dad told him he was God's gift to the world, and he thoroughly believed it. In a way I feel a little guilty talking about him because he's dead and I hate to talk about somebody who's passed away. But he *was* an awful problem on the set.

Alfalfa said to me once, "Reach in my pocket. I've got something for you." I reached in, and he had an open knife in there, and I cut a couple of fingers.

I was terribly scared for some reason or other of fish. I've never been able to touch them. Alfalfa knew it, and one time he talked the director into filling a pond in which we were going to do a scene with hundreds of little fishes. When we were all dumped in, I got hysterical.

Another time a scene called for Alfalfa and me to walk out of a theater together. As we came out, he pushed his fingernails into my skin with so much pressure that I started bleeding. That ruined the take, and the director blamed *me*! I told on Alfalfa, and he said, "I'll get you for that."

But he never did anything. He was just a misguided prankster. Maybe it wasn't Alfalfa's fault. Basically I think he was a nice boy, but his father was German and had drilled into his son that he was a member of the master race. The father treated the mother absolutely terrible whenever she came on the set.

I didn't know Hal Roach too well. None of us did. He was rather aloof. He would come on the set and stand off in a corner. He wasn't too friendly. But at Christmas time he was just fantastic. He'd have a whole soundstage blocked off for the Christmas party. The first Christmas I was there he asked me what I wanted and I said a dollhouse. What I had in mind was one of those small ones where you can open it and arrange the furniture any way you want. What I got was a huge three-room playhouse. They had to bring it to my house in a hired truck. Alfalfa wanted a horse, and he was given one. Still and all, it wasn't a buddy-buddy relationship with Mr. Roach. I was only in his office once, and that was with the rest of the Gang to pose for some publicity pictures.

I was told that Mr. Roach came up with the idea for the Gang comedies based on his own experiences as a kid in New York. He had a neighborhood gang, and they got into all kinds of trouble. They were always a bit on the outs with the police, but they never did anything bad. It was just good-humored stuff they did, and there was a fat kid and a colored kid in his gang.

In the late thirties Mr. Roach sold us to MGM. So we moved from the Roach studio to that marvelous Metro lot. It was a wonderland. When we weren't working, we were allowed to go round to all the sets. They were making Tarzan out there at the time, and we got to play on that set. We had more fun. And there was the Andy Hardy house and the train station where Mickey Rooney always said good-bye to his folks or to his girlfriend Polly Benedict when he was going on a trip. And I remember watching them shoot *The Wizard of Oz*, but I never got to know Judy Garland except to say hello.

Elizabeth Taylor came out to do *National Velvet*, and we got to be very good friends. We went to school on the lot together. She and I just hit it off real good. We just got along super. Her mother and brother Howard used to drive us down to the amusement part at the beach and follow us at a decent distance so we could giggle by ourselves and go on all the rides.

Elizabeth was just a wonderful little girl. She loved fairy tales. She loved me to read fairy tales to her. She always wanted the stories to end happily ever after. If I read or told her a story and it didn't end happily, she'd say, "Oh, don't end it that way. I want it to end happily." Unfortunately, it didn't work out for Elizabeth that way in her private life.

She never took herself seriously. She was sweet, not stuck-up or conceited. She lived in a dreamworld, and was charming, half child and half woman. When I saw her in *A Date with Judy*, which she made when she was sixteen, I said, "My God, look how grown up she is." She looked like a woman and I didn't. She'd grown up so fast. All of a sudden she seemed to mature.

The last time I saw or talked to Elizabeth was when she came to my twelfth birthday party. She gave me a picture which I still have. She wrote across the bottom: "To Darla, my best friend."

Mickey Rooney was the most adorable thing. He loved everybody, and everybody loved him. He sort of just took over the whole lot. He was welcome on any set at any time. He was always giving advice to everyone. There was the time when he married Ava Gardner. He kept walking around, saying, "Can you imagine that beautiful thing is marrying me. She's marrying me!" He couldn't get over it.

Lana Turner was going with Artie Shaw then. She always dressed in white and looked so beautiful. But she struck me as being conceited, although I shouldn't say that because I didn't know her, and it's kind of an awful thing to say that about anybody you don't know personally. But I thought she took herself awfully serious, and she wasn't very friendly to the kids in the Gang. When she was introduced to Artie Shaw, he wasn't impressed. He said, "That girl looks silly in that white outfit. I'd never have anything to do with her." Three days later they were married.

146

While I was in the Gang, I didn't know that I was a star. When people stopped me in the street for my autograph, I'd ask my mother why they wanted my signature. I couldn't figure it out because I didn't know I was anything except a little girl. I was making movies, and I'm on the lot with all these stars. It was like a game to me. Do you know that I thought all kids lived in that atmosphere. I thought that was the norm. I didn't realize till I got out of it that I'd been doing something different than other kids.

When I got too old for the Gang and I was released by the studio, I had a terrible time adjusting. I went to public school for the first time, but I didn't know how to talk to these girls. I couldn't do the things they were doing. I'd never played jacks or jump rope. I tried to impress them, but I came on too strong. No matter how hard you try to get away from it, if you've been in show business, you come on like Gangbusters.

I'd stand on the edge and wait for the girls to invite me in, which they wouldn't do. These kids had already been in school together, most of them for four or five years. So to impress them, I said I used to be one of the stars of *Our Gang*. They didn't even know what I was talking about because in California they ran double features in the theaters. Not many of the Gang shorts were seen out here until they were put on television. The Gang was most popular in the Midwest and back East, where the bill usually was one feature, a cartoon and a short.

I'd give these real lavish parties, and all the girls would come to those. I'd have a houseful of kids for the party on Saturday night, and when I went back to school on Monday, the same kids would all treat me like I was a stranger. So I had to learn how to become a member of a real gang and adjust to the real world. It wasn't until junior high that I got with it, and in high school I had a ball. I just loved it. I was on the student council, and I was just into everything.

I was married when I was seventeen. It lasted eight years. I've been married seventeen years this time, so I guess this one is set.

I've been working pretty steadily in the business since I was sixteen. I went into dubbing and sang for Linda Darnell in *Letter to Three Wives*. I also did dubbing jobs for *State Fair*, *Pajama Game* and *The Helen Morgan Story*.

Ken Murray hired me for his *Blackouts* show when I was eighteen. Then I went to New York with him, where I was his leading lady for three years on the television show he did for Budweiser.

After that I worked as a singer in Vegas, doing a single, and went on the road for several years performing at clubs. I've done a number of records, but none of them were hits.

The biggest money I've ever made came when I started doing television commercials. I've been on for Tide, Clorox, Mr. Clean, Kool-Aid and Kellogg's cornflakes. The bonanza commercial was the one I did for Chicken-of-the-Sea. I was the voice of the mermaid in those for years, and made twenty-five thousand a year out of that.

I guess all the Gang kids should have become millionaires or close to it. But none of us ever made it. When my mother signed the contract for me, she signed away all the rights to any medium that might be invented in the future. That cut me and the rest of the kids out of television residuals. Hal Roach has made millions from the Gang on TV. So has MGM.

The fate of the kids I worked with in the Gang has been good news and bad news.

Spanky spent years where he was just lost. He tried the restaurant business, but it didn't gel. Then he was a bartender, and he had a lot of other pickup jobs. "Once you've been in show business," he told me, "nothing ever comes up again to equal it. Maybe I was cute when I was a kid, but for a long time I didn't have anything to go on with. The Gang was a

148

curse; the fact that I'd been a star and was idolized was a curse. When the day comes when they let you out of the studio, God how your life changes." Spanky's okay now. He's working for Philco-Ford in Dallas as a sales manager in charge of the entire state of Texas.

I haven't seen Buckwheat in years, but I understand he's working for Technicolor and doing well.

Scotty Beckett was in the Gang before me. He was in the first few I made before they dropped him. He was the sort of good-looking snobbish boy of the Gang. Scotty ended in the actors' home out in Woodland Hills. He'd tried suicide once, so they put him in the home, thinking maybe they could straighten him out because he had a very strong drug problem. One morning in 1968 they found him dead in his bed of an overdose of drugs. He was only thirty-nine years old.

There was another kid in the Gang for a while. All he ever did was cry. His father was a gardener, and they came from New Jersey. In the Gang he was called Nicky. He's Robert Blake, one of the stars of *In Cold Blood*. He played Perry Smith.

Alfalfa wanted to be in show business when he grew up, but he never seemed to find the stature he had when he was in the Gang. He wanted to be a straight dramatic actor, which I think was a mistake for him because he had a natural comedic ability. He made a few pictures, then lost his way and started drinking, very heavily.

Alfalfa liked to hunt, and one day in 1959 he borrowed a hunting dog from a friend of his who was a movie stunt man. While he was on the hunting trip, the dog got lost. Alfalfa put an ad in the paper and offered a fifty-dollar reward for the return of the dog. Someone found the dog, and Alfalfa paid the reward. Then he went to his friend and told him he was owed the fifty dollars. His friend said that when somebody borrows something, it's the borrower's responsibility to return it. Alfalfa was out the fifty dollars, period.

Alfalfa left, went to a bar and got drunk. Then he returned to his friend's place and went at him with a knife. The guy shot and killed Alfalfa, and he got off by pleading self-defense. Poor Alfalfa, killed in a fifty-dollar argument in the prime of his life. He was thirty-three years old.

My father died thirteen years ago. He ended up as a branch manager of a bank. My mother is still alive.

I hate to tell you this because I love both my parents. But I really don't think they did right by me. At the time I started in the Gang they hadn't yet passed the Coogan Law.* In my last years in the Gang I was earning seven hundred fifty dollars a week. My folks got a lovely house out of it. I certainly didn't begrudge them that or any of the other things they bought with the money I earned.

Would you believe it—for all my years of work in the Gang I've never seen a single dollar.

---

*Officially known as the Child Actors Bill, it was enacted into law by the California legislature on May 4, 1939. The measure required parents or guardians to set aside at least half the earnings of a child star in a trust fund or some other form of savings and to provide an accounting to the court. When Jackie Coogan turned twenty-one in 1938, he discovered he was broke. He sued his mother and stepfather. Coogan claimed he had earned $84,000,000. His mother said the amount was $1,300,000. Coogan received what was left of his estate—$126,000.

14

Jesse Lasky, Jr.

AMONG OTHER MATTER, THE WRITING OF
THE TEN COMMANDMENTS

THE SON OF *one of the founding triumvirate of Hollywood
was born in New York in 1910. He came to Hollywood in 1913,
the year that the pathfinding* Squaw Man *was made by Sam Goldwyn, Cecil B. DeMille and his father, Jesse Lasky.*

*Jesse Lasky, Jr., is an impeccable man of 140 pounds, five feet
six, with silvery hair and beard. He's a thoughtful, forgiving man,
which is especially impressive because if events in his father's life
had transpired otherwise, he likely would have inherited millions.
As it is, he is "getting by" in England where he's lived for thirteen
years.*

*He was in town for a short visit, staying at his father-in-law's
home in mountainous Laurel Canyon above Hollywood. The rustic
house is situated on eight tree-choked acres. "There's something of
the charm here of the old Hollywood I knew and loved," he says as he
slides into a leather wing chair in the living room.*

My father had a film production company called the Jesse
Lasky Players. My earliest memories of Hollywood go back to
the beginning of the First World War. My father had formed
the Lasky Home Guard, which was a local militia regiment
composed of carpenters, cameramen, propmen, extras and
most of the other people who worked in his studio. I recall
parading down Hollywood Boulevard with the guard every
Thursday night. I wore an Army uniform and marched in

front of the band. The unit was available should the Germans invade Hollywood, which happily never came about.

I was more impressed with the guard than with the first movie stars I met because they wore dashing uniforms and carried rifles. I remember meeting Mary Pickford. I always thought of her as a very pretty little girl. She seemed a contemporary of mine because she had a child's voice and she always dressed like a little girl. I recall William S. Hart—he was impressive. He gave me an autographed picture, and he dressed like a cowboy off the set as well as on.

Far from encouraging me to go into the movie business, my father tried to keep me out of it. He'd come from an old California frontier family and was raised in a rather bucolic atmosphere around Sacramento and San Jose. He'd been a musician on the Barbary Coast in San Francisco and on the Bowery in New York. He went into vaudeville and toured the country and saw show business as a kind of sinister adventure. And always highly speculative.

Hollywood in its infancy was rather a typical small town that became the mecca for adventurers and all sorts of people who created an environment that was far from ideal for impressionable youngsters.

Those who were important in the film business then, Goldwyn, DeMille, Fairbanks, Chaplin, regarded themselves as a kind of aristocracy. And I suppose they were an aristocracy. Yet they wanted something better for their children, and they particularly didn't want their offspring exposed to the lower echelons in the film world. The extras of the time were a ragtag lot. They were thieves, perverts and prostitutes, the lowest scum of humanity. Not all of them by any means, but a great, great many. It was a rough world for a kid to grow up in.

In the spirit of the Rockefeller and Kennedy families, my father didn't want to spoil me. He sort of took the American position of the time among many wealthy men, which was not to hand out a very hefty allowance. So I was encouraged to work as soon as I could. I sold newspapers on the corner of La Brea and Hollywood Boulevard. I mowed lawns and washed cars. All of that was damned hard work. I found the easiest way of making money was to become an extra, which I did without my father's knowledge. In those days there was no Central Casting. You simply walked out in front of the studio and joined the usual big crowd. The director or assistant director came along and collected the people he wanted. If a kid happened to be needed, well, there I was. It was sort of a cattle pen operation. The extras had no dressing rooms. We dressed in enormous tents and were made up to look like Persians or whatever else was required.

After I'd had a number of jobs as an extra, my father discovered what I was doing. He was so horrified he shipped me out to a fashionable boarding school in the East. He wanted me out of Hollywood milieu, and I'm sure I wouldn't ever have come back if it hadn't been for the Depression.

I went to Blair Academy in New Jersey, then Princeton Prep, and after that the University of Dijon in France. I was training for the diplomatic service of the State Department.

My father went broke during the Depression. He'd merged his company with Adolph Zukor's Famous Players. From that came Famous Players-Lasky, which was one the most powerful companies in Hollywood until the end of the twenties and the early thirties. As the Depression rolled westward from New York, where it had initiated itself in the stock-market crash, it found Famous Players-Lasky overloaded with real estate. They'd bought vast chains of theaters in the United States and abroad. Though large numbers of people were patronizing them, seeking entertainment in the worst of times, the overhead on the movie palaces was dragging the company down.

The various partners were at each other's throats, the lot of them, Goldwyn, Zukor, DeMille. They clashed like titans.

Gradually the blame began to be focused on my father. The easiest way to describe it would be to say that when an army is losing a war, you change generals. The general who was the first vice-president in charge of production was Jesse Lasky, and he was blamed for losing the war. He was the general who was eased out. There was then a reorganization, new capital was found, and out of that came Paramount, which at first had been only a distribution facility owned by the studio.

My father became an independent producer for Fox, Warner's and RKO. His life became a series of terrible ups and downs. He lost fifteen million dollars during the Depression in the stock market, property investments, but mainly in Paramount stock. He had to take bankruptcy.

He'd pulled himself up again by 1941, when he personally produced *Sergeant York* with Gary Cooper. The picture was a smash success, and he was a wealthy man again, certainly not as rich as he'd previously been, but very well off. He was advised by his attorney Lloyd Wright, the son of the great architect Frank Lloyd Wright, to take a capital gain from the enormous profits generated by *Sergeant York*. Others had taken the same sort of capital gain and succeeded, but in his case it wasn't allowed. He lost in court, and it cost him more than a million dollars.

When he died in 1958, he was dead broke. But bitterness was strangely absent from his character, as was acrimony. He wasn't a tough character like most of the other moguls. He was an inspired man. A great dreamer, a great believer in the movie business. A man in love with life. He was always too excited about what he was going to do next to allow bitterness to color his feelings. He had many weaknesses, but bitterness was not one of them.

After my father's bankruptcy, I drifted back to Hollywood and drifted into becoming a reader, a ghostwriter and eventually a screenwriter. I'd always had something of a literary bent. Even in my schooldays I'd had some success with words. I was published as early as 1926, when I was sixteen. Before I was out of my teens, I'd had three books of poetry accepted in New York by important publishers. The books received very good reviews. Since I apparently had a flare for writing, I decided to pursue that career.

The first important writer I met was F. Scott Fitzgerald. He was among the many guests my father would have out to his beachhouse. My father liked Scott very much until Scott beat him at golf, and then he wasn't too pleased with him.

Scott Fitzgerald was the most attractive man, one of the handsomest men I've ever known. It wasn't easy for me to talk to him because in that period he was drinking very heavily. He was always pleasant, pleasantly plastered, I'd suppose you'd have to say. He was sort of in the midst of falling apart.

Scott did talk of himself as a Philistine because he was writing for Hollywood. But I think also that he was ill mentally in the sense of the liquor becoming a corrosive thing. He'd suffered terribly in his marriage to Zelda, and he was not the most successful writer in Hollywood. He must have felt, as most of us have felt at times, the anguish of failure and struggle. He drank, of course, because he was miserable.

Hollywood was a very cruel place at that time, and even today what's left of it is, I imagine, just as cruel. A failing writer, a failing anybody, a failing star like John Gilbert, whom I knew very well toward the end of his life after he'd been booted out of films when his voice didn't register properly in talkies, is shunned. Such people become pariahs. My father must have felt that pain many times in his life. You get to the place when all of a sudden you can't get a table in the Brown Derby, as it were. Hollywood has always been a success-oriented town, and there's little sympathy for failure.

The first of my sixty or so screen credits was a film called *Private Beach.* I wrote the play and some of the scenes in the film adaptation while I was a reader at Fox, where I was earning twenty-five dollars a week. Sometimes I'd pick up a little extra if I wanted to tire my eyes going through unsolicited manuscripts. The title *Private Beach* was changed to *Music Is Magic,* and it was made with Alice Faye as the star.

My breakthrough as a screenwriter came with *Secret Agent,*which was a film I did for Alfred Hitchcock in the early thirties. That led to a job as a contract writer with Metro.

The writers' table at Metro was astonishing. I was a very modest, quiet voice at that table because there were some pretty important people around it. Jack Kirkland, who wrote the screenplay for the Erskine Caldwell book *Tobacco Road.* I met William Faulkner at lunch a number of times. He seemed rather sardonic, and I was so much in awe of him that I hardly spoke to him. Faulkner seemed very friendly with Herman Mankiewicz, whom I've always considered the giant of screenwriters. Orson Welles may take credit, but it was Herman who wrote virtually all of *Citizen Kane,* perhaps the finest motion picture ever made. Bill Saroyan and Dorothy Parker were there. So were Julius and Philip Epstein who collaborated on such marvelous things as *The Man Who Came to Dinner, The Male Animal, Casablanca* and *Arsenic and Old Lace.* Dudley Nichols was in and out. He wrote *The Informer, Stagecoach* and *For Whom the Bell Tolls.* And Frances Marion, whose first important credit had been in 1920, when she did *Pollyanna* for Mary Pickford.

Given the enormous talent of all those scenarists, they were earning miserly money in comparison to the stars, directors and producers. It wasn't until years later that participation in profits became a possibility for writers. I've always felt and still feel that the screenwriter is the most underpaid and underhonored member of the creative pack. I think the screenwriter, the craftsman, the good carpenter, the man who can take a work of fiction or a piece of drama and convert it into a solid movie does a terribly important thing. So, of course, do those screenwriters who create original films.

In those days at Metro I'd say the top for a writer was

fifteen hundred a week, this at a time when many stars were earning five, ten, fifteen thousand a week. Fifteen hundred dollars was a very large salary for a genius like Dudley Nichols. And I'm not certain he made that much.

Newspapers liked to exaggerate the size of writer's salaries. We all heard that Ben Hecht had been paid fifty thousand dollars for writing a picture. The papers forevermore described him as a "fifty-thousand-dollar-a-picture screenwriter." Actually, Ben got that for probably only one picture. I believe he was paid that much for *Wuthering Heights.*

The average salary for a writer was about eight hundred a week. I wrote some very big DeMille pictures for five hundred a week, gradually progressing to eight hundred, then a thousand, which was my weekly stipend for writing *The Ten Commandments.*

Though DeMille had been my father's partner, their friendship had deteriorated to the point where it would have been preferable if my name had been Jesse Smith. I scored no points with him as Jesse Lasky, Jr.

After I had several screen credits, I wrote a letter to DeMille, telling him I'd like to be considered on my own merit as a screenwriter for him, that I would appreciate being given that opportunity. He called me in and asked me to write a few scenes for *The Buccaneer,* a Fredric March picture. He already had four writers on that, so he didn't need me except for the few scenes. But evidently he liked what little I'd done.

DeMille made me a promise. "The next picture I do," he said, "I'll call you and give you a chance at the beginning."

His next picture was *Union Pacific,* starring Joel McCrea and Barbara Stanwyck. I came into that at the beginning and survived. I then became a regular DeMille writer, and I wrote most of his major films, *Northwest Mounted Police, Reap the Wild Wind, Unconquered, Samson and Delilah* and *The Ten Commandments.* We had a row over money at one point, and I missed doing *The Greatest Show on Earth,* which was a pity.

DeMille was an inspiring man to work with. He was exciting, exacting, maddening, fascinating. DeMille didn't like to pay a great deal of money to writers. So we had that row and I left him to do two Gene Autry pictures in order to get my salary up. DeMille hired me back for *The Ten Commandments* and said, "If you write this picture, I'll pay you the same as you're getting for writing for Mr. Autry." There's a lesson or a moral somewhere in the fact that writing for a singing cowboy and writing for Charlton Heston playing one of the most noble human beings who ever lived was a matter of equality in DeMille's mind, at least financially.

From a writer's point of view *The Ten Commandments* presented a great many problems. One was how to take care of the unknown years in the life of Moses. The Bible, of course, only records that fact that he was discovered in the bulrushes. It does mention that Moses was raised in the court of Egypt. But there were those intervening years when we knew nothing about him. In the Bible that was a dark period in Moses' life. It's very strange, but many of the Biblical heroes, King Solomon and Christ, as well as Moses, have these long dark periods in their lives. You find them as children; then you find them suddenly emerging into the height of their careers.

Finding out what had happened to Moses after the bulrushes episode was solved, in a fashion, when I delved into the works of Josephus, who wrote a hundred years after the birth of Christ. I also consulted other sources of exegesis and Biblical history and the Koran. The Koran contained certain reference material that indicated Moses had become an Egyptian general, then had been unmasked as a Hebrew and made into a slave.

I worked terribly hard with DeMille to make the script as authentic as possible, to cleave it to the rock of solid information and history. And yet when it came out on the screen, it looked rather like a typical, overdone Hollywood spectacle.

Another difficult problem was the scene in which we showed the first feast of the Passover. About all I could learn was that the Passover feast began in Egypt. So how do you write about the celebration of a ritual occurring for the first time? The answer, of course, was imagination, which is what writers are paid for. I would have felt more comfortable, however, if there had been detailed and authenticated research material available. After all, you could take just so much liberty with the world's most revered book.

The biggest problem that had to be licked in the script was the rejuvenation of the children of Israel after they had crossed the Red Sea and the Pharaoh's army had been destroyed, gulped down and submerged by the Lord with this fantastic miracle of drowning the Egyptian enemy. The Hebrews had been brought to safety, but suddenly they are available for corruption. Moses has gone up to the mountain to receive the tablets. He's only been gone a relatively short time, thirty days and thirty nights, and the Israelites fall right into the worship of the golden calf and other forms of corruption. It seems they had totally forgotten the very recent miracle of the parting of the Red Sea and they had become idolaters.

To justify this change of face was the most difficult writing problem I could ever imagine. Because here you are—the Hebrews marching in triumph behind Moses, the submerged chariots of the army of Egypt behind them. They reach safety and glory, and Moses is on his way to obtain the Ten Commandments, and the Hebrews are suddenly rolling around in the worship of the golden calf.

How to explain such short-lived faith and such easy corruption was a hell of a job. Moreover, it had to be done in one speech because it was very late in the film, which already was running too long. The writing of that speech had to turn a great host who'd marched in glory, shouting hosannas, back to the path of righteousness, remove their doubts, rid them of their quickly acquired sins of debauchery and idol worship.

Thank God, we had a great actor to do it, Edward G. Robinson.

I don't recall the speech exactly, but the substance of it was:

"You've waited thirty days and thirty nights. Moses is seeking the Lord in the mountains. We must have faith that he'll come back and won't abandon us. But how do we know he'll find meat and drink? How do we know he'll find the Lord? How do you know there is a Promised Land? How do you know you won't die here in the desert? How do you know that the old gods you are embracing can save you? How do you know there is an invisible God who can save you? Faith! Faith! Faith! You must have faith! You must have faith in Moses and the Lord!"

Robinson, using all those arguments, almost succeeded in the film, although I wouldn't say completely. Perhaps there was too much of the fire-breathing evangelist in the speech. But it was a miraculous thing to bring off with as much of a splash as we did.

The Ten Commandments was a remake for DeMille. He'd made the first version in 1923. Somebody said, "God gave us Ten Commandments and left it to DeMille to give us twenty."

Many people in Hollywood privately accused DeMille of being a hypocrite for bringing the Bible to the screen while it was common knowledge that he'd had a succession of mistresses and interludes with many of his female stars.

I prefer to call DeMille a great actor and a great showman rather than a hypocrite. He had the capacity to absolutely believe what he was doing and saying while he was doing and saying it. If he happened to be talking about the virtue of the American home, he'd believe it at the moment, though he

160

was violating it in his personal life. If he happened to be making a film like The Ten Commandments in which one of the Commandments was "Thou shalt not commit adultery" he saw no conflict in that he himself was committing adultery. There was a dichotomy in his moral code, a comfortable, yet somehow sincere dichotomy.

With the possible exceptions of Brigham Young and Thomas Jefferson, and one can't even be sure of them, there have been very few great public leaders and celebrities who didn't keep their private life behind one door and their public life behind another. DeMille tried to be all things to all men, including himself. He never hurt people very much. He was very loyal. He took care of his worn-out actresses and hangers-on. He always took care of his people; he had that quality of *noblesse oblige.*

My career began sinking slowly in the West by the early sixties, when Hollywood was beginning to go. The old Hollywood had begun to fall to pieces, and I was getting pretty old myself in terms of being a dynamic screenwriter. DeMille had died in 1959, and I found no other employer to take his place.

The decision to move to England was made for me. When I had to write for television, and even those jobs were few and far between, I felt my career had slipped into utter hopelessness. Then a lucky phone call came from England. A producer I'd known slightly asked if I'd like to write a film in England. Well, how would I like to breathe? How would I like to go on living? I went to England, of course.

The producer gave me a two-picture deal, but he subsequently turned out to be what many producers are—I suppose unfortunately what they are forced to be—a promoter. But this one was a promoter who failed. My completed screenplay fell into the hands of his creditors, and my wife, Barbara, and I were left absolutely poverty-stricken in England. To be honest, we hardly had the money to come home.

161

And if we came home, we couldn't be sure we were coming back to much.

Then came a chance to do a little job for English television, and I clutched at it. A few more jobs came along in television, and I was earning a living, which gradually got to be a little better each year. Then, happily, Barbara got a bit of capital together in 1964 from one of her wealthy school friends and from her father, and we bought the rights to an English book. We developed a screenplay, and she formed her own small company with the money she'd raised.

We've been able to produce a few pictures, no smash hits you've heard of. But essentially we've been unlucky because of various things. A change in government in Greece killed one picture we wanted to make there, and that lost us quite a good deal of money.

I now write books and an occasional screenplay . . . and we are getting by.

I suppose I share one of my father's traits—I lack bitterness, too. Of course I've never made and lost millions, but I managed to make a decent living in the old Hollywood.

In its heyday Hollywood was a fascinating, a golden place. The cruelty was always there when you were between jobs or had bad reviews or if you were known to be in debt. You could be wiped out very quickly professionally, scrubbed from the slate, a figure to be avoided.

Nevertheless, the grandeur was there. Because you didn't have to do what exists today. Nobody had a courier out looking for money to make films. The great companies had money and they looked for the films, not the money. And the producers were showmen who could lift their eyes to vast projects. Their films may have looked like circuses at times, but still there was always a project. It wasn't a matter of scurrying around to get a few bucks together and somehow coming up with a package. They didn't have to operate that way. The old moguls worried about the film rather than the financing.

162

Suddenly the world changed—television, inflation, the spiraling cost of production due in part to the rising cost of the unions. Pictures became too expensive to make. The audience became more sophisticated because of cheap travel. A lot of the mystery, the adventure, the romance in the old movies was lost because people didn't have to go to a theater to see Morocco. They could get a package tour to Morocco and be back in a week. The shrinking of the world and the cynicism that set in after the war, the loss of the old simplistic idealism and the sense of fantasy were other factors that destroyed Hollywood. Film became less of a product and more an art form. And there is always a smaller audience for art than for product.

I look back on it all with great, great fondness. I don't delude myself about its seamy side, the abuse of power and the extravagance. But that was part of the sort of circus in which we lived.

But think about it—suppose the motion-picture camera had never been invented. Suppose my father and the other pioneers hadn't created Hollywood. It would have been a much sadder kind of world. I think motion pictures have been very important in alleviating the burdens of people. They have served, on a vaster scale, to perpetuate values, as the morality plays did in the Middle Ages. Films gave people an orientation and showed them the difference between good and evil, right and wrong.

The Hollywood I knew served its purpose magnificently. Today people are more sophisticated and things are changing and the world is becoming much more complex and horrific.

I loved the old Hollywood, and because it's gone, something of splendor has been lost by all of us.

15

Lew Ayres

THE JOURNEY OF YOUNG DR. KILDARE

BORN LEWIS FREDRICK Ayres III in 1908, he is still boy-
ish-looking. "I think there have been about a hundred films. I never
really kept count. Every once in a while I'm surprised to hear that
one I'd forgotten has cropped up on late, late TV."

He was one of Hollywood's most popular—and controversial—
leading men. Divorced from his first wife, Lola Lane, in 1933 on
charges of cruelty, he married Ginger Rogers the following year.
That liaison lasted two years. "I haven't seen Ginger in twenty
years." He did not marry again until 1964. His third wife is Diana
Hall, a former stewardess. They have a five-year-old son, Justin
Bret.

A reflective, introspective and private man, he seldom consents to
interviews. "There are so many important things to be thinking and
talking about. I really don't see how people can waste precious time
on such irrelevancies as discussing my life or the movie business."

The following interview, arranged through a mutual friend, got
off to a touchy start.

"I wasn't told there would be a tape recorder," Ayres said with
pique and suspicion.

Reassured that it was only a means of getting an accurate record
of the conversation, he thought a moment, then relaxed. "It's just
that I'm a very cautious man," he said, smiling and cooperative and
pleasant now.

His home is in gold coast West Los Angeles, in Brentwood, near

*the summit of a winding hill. The house is modern and rectangular,
supported by great graceful wooden beams. It has a spacious stone
driveway and huge sun-grabbing windows that filter glare and
afford a mile-long view.*

*In the library, the shelves lined most conspicuously with religious
books, Ayres is dressed in slacks and an alligator-speckled golf shirt.
Despite his self-declared caution, he talked with frankness and di-
rectness.*

My secret ambition as a youngster was to be an actor. But it
was a very well-kept secret. I included no one in that confidence, not my family or friends. I grew up in Minneapolis in
a very suburban kind of Midwestern society. No one talked
about things like being an actor. It was so farfetched in that
rather insulated time and place that was two thousand miles
from here.

The great stellar personalities I admired in my youth
were Valentino and John Gilbert. It was, it truly was, my secret ambition to be a part of their world. I tried to find a way
into it, and one of the things I did was to become a musician.
I learned to play the guitar, the banjo and several string instruments. I wasn't much of a musician, but as many youngsters do today, I managed to play with a number of small
combos.

I was thrilled when my family moved to San Diego. I was
about fourteen then, and that brought me closer to Hollywood. After finishing high school, I began playing with orchestras and finally played with some very good ones, nota-
bly Henry Halstead. He was one of the biggest bandleaders
out here, rivaled only by Paul Whiteman in popularity.

We were the first orchestra to play the Beverly Wilshire
Hotel in Los Angeles. Since I was now where movies were being made, I used my spare time to go to the casting offices of
the studios. I was very naïve and knew nothing about acting.
Hard as it is to believe, I thought that the casting director di-

rected films. I was not only ignorant but shy. I said very little in my interviews. Nevertheless, the casting director at Paramount gave me a test. It didn't come off. It wasn't suitable, and he discouraged me from entering the acting profession. I was eighteen or nineteen, and I was crushed; my long-held ambition had gone up in smoke.

To complicate matters, our engagement at the Beverly Wilshire had ended. I was out of work, or between jobs, as the saying goes. I went to the Roosevelt Hotel on Hollywood Boulevard to visit some musicians I knew who were playing there. There was an afternoon dance in progress, and the custom was that you were literally entitled to walk up to anybody who was free and ask for a dance. I saw an attractive young lady sitting at a table with an older woman, and I went over and asked for a dance. I had no idea who she was.

When the dance was over and I was leaving, a man stopped me.

"Are you an actor?"

"No, but I'd like to be. I'd like very much to be an actor."

"You danced very well with Lily."

My partner had been Lily Damita, who had just arrived from France to make pictures in Hollywood. She was quite a famous actress, who married Errol Flynn a little later.

The man I was talking to was Ivan Kahn. He became my agent; he was like a foster father to me until the day he died a few years ago. You aren't discovered that way anymore. At that time a man like Ivan would just stop anyone he thought might be photogenic, might be likely material for the screen, and take a chance on him. Thus my career began on that gossamer thread.

Ivan arranged a six-month contract for me at Pathé. I played bits for the most part. Such as it was, they had a school for acting. We did little plays, and our teachers were old actors from films and the stage.

When my contract expired, I was dropped. But the man who'd signed me at Pathé was Paul Bern, who married Jean

Harlow and soon after committed suicide. Bern had gone over to MGM, where he was producing Garbo's last silent film, *The Kiss*. He sent for me, and I got the role of the juvenile in the picture, quite a large and important part.

I was flabbergasted to find myself working with Garbo. She was the most glamorous woman. I remember her saying, "I'm a woman who's unfaithful to a million men." To this day I don't think there's been another star more glamorous than Garbo.

There was a mood orchestra on the set during all the scenes. Five pieces, including a violinist and a man who played a small organ. I found Garbo a gracious lady, and far more shy than I'd ever been. In the love scenes, which were considered quite intimate at that time, no one was permitted to watch her doing them except the director. That was Garbo's demand, not a request. She insisted on a screen that would hide her from the crew. She did that, not because she was temperamental. She was just embarrassed. She said she felt more relaxed doing her love scenes as privately as possible.

During that picture she originated the private dressing room for film stars. She was the first to insist that she have one. She was given a cubicle, just four wooden flats on wheels. I didn't work with anyone else for a long time who had a private dressing room. While making *The Kiss*, I would dress offstage, in a corner someplace, or I'd bring my wardrobe with me.

Garbo had very little to say. She seemed quite meditative. I don't believe she was an intellectual. She was a woman with a great talent who was very much wrapped up in her own thoughts.

The film helped my career, of course, but it didn't establish me as a star. Sound was coming in, and many silent actors were going by the wayside. Nobody knew if I could talk. Unlike so many others, when I got the opportunity, my voice seemed to register well on the screen.

It didn't seem to cut any particular ice that I'd made a picture with Garbo when I wanted to test for *All Quiet on the Western Front*. Every young actor in town was being tested for the picture, everyone apparently except me. I had to wait a long time for my chance, I'm not sure why. Finally, Ivan was able to arrange it solely because they'd been testing for months and still weren't satisfied.

When I went to the studio, I didn't expect a test for the lead in *All Quiet*. There were eight or nine good roles in it, and I would have been happy to play any one of them.

George Cukor was then a dialogue director, and I made my test with him. Cukor was assisting Lewis Milestone, who was going to direct the picture.

Milestone told me later that he wanted Douglas Fairbanks, Jr., for the part I got. But the day after I tested he received word that Fairbanks wasn't available. Milestone dreaded going back and looking at months of tests of so many actors. But he was under pressure and had to make a decision. When he went into the projection room, he simply asked the projectionist to run the film of whoever had tested the previous day. That happened to be me. And that's how I got the role. So there is a great deal of fate in whatever you do in life, which is a little frightening but also interesting.

I played the part of a young German soldier who learns about the bitterness and futility of war. At the start of the film he and his friends are all extremely patriotic, all eager to join in this great adventure of conquest. He is told that the war is a defensive one and therefore justifiable. But he comes to see the uselessness of war, that he and his friends are participating in something meaningless, that war has meaning only for the leaders of nations who could bask in the glory of it.

We were on the picture for five months, and I was saturated with Erich Maria Remarque's philosophy of the futility of war. I would not say that his was the background of my particular stand in World War II, but I wouldn't say it didn't have some effect.

The picture came out and won an Academy Award, and in the language of the press I was "catapulted to instant stardom." I suppose that was true, but my career became a roller coaster, with many ups and downs. To this day, and that was more than forty years ago, people seem to remember *All Quiet* and *Dr. Kildare* beyond any other roles I've done.

After *All Quiet* I made several very good, successful films. One was with Constance Bennett called *Common Clay*. A gangster picture I did, one of the earliest in that genre, had James Cagney playing a small role as my pal. That was called *Doorway to Hell*. Those two films plus *All Quiet* kind of clinched my acceptance. I then made quite a few that were unsuccessful, pictures that no one has heard of—*Iron Man*, *Up for Murder*, *Silk Hat Kid*, and many others of that ilk.

Some were quite bad, and my career went down for a while. And I feel it should have because I was really far too young and inexperienced to be shot into this big ocean of stardom that commenced with *All Quiet*. I wasn't prepared for stardom by apprenticeship or education. As time went on, I became aware of the paucity of my background. I'd never gone to college, and the writers, producers and directors with whom I was working as a star—well, I was unable to communicate with them, and it made me feel ill at ease. So the important thrust in my life became seeking an education. I embarked on a course of study that has never stopped to this day. The search for knowledge remains the greatest fascination of my life.

Under contract to various studios, two years at Fox, four years at Universal, two years at Paramount, a year or so at Columbia, I did a great many more pictures, largely undistinguished. I was pretty well known, but a little shopworn.

Then I did a picture with Katharine Hepburn and Cary Grant called *Holiday*, which turned out well, and that caught the eye of MGM.

They'd come up with the idea of doing the *Dr. Kildare* series. Here is a case of doing a role that I didn't want to do. Many actors in those days didn't want to do a series, and I was one of them. We thought a series was limiting, that it was best to do something fresh and different in each film. The old classic idea of an actor is one who plays a great variety of roles, who has scope and breadth, who can play roles in which he is young, old, rich, poor. Of course, there were the personality actors, Spencer Tracy, Gable and Gary Cooper, who more or less played themselves all the time. But they did exhibit some growth and showed different sides of themselves as they matured. There were others who were stars, and I won't name them, who did not grow. They lasted for a while, but we professionals got so tired of seeing them. I knew mood for mood, gesture for gesture, exactly how they would react to every situation in the script. They did their parts effectively, but it was a bore because you had seen it so many times. You became tired of them; you couldn't really identify with them or with the roles they were playing. They didn't expand and grow, but as time went on, the great ones did.

I have always had sort of a religious orientation, and my life has something of the mystical about it. I don't know if you can understand that. Anyway, when I am truly puzzled about a decision, I can suddenly turn and really ask the cosmos or whatever you want to call God, and I will get strong answers. I always get a definite yes or no answer. I was absolutely determined that I wouldn't do *Kildare*. But the studio was urging me into it. Finally, I stopped dead, and I asked, Well, now, should I do it? I dropped my own personal views about it. I simply opened myself for an answer, and I have never had more of a yes smack me right in the face as this one did. There was absolutely no evading it. Something just said, "You do it!" It's not a voice, just something within you that somehow registers a positive or a negative that is a very concrete thing. I've had a number of instances in my life, which are treasures to me, where I've had a communication of a kind from a voice that is stronger than I've ever heard from a human being. It's a silent voice, but it's tangible.

So I went into the series, and I was sorry in a way that the first one, *Young Dr. Kildare,* was quite successful. They all came running with the good news that the series was going to continue. We ultimately made about twelve, including *Calling Dr. Kildare, The Secret of Dr. Kildare, Dr. Kildare's Strange Case, Dr. Kildare Goes Home, Dr. Kildare's Crisis, Dr. Kildare's Wedding Day.* I can't tell one from another now, they're all hooked together in my mind. Each of them ran about an hour and a half. That is quite a bit of film. We had a doctor on the set at all times, who was the technical adviser. Each of the *Kildare* films dealt with some new medical discovery, and so I learned a good deal about medicine.

Lionel Barrymore, who played Dr. Gillespie, was thirty years older than me, but we had a wonderful relationship. He was far my superior in every way, in background and experience. But we shared offscreen interests in many things. We both painted and composed music. We became quite well acquainted, and we had a quiet relationship that consisted primarily of a great many serious, exploring conversations about the nature of art, of life and death, as well as films and theater.

When World War II came along, I became a conscientious objector. I said I wouldn't take up a gun and kill anyone, that war is the worst of all crimes. My position raised an enormous furor.* I went into the Army as a medic, and then I be-

Variety called him a "disgrace" to America. Thousands of letters poured into MGM from fans saying Ayres had been their favorite star but

171

came an assistant chaplain. Two years of my service was in the Philippines. I was with MacArthur's forces when we landed on Leyte and two other beachheads.

When I came back after the war, I thought perhaps my career was ruined. I wasn't hurt by the criticism. I was prepared for it. When you go counter to what practically everyone else feels, you must expect some people will be vituperative, and many were. But for some reason I was given some of the best films of my life. I worked with Olivia de Havilland in *Dark Mirror* in 1946. I did *Johnny Belinda* with Jane Wyman in 1947. I had gone counter to the general emotional feeling of most of the American people, I was surprised at their hospitality to me. And grateful that they seemed to understand the way I felt. They accepted me back not only as a person but as a movie actor. And that's the way it's been ever since.

I still have strong antiwar convictions. I'd rather not comment on the young Americans who fled to Canada and Sweden to avoid the Vietnam draft. I can't act as another man's conscience. Every man must do that for himself.

The highlight of my career, so far as I'm concerned, wasn't *All Quiet* or *Dr. Kildare*. For me, the outstanding thing I've done was a series of films I made on world religions in the 1950's. They consisted of nine documentaries titled *Altars of the East* and dealt with every religion except Christianity. They received excellent reviews, and I was delighted. They're still shown in universities and museums, and people seem to respond affirmatively to them.

Now I'm just an old motion-picture actor. I'm no longer one of the important players, but I choose whatever I do carefully. I turn things down all the time that I don't feel are

---

now they would boycott his films. He was labeled a traitor and a coward, and many theaters throughout the United States refused to show his pictures.

right for me or don't square with my convictions. I won't appear in trash. I feel that if a film doesn't make the kind of social comment with which I agree, I have no responsibility to participate in it.

I've had more than forty years of it now. I no longer have any particular ambitions regarding acting. I still enjoy it and am willing to go along so long as I get roles that are halfway decent or parts that I feel are interesting. I don't do walkons, just to be there. I have no hunger to smell greasepaint or to be in the atmosphere of acting just for the sake of being in that atmosphere.

I feel each of us should render to society in some measure that which we can. Somebody has to pump the gas and deliver the bread. If I can participate in a film that offers society something worthwhile, that is satisfying to me.

I do four or five roles a year now, and that's about it. The rest of the time I study. I am concerned with trying to understand more about life. I am trying to learn more about life.

You realize that reincarnation is a possibility that can't entirely be dismissed. If I were to come back, I'd like to be a teacher or a philosopher or perhaps a theologian dealing with things of the spirit. I would never want to return as an actor.

16

Ken Murray

HIS OSCAR WAS FOR THE BIRDS

IN THE DARKENED *living room of his Williamsburg-style home in Beverly Hills, the projector whirs and the screen kicks alive with rara avis footage. There they are—Hollywood's bright shining stars, frozen by Murray's camera in informal offscreen moments. Charlie Chaplin unsuccessfully navigating a high-wheeled bicycle, headed for a spill. Tom Mix handing sugar to his horse, Tony, in the only color film ever shot of the cowboy hero. Mix is standing in front of his white Auburn, the car in which he would soon be killed in an auto wreck. W. C. Fields, with the hat and cane he wore in David Copperfield, juggling dexterously and hilariously attempting to maneuver a cigarette into his mouth rather than his nose. Maurice Chevalier looking uncomfortable but still debonair as he feeds Baby LeRoy a bottle of milk. A boyish John Wayne playing Ping-Pong with a baby-faced Dick Powell. . . .*

After an hour or so the lights go up in the gemütlich *room, tastefully furnished by Murray's wife, Betty Lou, in authentic Early American.*

"I've shot hundreds of thousands of miles of film since I came out here in 1927," says this most amiable of men, a walking encyclopedia of Hollywood lore, as he seats himself in a captain's chair. "My collection is priceless. I wouldn't take a million for it, and I've been offered a million."

His home movies compose an unofficial forty-seven-year history of Hollywood. There isn't a major star, from Clara Bow to Ann-Mar-

gret, from Douglas Fairbanks, Sr., to Jack Lemmon, who hasn't posed for his ubiquitous camera.

Murray has been successful in every branch of show business—vaudeville, the stage, radio, movies and television. His first and abiding love, however, has always been the screen. "I'm superfan," he says. "You're looking at a man who's still star-struck, a guy who almost goes numb every time I meet a movie star."

It started for me as a kid in Kingston, New York, where I was born in 1903. There wasn't even a real movie theater in town. We watched pictures, which changed once a week, at the firemen's hall.

My father was a vaudevillian, and I can't remember having any other ambition except show business. I especially wanted to be a movie star. I figured the best route to that goal was vaudeville. My father, unfortunately, had a who cares, let's have another glass of beer attitude. Me, I was more ambitious. I was determined to get to the top. You must have that kind of drive to make it big. You had to think you'd be good enough one day to make the world forget about Fairbanks and Valentino.

By the time I graduated from high school I'd learned everything I thought a vaudevillian would need to know. How to spin a rope. Play the cornet and the clarinet. Dance the soft shoe, the waltz, the clog. How to sing. Juggle. Crack a whip. I can still slap a cigarette out of your mouth with a whip from twenty feet away. To my surprise, I also seemed to have a bent for comedy, which I honed. I learned timing, pacing and, hopefully, what was funny and what wasn't. Comedy is the most elusive material to deal with. In my entire career, I was never one hundred percent sure how or if a gag would play. A lot depends on the audience as well as the comedian. I like what Will Rogers said about comedy: "An onion can make people cry, but there's never been a vegetable invented to make them laugh."

I learned everything myself. There was no school to teach me anything. Even my father, God rest his soul, was too preoccupied to help me. He was on the road a lot, and when he came home, he wanted to forget about the business.

I got my first job in vaudeville in 1922 and played the tank town circuit. I reached the Palace in New York, that heaven for all vaudevillians, in an amazingly short time, by 1926. That was pretty good considering the competition in those days. Eddie Cantor. Burns and Allen. Smith and Dale. Eddie Foy. Bob Hope, thank God, was still on his way up. In 1926 I was making fifteen hundred a week topping the bill at the Palace. I played there in '27, '28 and '29 and worked my salary up to twenty-seven hundred a week, which isn't bad money even today.

The Palace was owned by RKO. I was approached by an RKO executive who offered me a seven-year movie contract. The contract said I could do pictures as well as vaudeville. I insisted on that clause because I wanted insurance. I was doing okay in vaudeville, but who knew how the picture career would go?

I came to Hollywood, and while I was waiting for the cameras to roll on my first movie, I played the Orpheum Theater in downtown Los Angeles. Opening night the place was filled with movie stars. Chaplin and Doug Fairbanks were there.

Fairbanks came backstage to greet Edmund Breese, a fine actor, who was also on the bill. I cornered Fairbanks and said, "I'm your number one fan. Can I come out to the studio and take some pictures of you?" He smiled and agreed. While we were standing there, somebody came up to Fairbanks and asked him to autograph a picture of himself. One of my amateur hobbies was reading handwriting. As Fairbanks signed the picture, I sort of interpreted his signature. It indicated a very decisive character. The heavy swirl said he was an optimist and a man who didn't care much for details.

I went to the studio the next day, and Fairbanks was gracious enough to pose. He even did a few leaps and somersaults for my camera. He was the first star I ever put on film in what became my home movie collection. I never thought it would become such a big thing, that one day I'd do a one-man show on Broadway featuring nothing but my film.

The home movies started because I hated to write letters. Before leaving New York, I'd bought a projector and left it with my parents. I took the camera with me, and every time I 'shot some footage of a star I'd send it back to the folks. Those were my letters, my postcards.

That first day on the set I could hardly believe that my dream of being in the movies had become real. My maiden effort, *Half Marriage*, was a comedy in which I was a playboy politely trying to seduce my leading lady. It was fairly risqué for its time. *Half Marriage* turned out to be an acceptable picture. It wasn't a tremendous hit like two other RKO films that came out around that time, *Cimarron* and *Rio Rita*. My costar in *Half Marriage* was a beautiful girl named Olive Borden. She chucked her movie career a few years later and went down to skid row in Los Angeles to devote herself to helping alcoholics. She could have done the same work among a lot of the stars in Hollywood.

Half Marriage was the first picture made at RKO under the regime of Joe Kennedy. He took the studio over as a stock manipulation, and he ran it in a cutthroat fashion. He took off his jacket, raised hell, cut salaries and canceled the contracts of a lot of important players. The studio had been in severe financial trouble, and Kennedy got it back on its feet by being ruthless. Once he drove the price of the stock up, he sold out and went home to raise a President and two Senators.

Kennedy was the toughest kind of businessman, the kind that scares me. There's tough, and there's tough. You know, you go into the office of a movie executive or a producer, and they disarm you by being charming and pleasant, though they're steel underneath. Kennedy wasn't like that. That wasn't his style. If Kennedy had any charm, he kept it hidden in his pocket. He was gruff and all business. He wasn't a guy for small talk. He didn't waste time saying hello. When it came to discussing contracts and money, he didn't give an inch. I'd say that Sam Goldwyn, Louis B. Mayer, Jack Warner and Harry Cohn were pussycats compared to Joe Kennedy. It may or may not be a good thing that Kennedy didn't stay in the movie business too long. Probably a good thing because he was the total businessman and he didn't have the feel for showmanship that the other moguls did.

Nevertheless, I got along with Kennedy. He picked up my yearly options without too much fuss. I made four or five pictures for him, and he used me in a very clever way. After each film he sent me around the country to play the stage show with the picture. RKO's theaters were dying at the time, and anybody who had a name helped the box office.

The second picture was *Leathernecking*. My leading lady in that one was a teen-ager who'd come out of a road company production of *Showboat* in Chicago. Her name was Irene Dunne. And she wasn't the typical young movie ingenue. Even then, she was a lady with style and sophistication, mature beyond her years. I don't think Irene Dunne was ever a little girl. That picture, by the way, which was made in 1929, had one little color sequence in it. They were already experimenting with color, and it was murder. The lights were so hot that there's one close-up of me where tears are coming out of my eyes. I wasn't supposed to be crying, but the hot lights induced the tears. They left the shot in, though it was out of place in the story. I was crying in a shot where I was supposed to be laughing. Everybody said, What the hell, the important thing is the color, not whether Murray's laughing or crying. They were right—the picture made a bundle, helped by the novelty of color.

In my next one, *Ladies of the Jury*, a girl named Jill Esmond played the lead. Outside the entrance to the studio on Gower there was a bench, and every night after work I'd see a young fellow sitting there. "What time do you think Miss Esmond will be finished?" he'd ask. And I'd tell him when he could expect her. They wouldn't let the poor guy into the studio, wouldn't let him on the set, even though his name was Laurence Olivier and even though Jill Esmond was his wife. Olivier was out here to do a picture with Garbo. He'd been signed to star with her in *Queen Christina*. But Garbo turned him down. She wanted to do the picture with John Gilbert, who'd bombed out when talkies came in. Garbo wanted to give Gilbert another chance, which was a lovely gesture on her part. And Olivier seems to have survived the blow of losing that role.

After Kennedy left RKO and David Selznick came in as head of production, he called me into his office one day and said, "We're going to keep picking up your option. But I really don't know what to do with you. I operate on the premise that a leading man looks like a leading man. A heroine looks like a heroine. And a comedian looks like a comedian. But you don't look like a comedian. You're taller than most of our leading men, and you're normal-looking. But we'll try to find a character for you, a screen personality."

I was then cast in a series of forgettable pictures where I played those fast-talking, press-agent-type guys. Finally, I thought, What is this? I don't want to spend my life shaking a cigar at the leading lady. I played out every day of my contract at RKO, and that was it. The character, the personality that Selznick talked about didn't materialize. Nothing great came along . . . that one pivotal role. As I look back, it was a blessing. And that's not sour grapes, though at the time I was shaken when I realized I wasn't going to be another Fairbanks. I discovered I was interested in a great many things, and I'll never live long enough to do all the things I want to do.

So making pictures didn't become my primary business, though I've often wondered what my primary business is. I've worked in dozens of pictures through the years. I did *You're a Sweetheart* at Paramount, *A Night at Earl Carroll's* for

Warner Brothers, and *Son of Flubber* for Disney. They were all light comedy parts, but the role I liked the most was playing a drunken doctor for John Ford in *The Man Who Shot Liberty Valance*, with Wayne and Jimmy Stewart. Sure, comics want to play Hamlet. That part was my Hamlet.

One of the first friends I made in Hollywood was Arthur Lake, who was Dagwood in the *Blondie* series.

"You've got to meet the Chief," Arthur said to me one day. When he saw the puzzled look on my face, he added, "I mean, William Randolph Hearst."

Meeting Hearst wasn't any big thing for me. But when Arthur told me about all the movie stars who visited San Simeon, that was another matter entirely. That would give me a chance to shoot a lot of casual and informal film of the biggest names in the business.

That first trip of mine to San Simeon was in 1933. Arthur and I drove up and arrived as it was getting dark. But I could see enough so that the place hit me with the same wallop as it does everyone else. Arthur said the whole spread consisted of two hundred and seventy-five thousand acres. I could see three guesthouses besides the main house, which looked like a castle. There were hundreds of animals roaming around.

Arthur and I went into the assembly room of the main house, where Hearst was milling around among his guests. To give you an idea, that room alone was eighty-four by thirty-three feet, and it was filled with priceless paintings and artifacts.

Arthur took me by the arm and guided me through the crowd to Hearst. "Chief," Arthur said, "I want you to meet my friend Ken Murray."

"Welcome to the ranch," Hearst said in that high-pitched voice he had.

Then I said one of those things that haunt you the rest of your life. "Mr. Hearst, you sure have got a nice little place here." Can you imagine? I wasn't trying to be funny. It just came out that way. Hearst must have thought I was an idiot.

Aw, I was so embarrassed that I've never told that story to this moment. I didn't even put it in my own book.* Hearst kind of smiled, one of those Coolidge lip-curler smiles.

To me that was a big incident. I guess it didn't bother Hearst because I was invited back frequently.

Hearst and I weren't bunk buddies or anything. We didn't sleep in the same room the times I was there. No one got to know him that well except Marion Davies. The quality that most impressed me about Hearst was his lack of phoniness. He was a realist. He didn't play it humble, and he didn't play it like he was a king. He simply accepted what he was and what he had.

I spent most of my time during my visits to San Simeon taking pictures. Hearst himself posed for me. So did Marion. One weekend I was there Hearst entertained Gable, Cary Grant, the shah of Iran, Hedda Hopper, Louella Parsons and Dolores Del Rio. The weekend before, Garbo had been a guest. Another time I was up there the guests included Constance Talmadge, Buster Keaton and Bill Tilden, the tennis champ. It was one great giant candy store for a camera buff like me.

There usually would be about sixty for dinner. Once I was seated next to Marion, who was a delightful, witty and wonderful girl. She was much maligned and underrated by a lot of people in Hollywood.

Concerning Hearst, all I can say is that he was a very cordial host and a very nice man. He wasn't a funny man, a great raconteur or storyteller. He seemed content to listen to his guests for the most part. He wasn't trying to prove anything. He didn't have to.

San Simeon was a great deal like being in a resort hotel. Guests were free to do whatever they wanted. You didn't see

*The Golden Days of San Simeon, published by Doubleday in 1971. As of this writing, the $10 book has gone through eleven printings and sold some 50,000 copies.

Hearst until lunchtime or dinner. You didn't have to be at the table for lunch, but dinner was a command performance.

As I said, he was a nice man. I never did business with him. Maybe he was entirely different when he did business. Maybe in business he was as tough as Joe Kennedy. All I know is he treated me well, and I told him a lot of stories that made him laugh. I was still trying to make up for that first gaffe.

San Simeon, you might say, was for me the pause that refreshes. My career was zigzagging through a picture now and then, radio and nightclubs. By now the old two-a-day vaudeville circuit was a memory. But I'd never lost my love for vaudeville, and neither had a lot of other people. So I took it upon myself to bring it back, dressed up in new clothes.

That idea translated itself into *Blackouts,* which I opened in 1942. Everybody in the business, including my agent, said I was crazy to put my own money into a vaudeville review. But the show was a smash hit from the beginning. Actually, it was like stealing money. Remember, that was wartime Hollywood. There was no Disneyland or Knott's Berry Farm or an organized tour of the Universal lot. There was next to nothing for the tourists and servicemen to do when they hit Hollywood. You could only get on a movie set if you knew someone. The only things the average visitor could see were Grauman's Chinese and Forest Lawn.

But it took more than a "captive" audience to make *Blackouts* succeed. It succeeded first and foremost because it was pure entertainment, filled with pretty girls, with Marie Wilson and all her wonderful nonsense, with sketches and fun. And I guess I didn't hurt it any.

Blackouts turned into a miracle. It became the longest running show in the theater.* It grossed over seven million dollars in seven and a half years.

Everyone came. Dick Nixon was a Congressman then, and

---

*3,884 performances. According to the 1974 *World Almanac,* the five most durable Broadway shows were *Fiddler on the Roof,* 3,242 performances; *Life* he was a big *Blackouts* fan. He saw the show maybe a dozen times and always brought a number of people with him. One night Nixon came backstage and told me, "I enjoy the show more every time I see it. Thank God for *Blackouts*. I don't know where else I could take a lot of these dull political people I have to entertain."

Garbo was in several times on the QT. We'd reserve a seat for her in the balcony, and she'd slip in after the curtain went up and leave just before the curtain went down. When there were stars in the audience, I'd usually introduce them. Hope would come on stage and do half an hour. W. C. Fields, Jack Benny and George Burns also came up and ad-libbed with me. Of course, I never put Garbo in that position. And I didn't do it with another star I spotted in the audience one night because he wasn't wearing his toupee, and I knew he'd be embarrassed. The next day I got a telegram from him which said: DEAR KEN. LOVED YOUR SHOW LAST NIGHT. AND THANKS FOR YOU KNOW WHAT. FRED ASTAIRE.

By 1947 *Blackouts* was cruising along like a ship on automatic pilot in a clear sea. But a successful show wasn't enough for me. I was restless, and I needed another project. To put it mildly, the project I chose made people question my sanity—just as they had when I opened *Blackouts*.

I had an act in *Blackouts* called "George Burton and His Lovebirds." He had fourteen birds, parakeets to doves. Every time I watched them I was entranced. To me they seemed almost like little people. George would talk to them; he would never touch them. He would talk to them, and they'd do all these amazing circus tricks. They'd do anything he wanted. So I thought, Gee, these birds would make a hell of a picture.

I wrote a script called *Bill and Coo*, and I wrote it as if the birds were people. Bill and Coo, my hero and heroine, lived

with *Father*, 3,213; *Tobacco Road*, 3,182; *Hello, Dolly!*, 2,844; and *My Fair Lady*, 2,717.

in a town named Chirpendale. The whole thing was that they were constantly being menaced by a crow called Himmy. I wrote in several big sequences involving a circus, a parade, a wedding and a fire. There were parts for three hundred birds. It was sort of a large-scale bird-land Western. It had scope, drama, passion, love, conflict. It boiled down to the classic fight of good against evil.

When I was finished, I thought I had an interesting, offbeat property. And I was breaking new ground. Up to this time even Walt Disney hadn't done a picture with live animals. All his stuff was cartoons.

I decided to produce the picture myself, and the first thing an independent producer does is try to find a studio that will supply facilities, financing and distribution.

I went to the majors. At Fox I talked with Zanuck, and he sort of looked at me if I'd just landed from Mars. "No," he said, "we've never done anything like this. Anyway, I don't think you can bring it off." MGM—I couldn't get past the guards to see Louis B. Mayer. I knew Jack Warner, and I talked to him about *Bill and Coo*. He said he'd do it as a short. But a short meant a onetime flat sum without owning a piece of the picture. Bing Crosby took me to see Y. Frank Freeman at Paramount. Freeman also saw it as a short. I got the same reaction at RKO. I'd tried the five majors and struck out five times.

In desperation I went to see Herbert J. Yates, the president of Republic. He sparked to the idea. He'd let me make it as a feature and in my own way. Yates said I could have cameras, a sound stage, a crew, and he would distribute the picture. After those charges were subtracted, I'd own *Bill and Coo*. Yates himself wouldn't put up any money.

But now that I had access to a studio, I figured the financing would be easy. My credit rating was first-rate. I mean, I could go in and sign a note for a hundred thousand dollars without collateral.

I went to a friend of mine who was vice-president of a

Bank of America branch in Hollywood. When he saw me, he jumped to attention like I was Howard Hughes.

"Sit down, sit down, Ken. What's on your mind?"

"Look," I said, "I need a little money for a picture I want to make."

"Fine. Don't tell me. You're going to make a picture out of *Blackouts*. With you and Marie, it'll be sensational. How much do you want?"

"Three hundred and fifty thousand."

"No problem. No problem at all."

"The picture isn't going to be a screen version of *Blackouts*. It's going to be a feature with birds, three hundred of them."

"Oh, yeah, birds. I suppose that could work. People love birds. Of course you're going to be in the picture. You're going to be the star."

"No, I'm not going to be in it. It isn't that kind of a picture. The hero and heroine are parakeets. The heavy is a crow. It's going to be one hundred and twenty minutes of birds, all birds."

"All birds?"

"All birds."

"That's very interesting."

He got up from his desk—you know, the move people make when they want to get rid of you, they get up first. He put his arm around me and said, "All birds, huh?"

"That's right."

"I'll have to talk to our loan committee. You know, Ken, you've been working awfully hard. You ought to take a nice long vacation."

He went out the door with me to my car. As I turned the ignition, he said, "Three hundred birds? And the heavy's going to be a crow? You're sure about that?"

"I'm sure. What about the financing?"

"I'll let you know when I've talked to the boys."

I guess I hadn't done much of a selling job. I guess I sounded ridiculous. Needless to say, I never heard from him.

185

I ended up financing *Bill and Coo* myself, in partnership with my lawyer, Dave Siegal. He'd also been the angel who put up half the money for *Blackouts*.

We had a tight thirty-day schedule to shoot the picture. As it turned out, the only bargain in the project was that we could feed our stars birdseed. Everything else was very expensive, and we went way over budget. We'd start at eight o'clock in the morning and work until five or five thirty the next morning, with me taking time out to do *Blackouts*. The crew was into golden time and double time.

As talented as George Burton was, he couldn't always control the birds. There was no air conditioning on the sound stage, and when we opened the doors one day during a break, Jimmy the Crow flew out. It took a day and a half to find him. One time Coo, who was dressed in a bridal outfit for the lakeside wedding scene, jumped into the water. The camerman wouldn't shoot her with wet feathers. "It would look just awful," he said.

"Then get a fan and dry her off," I said.

George Burton wouldn't hear of it. "You can't use a fan on Coo. It might give her pneumonia."

Somehow we finished on schedule. And when the picture opened a few months later, the notices were raves.

One date I'll never forget is March 21, 1948. I was in the Shrine Auditorium on Academy Award night, and my name was called. I ran up to the stage, and Ingrid Bergman and Jean Hersholt presented me with a special Oscar for outstanding and innovative achievement in the film medium. I'd won the Oscar that Disney won every year. That was the first year that Disney didn't win it.

The film eventually grossed between two and three million dollars, and it's still making money. It still plays all over the world and on television.

After *Bill and Coo*, I did another year of *Blackouts*. We finally closed to capacity in 1949. The only reason I had to fold was because I'd signed a three-year three-hundred-thousand-dollar deal to do a television show for Bill Paley on CBS. It had to be done in New York. At that time there was no cable, and in those days all the important live shows were done in New York.

I decided to do both the television show and *Blackouts* while I was in New York. Then I found out that Marie Wilson couldn't go with me. She'd agreed to do the *My Friend Irma* television show, which could be done out here because it was on film.

I had to find someone to replace Marie. I looked at dozens of girls, and no one was suitable. A friend of mine, an agent named Charlie Wick, called me one day and said, "I've got a girl you must see. She's terrific. She'd be a perfect replacement for Marie."

The girl came down, tried out, and she was fine. She was beautiful and had a marvelous feel for comedy. But there was one problem—she didn't fit Marie's costumes, which were very costly and a pity to throw away and replace. Marie had a thirty-nine-inch bust, and this girl was only thirty-six.

The girl looked like a startled bird. She was maybe sixteen or seventeen years old. I leveled with her and said I didn't have time to wait for her to grow into Marie's wardrobe. She looked at me, and her disappointment was obvious. I told her that she needn't worry, that she was going to make it in show business. And I meant it.

We walked out of my office in the Edgar Bergen Building. As we were going down the hall, we passed the offices of some of the other people. And they guys, you know, were staring at her.

She said, "They're never going to believe that we were just doing an audition."

When we reached her car, she began to cry. Big fat tears came rolling down her cheeks. She asked me again if she could have the part, if the costumes couldn't be redesigned. She said she needed the job, that this could be her big break. I told her that I was sorry, but it wouldn't work.

187

I ended up using Marie's understudy, a girl named Pat Williams, who was the same size as Marie. The name of the girl I turned down was Marilyn Monroe.

It was a lucky thing for Marilyn that I didn't use her. *Blackouts* ran for only fifty-one performances at Billy Rose's Ziegfeld Theater. The critics roasted it. What played in Hollywood didn't play on Broadway, according to Brooks Atkinson of the New York *Times,* Ward Morehouse of the New York *Sun* and the rest of them. I have no excuses for that failure though I've often wondered why such a big hit on the Coast couldn't make it on Broadway. Maybe I was tired, coming in off a seven and a half years' run. Maybe the chemistry in the cast was no longer right. Maybe not having Marie hurt. Maybe Broadway and New York audiences were different. Who knows?

In spite of the critics' disapproval, we didn't do too badly at the box office, an average of twenty-five thousand a week. Our break-even point was thirty-nine thousand. The last week we even showed a small profit, fifteen hundred dollars. I decided to close the show, though the gross was building. Billy Rose asked me to keep going. But I realized that doing an hour television variety series in addition to *Blackouts* would be more work than I could handle. I *was* tired, and I didn't think I could do both things well.

I concentrated on the TV show, which from the time it went on the air was consistently in the top ten.

I'd found a girl named Barbara Dobbins selling cigarettes in a New York nightclub. She was a lovely thing and had kind of a Judy Holliday voice. I made her the secretary on the show and the billboard girl, and I used her in sketches and in some of our big musical numbers. She had talent, and she was an asset to the show.

One day I got a phone call from Arthur Willi, who was a talent scout for Howard Hughes at RKO.

Arthur said, "Howard says he wants that girl, Barbara Dobbins. He thinks he can make a star out of her."

I knew Arthur and knew he was a reputable guy. I had doubts about Hughes, whom I'd met at parties in Hollywood. He never said much, just sat there in his sneakers. But now he had a reputation as a swinger. Still, he'd made Jane Russell a star and maybe he could do the same thing for Barbara.

I told her about the offer from Hughes. "No," she said. "I don't think so. I'm making a lot of money on your show. I'm doing modeling on the side. I'm doing very well. Besides, my boyfriend is in New York. I don't want to go to Hollywood."

I told that to Arthur Willi, and he told Hughes. The next day Arthur called me again and said, "Look, will you come up to my office tonight and bring the girl? Make it midnight, Howard is going to call from the Coast, and he wants to talk to you."

I convinced Barbara to at least listen to Hughes' offer. She reluctantly went with me to Arthur's office. It turned out that Hughes wouldn't speak to me on the phone. Maybe he thought I had germs. All the questions and pleas from Hughes were relayed by Arthur to Barbara. But she repeatedly refused to go to Hollywood. The conversation finally ended in an impasse.

The following day the phone rang in my hotel. Apparently I didn't have germs. It was Hughes.

"Ken, I want the girl."

"It's up to her."

"I really do have a part for her."

"I can't do anything about it, Howard. I can't make her go."

"Ken, I'd appreciate it very much if you'd talk to her again on my behalf. I'll call you back tomorrow."

That was on a Monday, and Hughes wanted Barbara in Hollywood the following Saturday.

I told her, "Look, this is the kind of thing you may regret for the rest of your life if you don't take a shot at it."

We talked for a while, and Barbara changed her mind. She said she'd go.

189

When Hughes called back, I said, "Barbara's coming out."

"I have to test her first," Hughes said. "If it works out, will you give her a release from your show?"

"Certainly. I won't stand in her way."

"Ken," Hughes said, "I appreciate this. I know she's important to your show. You're making a sacrifice. How much do you want for your trouble?"

"Howard," I said, "I'm not a flesh peddler. I don't want anything. And I don't think your suggestion is the most tactful offer I've had in my life."

"Sorry, Ken," he said, hanging up with what I hoped was a blush, if not an apology.

Barbara went out there, and Hughes used her in a couple of pictures. One of them was *The French Line*, with Jane Russell. Then Hughes sold the studio, and Barbara's motion-picture career was over. She went back to New York and married her boyfriend.

My show for Budweiser lasted three years. I was in the time slot, Saturday night at eight o'clock, that Jackie Gleason took over from me and that *All in the Family* has now. The only reason my TV show went off was that Budweiser at the time had only one brewery, in Newark. We were selling so much beer for them that they couldn't meet the demand. No one sponsor could afford to buy an hour show every week.

After my TV show ended, I played Vegas for several years, did a few pictures and television guest shots. Then one day I sat down with my wife and I said, "Who needs all this? We can't keep the money anyway." I was paying an estimated income tax of forty-eight thousand dollars a quarter. I told Betty that I'd been away from home long enough. Now I wanted to see my daughters, Pammy and Janie, grow up. I wanted to take them trick or treating on Halloween. I wanted to join the PTA. I wanted to help them with their homework. I wanted to be with them on Thanksgiving and Christmas and birthdays. I'd never had any family life to speak of. I decided to change that, and I did. Now Pammy's married to a great guy. And Janie is a student at Occidental, majoring in drama. She's played leads in every thing from Shakespeare to Noel Coward, and I'm always there. I'm her biggest fan.

I've enjoyed the last fifteen years or so more than any other period of my life. Show business is okay. It's been good to me. I'm not a millionaire—there were some bad investments I made along the way. But if I'm not rich, I'm comfortable.

I've learned that in the last analysis the only thing that's worthwhile, that's lasting, is your family. When you get on in years in this business, it can be very sad. In a lot of cases it's been pathetic for some of the former stars I know. They've ended up unwanted professionally and divorced and alone. You get older, and no matter how big you've been, all of a sudden everybody you call is busy. No one gives a damn, except your own family. Particularly as a straight actor, you're in a terrible position. You're always waiting to be bought.

I didn't have to be a genius to figure out early in my career that this was a very, very insecure business. That's why I've done so many things. I never wanted to do the one thing with the cigar. I never wanted anyone to say, "If I see Murray come out on the screen or the stage one more time with that cigar, I'll go out of my mind." But when you do a lot of different things, nobody can say, "I'm sick of that guy."

I'm writing a new book on comedy. Right here in my own lab in my own house I made a series of shorts, with film culled from my collection, that are playing in theaters all over the country. Occasionally I do a show in Dallas or Minneapolis built around my home movies. But I'm never gone for more than a week. I must tell you that all these people who are constantly hanging crepe for Hollywood are wrong. I don't think Hollywood is dead. The business is just changing. There's more film being made today, including television, than at the height of the golden era. There's always going to be a Hollywood. God knows, Ken Murray isn't Clark

191

Gable or Spencer Tracy or Dean Martin. But I'm on the movie star maps, and there are people who come to my house every day who ask for autographs. If they do that with me, you figure what they're doing with the superstars, Redford and Paul Newman and guys like Burt Reynolds, Gene Hackman, Warren Beatty and Jimmy Caan.

I didn't want to end up as a one-dimensional man. And I don't think I have. There have been disappointments, sure, but I've had a great career, a wonderful life. I'm still busy, and I find that I'm still wanted.

I'm the luckiest guy in the world.

17

Ann Rutherford

WELCOME HOME, POLLY BENEDICT

ANDY HARDY'S ERSTWHILE girlfriend is a chic, vibrant woman who was born in San Francisco in 1920. "My father and mother had separated, and with my grandmother we moved to Hollywood when I was about eight years old."

She's been married for twenty-one years to television producer Bill Dozier, whose credits range from Playhouse 90 *to* Batman. *They have two children, both from previous marriages. Gloria, twenty-eight, was born while Miss Rutherford was married to department store heir David May. Twenty-five-year-old Debbie is Dozier's daughter from his marriage to actress Joan Fontaine.*

They live with a family of four Chinese servants in a half-million-dollar English Georgian home on Beverly Hills' Greenway Drive, across the street from the Los Angeles Country Club. One of their neighbors is Debbie Reynolds.

In her yellow and brown living room, Miss Rutherford, dressed in tailored overalls, still appears young enough to be Andy Hardy's girlfriend.

I fluked into the business when I was twelve. I'd skate home from Virgil Junior High, and on my way I'd pass a radio station. One afternoon I got daring and went into the lobby and rode up in the elevator. They had a place where an audience could sit, a sort of glass booth with a sofa or two and two overstuffed chairs. Through the glass you could see the actors performing at microphones the size of saucers.

I was fascinated, and I'd visit the station almost every day. It was a fun thing to do. Sometimes I'd just see a man reading the news or a dramatic show like *Calling All Cars* or *The Witches' Tales.*

One day I was very cross, in a snit at one of my teachers because she'd caught me writing poetry in class. I was going through the Edna St. Vincent Millay stage, and I was in love with Dorothy Parker's writing, and instead of studying about the ancient Phoenicians, I scribbled poetry. The teacher not only caught me, but read my verse aloud, and read it badly.

I was really ticked off when I skated myself home from school that day. I mumbled to myself, "Boy, I'll bet if you had a job, you wouldn't have to go back to that miserable old teacher." Suddenly there on the horizon loomed the radio station.

I unstrapped my skates, slung them over my shoulder and marched into the lobby, where I asked the girl at the desk, "Where do you go to apply for a job?" It's funny how kids get this kind of *chutzpa.* The girl directed me to an office and a very nice man said, "What have you done?" I found myself naming the names of every play I'd seen or read that had a child in it. Whether the child was a boy or a girl, it didn't matter. I just rattled off names, dropped them like marbles, and said I'd played in every one of them. I was so convincing that pretty soon I was believing it myself.

It just so happened that they were looking for kids for a series called—are you ready?—*Nancy and Dick in the Spirit of '76.* It was sponsored by the Broadway department store and the Daughters of the American Revolution. Without an audition, I got the job as Nancy for five dollars a week, and I'll have you know that the boy who got the part of Dick is now Richard Quine.*

---

*Among his credits as a director: *My Sister Eileen; The Solid Gold Cadillac; Bell, Book and Candle; The World of Suzie Wong; Hotel.*

It didn't take the people at the station a minute and a half to learn that all I knew was which end of the microphone was up. But they were dear and patient, and I lasted. After three or four years of playing in *Nancy and Dick* and branching out into other parts, one day there was a little bitty publicity picture of me in a radio column. Incredibly, I resembled a young girl named Anne Darling, who had just eloped and left Republic high and dry for a leading lady. So Republic signed me to replace her in a picture called *Waterfront Lady.*

I did about eighteen pictures in about eight months. I have the dubious distinction of being Gene Autry's first leading lady. I did like nine pictures with John Wayne. That was before he did *Stagecoach,* when he was still known as Marion Morrison.

From Republic I segued directly to MGM, mostly because I was taller than Mickey Rooney. They were starting the Andy Hardy series, and the producer thought it would be funny if Mickey played opposite a taller girl.

I was signed for the role of Polly Benedict, and I became Mickey's girlfriend in what turned out to be seventeen or eighteen Hardy pictures. From the first one I did, *Love Finds Andy Hardy,* the series was a super supersmash hit.

God, it was wonderful being part of that incredible enterprise known as MGM. I was still quite young, and all I really knew about the picture business was that you had to save your money. I'd learned that in the first picture I did, that *Waterfront Lady* thing. Jack LaRue was in it, and to me he was a big movie star. Along with all my chums in junior high school, I thought he was the greatest thing since the zipper. And suddenly I realized he was only working for three days and I was working for ten, twelve days on a two-week picture. Suddenly I'm the star of the picture, and here's Jack LaRue playing a very small part as a bartender.

I said to the nice assistant director, "Why is a big star like Jack LaRue playing this little part in the picture?"

He said, "Because he didn't save his money."

"What's not having his money got to do with it? A big star like that can always make money."

"Big stars often become little stars. LaRue didn't save his money, and if you don't save your money, you don't eat. He has to eat, and that's why he's playing a bartender, and grateful to get the work."

That made quite an impression on me. I was under contract at MGM for maybe three years before I bought a car, a fur coat or a house. I went to work on the bus. The Jack LaRue lesson was reinforced on the MGM lot. I saw dozens of girls with mink coats and fancy cars who cried hysterically when their options were dropped. They ranted, raved and said they were going to kill themselves. I decided that wouldn't happen to me.

MGM started me off at three hundred a week, and I thought that was grand because I'd been making only one hundred fifty a week at Republic. My next jump went to four hundred, then five hundred, then seven hundred and fifty. Whenever option time came up, Mr. Mayer wouldn't call my agent. He'd call me, thinking I could be intimidated. That was rather tacky, but I suppose if I ran a business, I'd probably do the same thing. I'd be summoned to Mr. Mayer's office, and he would say, "We've got big plans for you. The exhibitors love you. We love you. And we want to keep you, but we can't give you that next salary jump."

Under my contract, I could go to twelve hundred a week, and I wasn't about to miss any of that or delay it. I had a little routine that I used to do for Mr. Mayer. I'd wave my bankbook at him and say, "Mr. Mayer, I've saved my money." I wasn't burdened with great ambition and was prepared to chuck the career if need be. But my bankbook ploy always worked. Mr. Mayer always gave me my raises.

The Hardy pictures not only made a huge amount of money for MGM, but the studio found they were a marvelous showcase for new talent. Esther Williams, Donna Reed, Lana Turner, Judy Garland cut their teeth in a Hardy picture.

Besides playing Polly Benedict, I was also doing a series with Red Skelton, *Whistling in the Dark, Whistling in Dixie, Whistling in Brooklyn.* You name it, we whistled in it. In order to make those I sometimes had to be written out of the middle of the Hardy pictures. In the beginning I'd go away on vacation with my family or leave for school. That would give Mickey the chance to have his dalliance with Lana Turner or Judy Garland, but I always got him back in the end.

To me the Hardy pictures exemplified what a family should be. For instance, Judge Hardy, played by Lewis Stone, had a maiden aunt living with the family, and she was *part* of the family. That was Aunt Milly, and the part was done beautifully by Sara Haden. Maiden aunts do not live with their families today. Now the relatives probably call them old lesbians and shunt them off to institutions for the retarded or homes for senior citizens.

People say today that the Hardy pictures mirrored an unreal world. But it wasn't an unreal world. In my growing-up years there was much of Polly Benedict in me. And I knew a lot of boys who were similar to Andy Hardy. In my peer group, I don't recall any of my friends running around and saying, "My mother doesn't understand me, my father doesn't understand me." We had no such complaints. At least my friends and I didn't. Perhaps that was because it was the tail end of the Depression years. My own family and the families I knew were all in the same boat. What was there for kids not to understand? What we all tried to do was get through each day and make tomorrow better than today and today better than yesterday.

The incredible appeal of the Hardy pictures was that they touched a nerve among people in all walks of life and all ages. They could identify with those pictures. Maybe not everybody. If you were poor, it was an ideal existence. If you were middle-class or happened to be rich, you wished your life was that uncomplicated, that simple.

I saw one on television recently, and there was a scene where Andy comes to see Polly, who is entertaining a young naval lieutenant on her porch. Andy leaps gleefully over the hedge. He's jealous, but he's a gentleman. And he's clean. His hair was wet-combed, and his shirt and sweater were immaculate. And you knew when you looked at Polly, that she had dabbed a little cologne back of her ears, and you saw her with a sparkling bow in her hair. Her shoes were shined, and her dress was fresh. She liked being a girl.

The boys I dated in high school looked as nifty as Andy Hardy. Maybe they didn't always wear neckties, but their shirts were starched. You could tell that they thought it was important to look their best. Boys looked like boys. My girl-friends and I wore Tangee lipstick, and we had clean finger-nails and nail polish. It was neutral-colored, of course, because our mothers would get after us if we wore red. Red looked like claws or talons or looked cheap. We were girls, and we looked like girls, and it had nothing to do with money. The boys I dated had little or no money, but they had pride in their appearance. What, I ask you, was wrong with that? There was none of this grubbiness that kids seem to favor today.

So you can see, as far as I'm concerned, the Hardy pictures to a large extent *were* a representation of real life. And audiences obviously enjoyed seeing a family presented on the screen who loved each other in a wholesome, caring way. That was the reason for the popularity of the series and that was why we did one after another. There was *Out West with the Hardys, The Hardys Ride High, Andy Hardy Gets Spring Fever, Judge Hardy and Son, Andy Hardy Meets a Debutante, Andy Hardy's Private Secretary, Life Begins for Andy Hardy, The Courtship of Andy Hardy, Andy Hardy's Double Life.* They used every plot except Andy Hardy Gets Bar Mitzvahed.

They were the largest grossers that MGM ever had. I forget how many millions they made, but when they began shooting them, I think their original cost was around two hundred and fifty thousand to three hundred thousand dollars. It was just unbelievable how much money they made. When the studio finally got the message from the exhibitors—they were clamoring for more, more, more Hardy pictures—MGM just couldn't supply the demand.

After we made six or seven of them, the brass decided well, boy, if the Hardy product could earn that many millions of dollars with this little outlay, we'd better give it the A treatment. So instead of making them in three weeks, they pulled out the schedule to three months and poured more money into the budget.

They brought in Woody Van Dyke, who'd directed a couple of successful Gable pictures. Okay? So now they have Woody Van Dyke, and they remove dear, gentle George Seitz, who'd done all the first ones. Well, Woody Van Dyke was a very commanding gentleman, a dear man, but whatever he said was law. He totally intimidated Mickey. Mickey had called George Seitz Uncle George. He'd kind of tug at Seitz's sleeve whenever he had a suggestion to make for how a scene might play better. Mickey had invented all sorts of shtiks that played brilliantly in the pictures. But Mickey couldn't bring himself to say Uncle Woody. Mr. Van Dyke liked to be four days ahead of himself. As fast as a scene was shot, he'd say, "Print it." And when Mickey tried a couple of times to make suggestions to him, he'd say, "Go away, kid, you're bothering me. I'm ready for the next setup." Mr. Van Dyke kept moving on at this clip for ten days. Then every foot of film he'd shot was scrapped, and they took dear Mr. Van Dyke off the picture and called George Seitz back. After that, we never looked behind us.

In 1938 I was borrowed by David Selznick to do *Gone with the Wind.* I just read for him, and he said, "Honey, go to wardrobe."

I had the part of Carreen O'Hara, Scarlett's sister. It was a small role, and I didn't have as many lines as I would have liked. I was playing leading ladies, and I didn't want to do a minor part. but I'd read the book and fell in love with it, and I went ahead and did the picture without saying boo. Which only goes to prove that actors shouldn't have a say in what parts they play. If I'd been given a choice, I would have blown the opportunity, which would have been a tragedy. After seventy-eight motion pictures nobody remembers anything I've done except the Hardy films and *Gone with the Wind.*

Mr. Selznick, of course, didn't stint on anything. My wardrobe was astonishing. Gorgeous dresses with six petticoats under them adorned with layers and layers of lace. Mr. Selznick brought in this little fag Italian bootmaker from New York, who became a very dear friend of mine when I could afford his shoes. He was doing the most enchanting shoes, with scallops, patent-leather things and lots of little buttons that ran clear up to here. I thought if you did a costume picture, you wore Mary Jane pumps. That's what they always did in the Westerns I'd worked in at Republic.

Being frugal myself, I decided I was going to save Mr. Selznick scads of money. I went to him and said, "Nobody will ever know I have these expensive petticoats and shoes under my dresses."

"You're a rich plantation owner's daughter," he said. "*You'll know!* The wardrobe will help you in the part. It will make you stand taller, prouder."

Mr. Selznick took tremendous care with every aspect of the picture. The casting. The sets. The many months of preparation before a foot of film was shot. The best was none too good. Money was absolutely no object.

Most producers riffle through a script and hand it to the director and expect him to turn it into the best possible picture. But Mr. Selznick knew every if, and, or but in that script. God help anybody if they so much as interjected an article. He would hiss and scream, and it was done over. It had to be exactly the way he'd sent the script down. There were no liberties taken whatsoever. It was totally Mr. Selznick's picture, and to prove it, he replaced two directors. He clashed first with George Cukor, who was already known as a woman's director. Mr. Selznick thought George was throwing the picture to the women. Then came Sam Wood. His temperament and that of Mr. Selznick were in opposition. So he was replaced. Victor Fleming ended up directing most of it.

Mr. Selznick's insistence on realism was beyond belief. There's one brief scene at the very end of the first section of the picture where Scarlett pulls a radish out of the ground and eats it. Then she says, "Tomorrow I'll beat this world. I'll come back. I will have Tara back." While she's saying that, there's a shot of me and Evelyn Keyes, who played Suellen O'Hara. We're the downtrodden sisters, and we're out in the field picking cotton, which prior to the onset of hard times at Tara was done by the family's slaves.

Well, one day Mr. Selznick was on the set, and he noticed Evelyn's hands, which were beautiful, long and tapering, like lotus blossoms. My own hands were in pretty good shape, too. Mr. Selznick said, "We're going to have to do something about those hands." The next thing we knew we were out picking cotton for five days. We were driven to a cotton field in Calabasas, twenty-five miles from Los Angeles. Mr. Selznick had arranged with the man who owned the land to plant three rotating cotton crops. One had been put in ten months before, one seven months before, and the third five months before. Mr. Selznick was protecting himself against bad weather or the need for retakes.

So Evelyn and I picked cotton until our hands were covered with scratches, until we looked like we really were cotton pickers, which by now we were. And all of this enormous expense and and trouble for one scene in the picture that couldn't have run thirty seconds.

It's not just in retrospect, but from the very first day of shooting there was an electricity that permeated the atmosphere on the set. We knew we were part of something very special. How special we couldn't know. We couldn't know that the picture would gross more than a hundred million dollars and last forever.

Vivien Leigh was the dearest, most enchanting sprite of a lady, absolutely delicious and so beautiful. You looked at her, and you just couldn't believe how beautiful she was.

The cutest thing she used to do was to keep checking the time. Whenever she had a break for a few minutes, she'd run to the phone and call George Cukor, unbeknownst to Mr. Selznick. George was coaching her on the phone and at night. In those days we still shot on Saturday. You only got Sundays off. So you slept fast. The unions didn't really protect you. Sometimes you wouldn't get sprung until midnight, and you would get a call to be on the set at eight the next morning. That's what I call fast sleeping. But Vivien would find her way up to George's house in Beverly Hills every night and go over her scenes for the next day with him. George had the insight to help her. He had a fix on the character, and Vivien knew that, and she knew she wasn't getting any of that from Victor Fleming. Vivien needed that personal, quiet instruction, that little final fanning of the thought waves. And she got it from George. Obviously, George and Vivien knew what they were doing. Vivien won the Academy Award for her performance as Scarlett.

Clark Gable was the dearest, warmest, best-liked person on the set. He was adored by everyone who came in contact with him, from Mr. Selznick to the cop on the gate. Between scenes Clark spent his time with his best friends, the grips, propmen and electricians. And, of course, those were the golden days, when you did have time between scenes. You could really make a needlepoint pillow a week between scenes.

Clark and his friends would straddle a couple of those long pewlike benches, and they'd quietly play gedunk, which was some short-circuited version of either gin rummy or poker. He was unfailingly a gentleman, delightful, funny and whimsical and just altogether dear. They called him the King, and he was the King. Wherever he sat was the head of the table, though he never strutted or swaggered or displayed temperament or did the I-am-the-star, I-am the-king bit. It was an accolade others bestowed on him.

Most big stars then had gofers. Not the King. When they rang the bell for lunch, dinner or a coffee break, he'd stand in line like everyone else. He didn't send anyone to go for his meals. The night they burned Atlanta Carole Lombard drove out to watch. She brought a picnic basket and handed it to him, and he shared it with a couple of grips.

When the picture opened in 1939, I went to all four premieres, Los Angeles, Chicago, New York and Atlanta. In Atlanta I rode with Mr. Selznick to the airport to meet Clark and Carole. Mr. Selznick wanted to hug himself with glee because he had pulled it off and he knew he had a winner.

You know, when they have these things today like *Last Tango in Paris* and you think of the hush that fell over the theater in Atlanta when Clark said to Vivien, "Frankly, my dear, I don't give a damn," it's wild, just wild. How things have changed. But I'm very hopeful it will swing back.

Every ten years I can count on being propped up and wheeled out and taken to Atlanta where they celebrate the magic night that *Gone with the Wind* opened. There's dancing in the street, a parade, parties, and the film is reshown, and people remember the glory that surrounded and still surrounds *Gone with the Wind*. Some of my friends tell me I shouldn't go to Atlanta because the picture's a jinx. So many in it are dead. Clark. Vivien. Leslie Howard. Mr. Selznick

203

and Victor Fleming are gone, too. But I pooh-pooh that kind
of talk. Time decimates everything, but that's no reason for
me not to accept each time they invite me. Every time I go it
rekindles marvelous memories and gives me pause to thank
God that I was in the picture, that I was obedient, that I was
loaned out, that I became part of something stupendous,
that I was was part of a picture and an era the like of which
won't ever be seen again.

It *was* a beautiful era at MGM. They truly had more stars
than there are in heaven. It was exciting, just to walk down
the street there. I cannot tell you how depressed I was when I
went back in 1972 to shoot this picture, *They Only Kill Their
Masters,* with Jim Garner, Katharine Ross, Peter Lawford and
June Allyson. I hadn't set foot on the lot since 1943, and
when I saw it again, I could have cut a vein.

While I was there in MGM's heyday, anywhere from sixteen to eighteen pictures were being shot at one time. There
were thirty-five, thirty-six sound stages on which something
was always happening. They were either shooting or preparing to shoot on every sound stage. They were building those
marvelous giant wedding cakes for chorus girls to dance on.
Nelson Eddy was screaming his lungs out to Jeanette Mac-
Donald. You could stick your nose into any rehearsal hall or
sound stage, and it was just teeming with life.

It was a vision and a glory to see Jean Harlow come sweeping out of her dressing room with her maids and retinue behind her. You gasped and held your breath.

There was Norma Shearer, Marie Dressler, Lana Turner,
Gable, Spencer Tracy; you name the best, and they were
there. It was just a special kind of thing, an astonishment in
the air, so many people who were so important.

The stars had a non-flesh-and-blood glamorous quality
about them. But, of course, they were flesh and blood. They
laughed; they cried; they hurt.

I never really witnessed any big temperament except for Luise Rainer, who fainted a great deal whenever she disagreed with the director or something in the script. But she never really turned pale, and after a while Mervyn LeRoy stopped calling the nurse or the doctor. Luise knocked off two Academy Awards.* But the last picture she did, *Dramatic School,* knocked her right out of the business. God love her, I think she was still upset from playing in *The Good Earth.* If I were from Vienna and had an accent, I guess if somebody tried to make me look Chinese, I'd be upset, too.

MGM was always known as the White House. And there was just no competition. Warner Brothers had its stock company, sure, but who wanted to rub elbows with Guy Kibbee and Hugh Herbert, bless their hearts? Joan Blondell, who was queen of the Warner lot, was darling, but she did have a thyroid condition. Warner's kept making the same movie over and over and over. MGM didn't. They had the glorious *Min and Bill* pictures. And they had Margaret O'Brien doing something tearfully dramatic and Norma Shearer who could suffer marvelously or just be so terribly soignée. She was the first woman I ever saw who combed all her hair over to one side of her head. Norma was just great.

Most of the contract people at MGM stayed and stayed and stayed. Why? Because the studio looked after them. Warner Brothers wouldn't—they were always spanking somebody or selling them down the river. From the time you were signed at MGM you just felt you were in God's hands. Somebody was looking after you. I kid you not when I tell you I must have been twenty-six before I had the nerve to drink anything except Coca-Cola. I was about thirty before I smoked. Though nothing was said about smoking or drinking, I somehow had the feeling that Big Brother was watching and he would disapprove of those alleged vices.

*The Great Ziegfeld, 1936, and The Good Earth, 1937.

They cared about you. If they thought you showed talent in something, they would weed, hoe, winnow and water you in that department. They would push you as far as you wanted to go. They tried everything with everybody.

I will never forget the first time I laid eyes on Ava Gardner. That was before she did the test that resulted in her maiden role in a Hardy picture. It was in the makeup department, and here was some lovely, half-wit makeup man valiantly trying to plug up this beautiful cleft in Ava's chin. But, you see, they were surveying her from all angles. She had a Southern accent you couldn't cut with a knife. She hated to wear shoes. The first thing they did was to try and find the real Ava, which proved impossible.

They did try to make everybody conform to a mold, but when they discovered that you could resist that mold, that there was something unique about you that shone through, they would pull out all the stops and let you take the bit in your teeth and run.

They would chide you if you went out with someone that they deemed not good for your image. Not good for your image meant dating a gentleman who was too old for you or someone who was living in an unsavory way or someone who was a lousy or an unimportant actor. They were right. I know of quite a few young actresses who really screwed their lives and careers up by dating the wrong men, by disobeying the front office. Those girls made bad mistakes. By the time they realized the studio had been right in the first place they couldn't get back in the door, they couldn't get their foot inside the lot again.

Young players then had to make up their minds about what took precedence in their lives. If you were smart, you put your personal life aside. That could wait because this life was so yummy. Why louse it up? Where else could you work where you would be able to travel, be able to go to Washington and visit the White House and meet President Roosevelt, as I did, go on bond tours, have people pay attention to you and give you darling bonuses and large raises? It was a fun life. If you were not doing that, you might have been stuck in college someplace or you might be a dental assistant, which would be dumb.

When I went back to make *They Only Kill Their Masters,* I was greeted in a lovely way. They did the dearest thing. Over the main gate was a twenty-four-foot canvas sign with huge letters that said: WELCOME HOME, POLLY BENEDICT. They'd dug out Andy Hardy's old car. Mickey wasn't in it, unfortunately. But it was the old convertible that I had done all those scenes in, and they'd given all the people on the lot who weren't shooting forty-five minutes off to come and make a crowd for me. I learned in the next few days that ours was the only picture that was shooting on the lot, so the crowd that welcomed me didn't have much to do anyway. But still it was dear, very dear of Jim Aubrey, who was then running the studio, to foregather the MGM employees in my honor. They rolled up that marvelous canvas sign and gave it to me.

That was truly euphoric. Then came the terrible jolt when I saw the lot was only a shadow of what it once had been. And I really came to earth when I received my marching orders for the first day of shooting.

"You must be on the set in wardrobe for a walk-through with the cameraman at seven fifteen in the morning," the young assistant director told me.

"I beg your pardon," I said. "Do you mean I'm to be on the set at seven fifteen with my makeup in place and my hair done and ready to shoot?"

"No, just with your wardrobe for a camera test. Then your stand-in can take over."

"Well, when do I go to makeup?'

"There is no makeup department."

"What happened to our beautiful makeup department?"

"Can't you smell it from here, honey? It's all in mothballs.

We have a makeup man on the set. He's got a table—"

"A table! One of those tacky things with a mirror and those horrid light globes around it?"

"Yeah, but he's very good."

"You mean I have to be made up out there in front of God and everybody?"

"That's the scene."

"What time do I report to the makeup man?"

"Seven thirty."

"Now let's get this straight. At seven fifteen I'm in wardrobe. And I have to come on the set barefaced. Well that's all right, I'll come barefaced. Then I walk over to the cameraman and the makeup man. Okay. But when do I get my hair done?"

"There's a hairdresser on the set. She'll do your hair while the makeup man is doing your face."

"Really? And what time am I due on the set ready to shoot, ten o'clock?"

"Oh, no, honey, you're in the first shot. You start working at seven forty-five."

"That's half an hour. Young man, I can't pull myself together in half an hour to go to the supermarket."

All I could think of was that in my day, and I'm beginning to sound like a Floradora girl, you would check into the makeup department in the morning and, oh, it was beautiful. It smelled lovely. All of Max Factor's best scents were drifting out through the walls. You would hit makeup about five till seven, and somebody darling shampooed your hair, and they would give you darling movie magazines or they would cue you in your lines whiile you sat under the dryer. And then you were locked up into your own private darling pink booth where your own darling makeup man did your face. You could take a mental nap in his chair while he would do just the most divine things with your face.

If your nose felt fat that morning, he would make it feel thin. Did you want a dimple? He would put a dark brown thing on the side of your face. If you were cross-eyed, never mind, he'd put eyelashes on you that would distract attention from that particular affliction. But for an hour you really felt like a blonde with a turned-up nose. Meantime, they would give you intravenous feedings of black coffee and somebody would hover with a Danish.

About five minutes of nine you'd wander over to the set still in your robe or a smock or whatever was comfortable with a makeup man atwitter behind you who was carrying an extra pair of lashes in case you lost one.

You'd get to the set at nine for the walk-through with the cameraman. Then you would repair to your dressing room and start on your needlepoint or knit a sweater. Sometimes it would take an hour to light the set. By then it was like ten o'clock. Actually no civilized cameraman exposed a foot of film before ten thirty. I think it's terribly tacky to photograph people before they're truly awake. I think it's awful.

Between every scene they would strike the set and change all the lights around, and your stand-in would go stand in. It was a marvelous and leisurely way of doing things. You had a feeling of being pampered, and even though you then had to shoot on Saturday, it didn't really matter because you felt special. They did look after you, and the whole thing was just a great, larky adventure.

Many of the interests and hobbies that I've embraced in my life started at MGM because you were exposed to tasteful things and you had the time to learn about them and appreciate them. I remember I did a picture with Greer Garson called *Pride and Prejudice* from that wonderful Jane Austen story. Laurence Olivier was in it, too, and I fell in love with him. That was before *Gone with the Wind*. I thought he was the most beautiful man I'd ever seen. Vivien Leigh married Olivier right at the tail end of *Gone with the Wind*, and she broke all our hearts.

They spent two years preparing for *Pride and Prejudice*. They had the art department all over Europe buying bunches of beautiful French-type furniture and these marvelous, delicately wrought tables, little spindly things. On top of the tables were these marvelous porcelain statue pieces, heavenly things. From that picture I developed my interest in collecting antique porcelain.

It was an incredible life for young people if they could hang in there and keep their heads and if they had wise mothers or good families who didn't push or exploit them.

The unkindest blow of all when I went back occurred in the commissary. In all the years I was at MGM every day for lunch I had a bowl of Mr. Mayer's matzo ball chicken soup. It was his mother's recipe. His mother gave it to his wife and his wife gave it to his secretary and his secretary gave it to the chef. God forbid, he shouldn't have homemade matzo ball soup, his Jewish penicillin, as everyone called that glorious dish. To me that soup was almost the only magnet that drew me back to MGM. I couldn't wait to taste it again.

But when I ordered the matzo ball chicken soup, the waitress said, "The what?"

I said, "Mr. Mayer's matzo ball chicken soup. I understand you still have it."

"We have chicken soup," she said, "but confidentially it's the instant noodle."

That was truly the unkindest blow of all. That, and seeing the ghostly wardrobe department. Every female likes clothes; they love costumes; they love anything to do with clothes. I used to adore the wardrobe department. It was, well, the whole center of the lot for me. It wasn't just floor after floor of clothes. It was ringed with a cast-iron balcony so that you could stand there and look at these marvelous racks brimming with costumes. You could see pirates. You could see Marie Antoinette. You could see every costume and style under the sun.

The wardrobe department was an empty shell that echoed and reverberated with these naked iron racks and clattered with forlorn wire coat hangers.

As you progressed up the salary rank and into better pictures, you stopped going into a regular fitting room. You wound up either in Irene's or Mr. Adrian's fitting room. Mr. Adrian's fitting room was nirvana. He had white art deco sofas and marvelous sketches on the walls, rugs deep as the middle of the ocean, and he served tea and things. There was a maid in uniform to help you in and out of your clothes.

All that was left of this glorious room that was once Mr. Adrian's were these two moth-eaten sofas. They'd even sold his sketches off the wall at the MGM auction.

Shortly after I did *They Only Kill Their Masters,* MGM went out of the movie business.

That great and special and divine and magnificent place of my youth was gone.

The horn of plenty had run out of plenty.

18

Sue Carol

THE MAKING OF ALAN LADD

SMILING AND HAT tilted back, a painting of him as Shane hangs in the hall off his bedroom-office suite where everything is as he left it: the belt he wore in Shane; leather-backed comb and brush; an open script turned to page sixty-four. . . .

The house sits on a wide swath of land in Holmby Hills, the ne plus ultra of movie star enclaves, more fashionable, expensive and exclusive than neighboring Beverly Hills or Bel Air.

The endless rooms are strewn with Utrillos and Braques. A Picasso hangs casually in the breakfast room near a vault holding a print of the fifty-one pictures in which Ladd starred.

Ladd's estate included the $500,000 home, an office building on Wilshire Boulevard in Beverly Hills, a ranch in nearby Ventura County, and a home in Palm Springs, where he died under circumstances still not entirely clear.

Sue Carol, round-faced, friendly, hospitable, is a former actress turned agent. A woman of unflagging determination, she was the deus ex machina who discovered, married and made possible the career of Alan Ladd. In the warm October evening she sits at a modern cream-colored coffee table in the living room. The lighting is low, and behind her back a slight Santa Ana wind rustles the banana trees and other jungle foliage in the luxuriant garden.

I came to Hollywood from Chicago to visit a girlfriend. We were out horseback riding one day with a couple of people, one of whom happened to be a casting director at Fox. He asked me make a test for the studio. I was nineteen years old, and it had never occurred to me to be in pictures. I guess I was flattered and I did the test, which got me a part in *Slaves of Beauty*. From there I went into one picture after another, *Is Zat So?*, *Girls Gone Wild*, *Dancing Sweeties*. I played straight leads, flappers, the same sort of roles that Audrey Hepburn did later.

At one point the studio was grooming me as competition for Clara Bow. She was doing so well as the It girl that Fox wanted an It girl, too. They looked for a catchy tag for me, similar to the It Girl or the Oomph Girl title that Warner's gave Ann Sheridan. But they never found the gimmick that would have brought me the publicity that Clara and Ann received thanks to those labels.

I never made much of my career—it wasn't important to me. My stardom ended when I was supposed to do a picture on loan-out to Warner Brothers. It was called *Nickie and Her War Birds*. They brought in this director from Germany, William Dieterle. We were practicing some dance sequences on the set when he walked in with white gloves and a cane. He kept knocking the cane on the floor, saying, "Faster, faster, faster. Tempo, tempo, tempo." It just scared me so much that I went home in tears and never went back.

A friend suggested I go into the agency business. It seemed a natural, easy, obvious thing to do. I knew everybody in the industry, and while I'd been an actress, I'd helped several people get jobs. I enjoyed doing that.

I opened an office in the Norma Talmadge Building on Sunset Boulevard in 1939. Alan became one of my first clients. Some of the others were Milburn Stone—that was years before he got the part of Doc in *Gunsmoke*—and an attractive actress named Sheila Ryan. Later there was Rory Calhoun and the English boy at Metro who married one of the Kennedy girls [Peter Lawford]. Milburn Stone still tells me I was a pretty good agent until I met Alan. Once that happened I devoted most of my time and energies to his career, trying at the same time not to neglect the others.

Someone said I should listen to a radio show that had a talented fellow on it. He was so versatile that he played two parts, an old man and his grandson. I was intrigued, and I tuned in. That was the first time I heard Alan's voice. I thought he was remarkable. I had no idea what he looked like, what his personality was like. I didn't know a thing about him except that he was a very good radio actor and I wanted to meet him. So I phoned the station and asked him to drop by the office.

He was really so attractive when he walked in, not that it was love at first sight on the part of either of us.

"You've got the voice and looks to be in pictures," I told him.

"Universal didn't think so," he said. "I was under contract there a couple of years ago, playing bits. They dropped me, and they dropped Tyrone Power."

By this time Ty Power was a major star. He'd already done *Lloyds of London, In Old Chicago* and *Alexander's Ragtime Band.*

"I think you can make it as big as Ty," I said.

Alan grinned. "Never. I've tried, believe me. Producers tell me I'm too blonde, too short, too this or too that."

"Why don't we take a shot at it?"

"No, I'm not interested. I want to stay in radio."

"Think it over. If you change your mind, let me know."

About two weeks later he came strolling into the office and we talked some more. He *had* thought it over. He was somewhat reluctant but willing to give movies another try. He told me I could represent him so long as nothing interfered with his radio work. He said he'd had it pretty rough getting as far as he had.

I was interested in his background and encouraged him to

tell me about his life. He told it straight, without self-pity.

"I had a job on one radio station where they had a five-dollar budget for nine people. I worked nineteen shows a week, playing everything from fish peddlers to an old invalid and sometimes I got salary checks as low as fifty cents." He'd literally almost starved to death. For a couple of years he lived on candy bars and doughnuts until he reached the point where he was making a modest living in radio.

Alan said he'd been born in Hot Springs, Arkansas. His mother had been widowed and remarried. He didn't know a lot about his real father. His mother and stepfather, who was a house painter, had come to the Coast when he was six or seven in an old jalopy. His stepfather had painted people's kitchens on the trip out so they could eat and buy gas. Alan said he'd worked as far back as he could remember, sweeping floor in a candy store, as a bricklayer, a caddie, a swimming instructor.

Other than his potential, the thing I sensed most strongly about Alan was that he was terribly unsure of himself, that his childhood poverty and the unhappy relationship he'd had with his mother and stepfather had given him the insecurity that would stay with him all his life even after he became a star and millions of people adored him. I'm no psychiatrist, but it was obvious to me as we talked that day in my office that Alan was searching for something. He felt rejected, and maybe he was searching for an anchor of some kind. Life hadn't dealt him a very good hand, though he didn't complain and wasn't bitter. Alan always held much of himself back. He was friendly with people but didn't confide in them easily. I think he also had a premonition that he would die young.

Alan was then twenty-six years old, a little late to be starting a career as a leading man. But he didn't look his age, and I thought he was great. I never doubted that he'd be a star. But it was a struggle.

I made the rounds of the studios, talking him up. I sent him out on interviews. Producers were still saying he was too blond and especially that he was too short. At that time they wanted leading men to be at least six feet tall, like Wayne, Cooper and Jimmy Stewart. Alan was five feet nine.

There were other setbacks. One producer told me, "He looks like a freak with those green eyes, dark eyebrows and light hair." Another said, "That young man has no sex appeal." This was a short time before Alan hit it in *This Gun for Hire,* and became a male sex symbol.

In two and a half years I'd managed to get Alan a few bit parts and then leads in B pictures that were nothing important. He did things like *Captain Caution,* where he played a slave that was trying to incite the others to rebellion. He played in a picture called *Hitler, Beast of Berlin,* because they wanted someone who looked like he could be German.

Bill Meikeljohn, talent head of Paramount, told me that Frank Tuttle, the Paramount director, was looking for a leading man for *This Gun for Hire.* Alan and I went over to see Frank. He said Alan looked like someone who'd say, "Tennis, anyone?" He'd be perfect for a part like that, Frank said, but this script needs an actor who can play a cold-blooded killer and still come off sympathetically.

Luckily I'd brought along some mood stills of Alan, you know, with him looking sinister, smoking a cigarette with the smoke curling out of his nose. They were quite effective— Alan always photographed beautifully. Frank Tuttle studied the stills for a few minutes. Then he looked up at us and didn't say anything for what seemed like ages. Finally he said, "Let me test him."

Before the test they put him in a little glass cage. It was like a stage. You couldn't see out, but everybody could see in, and that's kind of a frightening thing. The whole hunk of Hollywood meat thing, like Alan was an animal in a zoo. But Alan made it under those conditions, and then they made the test and everyone was very impressed. He was sansational. Frank

Tuttle said, "This picture is going to make your client a star."

Paramount signed him for low money, three hundred a week. That's what he made *Gun* for. I had this price up to seven hundred fifty a week by then, and that wasn't much, even for straight leads in B pictures. But the seven fifty was touch-and-go. Alan was still free-lancing, he didn't have a contract with a studio . . . money coming in every week.

By coincidence the same day Paramount signed Alan, we were offered a contract from RKO at five hundred a week for fifty-two weeks a year. Alan had done a little picture there called *Joan of Paris* and made quite an impression.

But I'd read the script of *Gun*. I didn't care if Alan had to do it for nothing. It was an A feature, a dream part, and I'd battled for a long time to get him this opportunity. So we decided to gamble, and we took the Paramount deal for short money. I didn't even try to pit Paramount against RKO to get his money up. I guess I wasn't a good agent, but I desperately wanted Alan to make *Gun*. I agreed with Frank Tuttle that he'd come out of the picture a star . . . . and of course he did. The gamble paid off.

Even before *Gun* was released, the studio was wild for Alan. They knew they had a hit and a new star. Suddenly he was their fair-haired boy and they were planning picture after picture for him.

Alan and I had been dating for about two years, and we decided to get married just prior to *Gun* going into the theaters. The studio didn't want Alan to get married. They felt they had a new glamor boy, and a wife would hurt his image. I was all for furthering Alan's career, and I told him that maybe we should wait. Alan got furious when I said that.

"To hell with them," he shouted. "To hell with the career. We're getting married."

We ran down to Mexico City for the wedding ceremony. There was nothing the studio could do, and our marriage didn't seem to hurt Alan's career.

We went to New York for the opening of *Gun* at the Paramount Theater. The first night we were in town we walked down Broadway and looked at Alan's name up in lights. We stood there a long time . . . looking . . . looking. It sounds corny, but we were like a pair of kids set loose in a candy store.

The picture was a blockbuster in New York, and Alan was mobbed every place he went. But crowds scared him. The studio publicity department set up so many interviews for him that he just got to hate New York. He should have loved it, he should have enjoyed his stardom, but it frightened him. He did the interviews, he was gracious, but inside he was in turmoil. That childhood insecurity was still there. He'd wanted to be a star, but he never expected to make it. When it happened he couldn't handle it easily. Every picture he made from then on he said was going to be his last one.

I didn't renegotiate Alan's contract for a good year or more. And it wasn't a very successful renegotiation. The studio gave him a five-thousand-dollar bonus for *Gun* and raised him to seven hundred fifty a week, which was far less than he deserved compared to other stars. I felt sort of helpless because I was married to him, and it was difficult for me to be his wife and his agent.

I told Y. Frank Freeman, one of the heads of the studio, "You've just renegotiated Sterling Hayden's contract. You've given him twelve hundred fifty a week and a fifty-thousand-dollar bonus and I don't see that Hayden has made the impact that Alan has."

Freeman said, "Sue, Sterling Hayden is a different matter entirely. Hayden doesn't like the business. He doesn't want to be in it. So we had to give him that incentive. Alan loves the business. It's his lifeblood." I felt that was very unfair.

I just sort of went to pieces, and when I got home, I started to cry as I told Alan about the studio's new deal for him.

Alan said, "If you're going to take everything to heart like this, you have to let somebody else handle it. Sell my contract. But I want you to keep half of it so that you're always in a position to help me decide what to do." I sold fifty percent of Alan's contract to MCA and we were able to build our lovely home with the money. They were investing in Alan's future, and it proved a good investment.

Gun had cost almost nothing to make, four or five hundred thousand, and it grossed ten or twelve million. Right after *Gun*, he did three pictures in 1942, *The Glass Key, Lucky Jordan* and *Star-Spangled Rhythm.* Frank Freeman told me Alan was making more money for the studio than any other star on the lot. Alan then went into the Army for a year and a half. He was supposed to be sent overseas, but the doctors discovered that he had a double hernia. So they kicked him out.

Alan came back and resumed his career and was more popular than ever. He made two big hits in 1946, *Two Years Before the Mast* and *The Blue Dahlia.*

Finally, Alan got a good contract, and he got it himself. He was given a script for a Western called *California.* Alan liked Westerns, but he didn't like that one. And he wouldn't do it. They got Ray Milland to make it.

Alan sat home and told the studio he was quitting movies entirely. He wasn't a fool by now. He knew the kind of money that he was making for Paramount. He'd gotten a few small raises, he was up to twelve hundred fifty a week on a straight player's contract. But he knew other stars whose pictures weren't doing as well at the box office as his were, and they were making one hundred fifty thousand to two hundred thousand a picture. It didn't seem fair to him. Also, he had no privileges, no approval of story, cast, director. He had nothing to hang his hat on except that straight player's contract.

The studio came around, and they jumped Alan quite a bit. That was the start of the big money for us.

When Paramount was making great money on him with

the cheaper contract, they treated him like a little boy that had never grown up. Now he was given the treatment he deserved, the dignity and respect that was his right as a star.

Alan stayed at Paramount for eleven years. During that time he made *The Great Gatsby* and *Shane* for them. He loved doing *Shane*. It was another blockbuster and made a fortune for Paramount. *Shane* cost three million two hundred thousand and it grossed considerably more than fifty million. The picture's a classic.*

Paramount wanted to re-sign Alan when his contract expired. They offered him a deal where he would own part of the pictures in which he starred. But they didn't want to give him as good a deal as others were getting. So he left and went to Warner Brothers.

The deal at Warner Brothers gave Alan ten percent of the gross on the pictures he made for the studio, this at a time when ten percent participation in profits for a star was considered extraordinary. Warner's also allowed Alan total ownership of every other picture he made, which allowed him to form his own production company and make those pictures independently. Alan became the producer of his independent pictures, but he hired someone to do that for him.†
Alan made a number of pictures that he wasn't in. One of them was *Cry in the Night* with Natalie Wood, Eddy O'Brien,

---

*The critics agree. Leslie Halliwell in *The Filmgoer's Companion* says, "George Stevens directed it with great feeling and turned it into a classic." Bosley Crowther of the New York *Times* called it "towering . . . Hollywood at its Western peak . . . a fine cast headed by Alan Ladd . . . has wrought a thrillingly real, deeply penetrating outdoor drama." Steven H. Scheuer told readers of the 200 newspapers that subscribe to his motion picture column: "*Shane* is truly an epic Western, among the best ever made." Besides Ladd, the cast included Jean Arthur, Van Heflin, Brandon De Wilde and Jack Palance.

†See the interview with Martin Rackin, Chapter 20.

Brian Donlevy, Laraine Day, and this man who plays *Ironside* on television [Raymond Burr].

The Warner's deal was a great one, maybe the best in the business. But Alan still wasn't a totally happy man. One of the things that bothered him was the story about how short he was. Some stories had him as short as five feet. But he *was* five feet nine. I can show that to you on his Army discharge. James Cagney, John Garfield and Richard Barthelmess were much shorter than Alan, but it never became a big deal for them. I don't know how the stories started about Alan's height. Maybe because he worked with tall girls like Sophia Loren.*

His last picture was *The Carpetbaggers,* and he went back to Paramount to do that one. My favorite of all his pictures was *The Great Gatsby,* and I don't think the remake (in 1974) with Robert Redford compared to Alan's *Gatsby.*

Alan and I had no conception that we were living through a so-called golden era. We always felt that the old-time stars like Gloria Swanson and Clara Bow lived much flashier lives. Our lives were very quiet.

In his last years Alan thought the parade was passing him by. He could see the changes in the business like anyone else, the popularity of television, the breakup of the big studios, attendance going down in the theaters. Maybe it wasn't that the parade was passing him by. He just didn't feel the urgency to work as hard as he had. But he was always looking for *that* script, another *Gun* another *Shane*. It didn't come along.

At the end of January in 1964 Alan went to our place in Palm Springs for a couple of days of rest. We always went to

*After shooting *Boy on a Dolphin* with Ladd in Greece, Miss Loren said she'd had to walk in a ditch in a number of scenes to accommodate Ladd's height. Such quotes guaranteed newspaper space. When this writer, who is five feet nine, met Ladd in 1963, the star appeared to be about the same height.

the Springs together, but this one time I couldn't go because a man from the Internal Revenue Service was coming over to talk with me. We had a business manager, but the IRS man wanted me there, too. Alan hated things like that. So he went along, and I said I'd join him as soon as I could.

While I was sitting with the man from Internal Revenue I got a phone call, and I was told that Alan was dead of a heart attack. If you don't think that was a shock. . . .*

It was a very big funeral. There were more than two thousand people at the church and thousands of his fans outside.

I remember Eddie O'Brien's eulogy. "Alan was so good, so damned honest. He should have been a farmer and never come to Hollywood." Maybe Eddie was right . . . I don't know.

I keep as busy as I can, watching over our business affairs. We own a hardware store, a very large one, in Palm Springs. I must tell you the story of how Alan got us into that.

After we moved into our home there about twenty years ago, Alan went to the hardware store in town and bought about five hundred dollars' worth of brushes, mops, pails and other stuff we needed. When he asked to have the order delivered, the man said, "Sorry, we don't deliver." Alan had to rent a truck to get everything out to the house. He was an-

---

*Sensation mongers have persisted in calling Ladd's death a suicide despite the lack of official evidence. Writer David Hanna, who covered the movie colony for the *Hollywood Reporter* for a number of years, has said Ladd ended his life with a combination of barbiturates and alcohol because he "could no longer bear the torment of being pathetically small." Riverside County Deputy Coroner Robert Drake said Ladd died from "something he ate or drank that attacked his central nervous system." Palm Springs Police Chief August G. Kettman said, "There would be no further investigation of Ladd's death because there wasn't any exterior evidence of foul play." Whether or not Ladd died by his hand—at the relatively young age of fifty-one—is a secret he carried to his grave. An autopsy was not performed.

noyed, and he asked one of our neighbors, "How do they do any business when they won't deliver?" He was told it was the only hardware store in town. So Alan said, "Starting next week, there are going to be two hardware stores in Palm Springs, and one of them will deliver."

The four children also keep me busy. There's Alan, Jr., David, Carol Lee and Alana. Alan, Jr., was his son from a former marriage, and Carol Lee was my daughter from a former marriage. The two others we had together.

I'll never remarry. Alan would be quite a tough person to follow. I'm still in love with him. This man had so much more talent than he ever showed, even in his most successful pictures. But after he got to be a star, he became more and more self-conscious about his performances or the pictures, perhaps because the scripts hadn't been great to begin with.

I'm luckier than most widows. Because I still have Alan with me. I can turn on television almost any night and see him in one of his pictures. I sit up in bed, and all of a sudden I hear his voice, see his face.

I run his pictures all the time. I just ran *Shane* last week. And there he was, blond and green-eyed and handsome and I thought back to the day he first walked into my office. Alan was the tallest man I've ever known.

19
Edith Head

THE FIRST STAR SHE DRESSED WAS AN ELEPHANT FOR CECIL B. DEMILLE

SHE'S BEEN NOMINATED for Oscars an incredible thirty-two times and won on eight occasions.* The parade of golden statuettes in the vestibule of her Universal bungalow is the first overwhelming sight that greets a visitor. "It's called applied psychology," she says. *"It's impossible for potentially difficult actresses and actors to tell me, 'Now look, Edith, I think we ought to do the wardrobe my way.' When they see those eight Academy Awards, it may occur to them that perhaps I'm where I am for a reason, that I know what I'm doing."*

She came to Universal "after Paramount stopped putting people under contract. Paramount no longer wanted a designer. I prefer to be under contract and have a home base."

A lively sixty-seven, she wears severely tailored suits of her own design. The ubiquitous bangs and black-rimmed eyeglasses are trademarks. Edith Head looks much like the stereotype of a schoolteacher, which is what she trained to be. After receiving an MA at Stanford, she taught Spanish and French for several years before becoming a designer. "Teachers made no money at all in those days."

Married to architect Bill Ihnen for thirty-three years (no children) she's a thimble taller than five feet, weights 105 pounds, has brown eyes and "dark hair turning gray."

*For *The Heiress*, 1949; *All About Eve* and *Samson and Delilah*, 1950; *A Place in the Sun*, 1951; *Roman Holiday*, 1953; *Sabrina*, 1954; *The Facts of Life*, 1960; and *The Sting*, 1974.

"Are there any other vital statistics you'd care to know?" she asks with a lemon-and-candy grin. "Obviously I haven't survived because I have long blond curls and dimples."

The bungalow is a loping three-room suite. Yellow chairs. Mahogany paneling. Various shades of brown furniture. Several cluttered marble tables, one of which holds a collection of some thirty antique sewing machines. "It's an impressive office, isn't it?"

I got my job at Paramount by being dishonest. I answered a newspaper ad which said the studio was looking for sketch artists to help design the clothes in a forthcoming DeMille epic. I don't recall the name of the picture, it may have been *The Golden Bed.* That was forty-two years ago, and there have been hundreds of pictures since.

I showed the sketches I had with me to Howard Greer, who was the studio's head designer. He did the clothes for Pola Negri, Carole Lombard, Marlene Dietrich and all the great stars of Paramount in what we now call the golden age, when we had fabulous pictures and fabulous clothes.

"I've never seen so much talent in one portfolio," Greer said. He hired me and ten others. Five of us survived.

Howard found out soon enough that I didn't have much talent, but being a charming man with a great sense of humor, he kept me on and taught me how to be a designer. I'd been studying art in the evenings at Chouinard. When I applied for the job, I borrowed the sketches of the most brilliant students in the school. I was young and naïve and didn't think I was being dishonest. I was also unbelievably shy and tongue-tied. Looking back, I can't imagine doing such a thing because I wasn't at all a pushy type.

Also, I wasn't a movie fan. With classes in the daytime, studying art and correcting papers at night and on weekends, I didn't have time to go to the movies. I'd simply applied to Paramount because a career as a designer seemed to offer an opportunity to make more money than teaching.

I sat in a little room and turned out hundreds of sketches. I never saw anybody except Howard Greer, who'd come in occasionally, look at my work and offer suggestions. I never went on a set. I was only one of more than a dozen sketch artists.

There was a caste system in the design department. Greer and his top assistant, Travis Banton, would do the stars; the lesser people would do the second leads, the character actors, the bit players, the extras who played slaves or eunuchs or whatever. I was at the bottom of the totem pole. The first "star" I dressed was a darling elephant. Actually you don't just go and dress an elephant. First you did a sketch, in fact, many, many sketches, all of which were shown to DeMille, who was known around the studio as the Great Man. Everyone was in awe of him, especially me. He *was* a great man, an incredible moviemaker. DeMille approved one of my sketches, and I was so elated I wasn't sure whether to kiss him or the elephant. I kissed neither.

I quickly learned a great deal about elephants. After you dress an elephant, you can dress anything or anyone.

I didn't personally put the wardrobe on the elephant. That was done by his trainer. I stood there with my sketch and gave him instructions. I covered that elephant with wreaths of red roses along his flanks and around his ankles. I had real fruit of various types hanging all over him. And I designed a smashing tassel headdress. The problem was that the elephant ate everything that was put on him except the tassels. But it worked out. That elephant may have been responsible for my entire career. It was the first time I saw something I'd designed reach the screen—the headdress and the inedible wooden flowers and fruits I'd substituted and had painted so that they looked more genuine than the real thing.

I never had one big breakthrough. I mean, I didn't suddenly become a great star of design overnight. I worked as a sketch artist for years and years and years until I finally became an assistant designer. In all those years I did everyone except the stars, who were the province of Greer and Banton. I'd do the grandmothers, the extras, everybody except the principals, obviously with no credit.

When Greer left to open a salon of his own, Travis Banton became the head designer. He had a clause in his contract that allowed him a trip to Europe once a year. While he was on one of those trips, the studio suddenly signed Mae West for a picture called *She Done Him Wrong*. Cary Grant was in it, too—he was coming on fast, but he was not yet a superstar.

Because Travis was gone, I was given the chance to design Mae's clothes in *Wrong*. It was my first solo attempt with a star. How did I dress Mae West? I didn't. Mae West is Mae West. You don't really try to dress her or design for her. You don't try to change her. She's a fashion language of her own. She makes her own rules. Mae still wears long clothes in the daytime. Even when we did the picture, which was a great success as was the wardrobe, nobody would be caught dead wearing a long dress in the street . . . except Mae. She wears what she wants when she wants and how she wants. She's very sure of herself, which is a good motto for anybody. Be sure of yourself when you dress. So many people, you know, have the feeling when they put something on, I wonder if this is right, what are people going to say about my outfit?

I didn't dress Cary Grant in that picture. I dressed him later in *To Catch a Thief* and other films. Incidentally, it's far simpler to dress a male star than a female star. There are less things to do unless you are doing a period piece, and even that's relatively simple because period clothes are more or less reproductions that have already been designed. There are so few basic wardrobes for the male. These days I'm not quite so sure. But it used to be trousers, vest, shirt, tie, coat, sweater and jacket. With women there are literally hundreds of styles from which to choose. Another thing, men are much more objective than women. They don't care if the neck of

227

the shirt or sweater is square or round. They just want something that's comfortable. And male stars are far less vain than women. I've never found vanity in any male star with whom I've worked, and that includes Marlon Brando, Cary Grant, Paul Newman, Robert Redford and Steve McQueen. None of them had an ounce of vanity.

After the Mae West picture I went back to doing second leads because Travis had returned from his trip. When he left Paramount a few years later for a more remunerative job at Fox, I succeeded him.

My first Oscar came as the result of the easiest picture I've ever done. For *The Heiress,* which starred Olivia de Havilland, the director, Willy Wyler, wanted an academically perfect period piece. He said, "I don't want anything that you make up or imagine or substitute." Nothing is easier than reproducing something that's already been done. I went to New York and visited museums to research the clothes. In wading through a mass of books, I found sketches of everything Olivia was to wear in the picture, corset, petticoats, the shoes, the hose, the dresses. Now that wasn't difficult to do. The only real work involved was to adapt the clothes to Olivia.

Actually I thought I should have won the Oscar the year before for a picture I did called *The Emperor Waltz,* with Joan Fontaine and Bing Crosby. It was full of fabulous ballrooms, fabulous women in great evening gowns, jewels and fans. It was a lush, lush picture. It never occurred to me that I wouldn't win, I was that sure of myself because I'd done a superb job. But the award went to Dorothy Jenkins for *Joan of Arc,* who did a very fine academic job. *Joan of Arc* was suits of armor and a lot of French peasants, and though Dorothy had handled it extremely well, I was absolutely crushed when I lost. Later, when I thought it over, I realized I'd been fortunate. I shouldn't have won for *The Heiress* because it was only a reproduction. Still and all, suits of armor and French peasants couldn't compare to my fabulous clothes in *The Emperor*

Waltz. But, of course, every designer who's up for an Oscar thinks that her clothes should win.

Winning twice in 1950 was an unprecedented achievement. The two Oscars were *All About Eve* in black and white and *Samson and Delilah* in color. It will never happen again— two Oscars in one year—because we don't have a black and white award anymore.

If I had to name the most exciting actress in the world, not necessarily the easiest, it would be Bette Davis. She's fantastic. Why? I have no idea. She was born that way, I suppose. A lot of female stars stand in front of the mirror and look at the dress. But Bette would *move* in the dress. I remember once during the fittings for *Eve* she suddenly ran across the room and threw herself on a sofa. I was a little startled. Bette explained, "Edith, that's what I have to do with the dress in the picture. I wanted to see if the dress worked." Smart girl, a pro.

For a DeMille picture you did what Mr. DeMille wanted. In *Samson and Delilah* he wanted beautiful lush clothes. Unlike Willy Wyler, he didn't have a passion that everything be academically perfect. In other words, DeMille wanted things that were more imaginative, more exotic. A DeMille picture was never what you'd call a pure period piece. *Samson and Delilah* proved to be a complex assignment because there was no research available about how people actually dressed in Biblical days. I went back as far as I could, to Mesopotamia in the middle of Asia, which supposedly was the cradle of civilization. Then I found that I couldn't use their clothes because the women had nude breasts. Censorship was such in those days that you couldn't even show a female navel. If we had a belly dancer, we'd have to put a belt around her middle or a jewel in her navel. The censors had this strange thing about the female navel, that it couldn't be shown. But male navels seemed to be all right. I could never understand the discrimination.

The evening I won the two Academy Awards should have

been a stunning occasion for me. But I was still an oyster. I never said anything. I clutched the Oscars and ran off the stage without a word. I disappeared so quickly and with inadvertent rudeness that Bob Hope had to apologize for me—"Edith Head says thank you." I didn't learn to talk on my feet until a few years later when I started doing television appearances on Art Linkletter's *House Party* show. Art taught me how to talk, how to feel at ease in front of the public. He gave me confidence. "Speak up, girl," he'd say. "Don't be afraid." Art was an excellent teacher—I've been speaking up ever since.

I hit the jackpot again in 1951 for *A Place in the Sun*, which starred Elizabeth Taylor. That made it four Academy Awards in three consecutive years. But I never thought about it in those terms; you don't think of things like that. The Oscar is a competitive thing, and you reach the point where you hope you'll win. If you do, you're very pleased. If you don't, you're not very pleased.

A Place in the Sun was one of Elizabeth's early pictures. There was a schoolteacher at all her fittings, which was an interesting innovation. Elizabeth has a great passion for animals. At the fittings we always had cats or dogs or birds, scads of them, so I had to work in a rather crowded and hectic atmosphere. It was never dull. Elizabeth is an enchanting creature and a pleasure to dress.

Two more Oscars came in 1953 and 1954 for pictures I did with Audrey Hepburn, *Roman Holiday* and *Sabrina*.

Audrey is charming, intelligent, cooperative, quiet, gracious. She does her fittings and gets out. She wears clothes better than any actress I've known. If she wasn't a star, she'd be a model. Audrey is one of the few people about whom you can never tell a story. She's very self-contained and businesslike. I don't think she'd permit an anecdote to happen to her.

As a small-busted girl Audrey did extremely well for herself, winning an Oscar as best actress for *Roman Holiday* in the period when Marilyn Monroe was gaining prominence. I never dressed Marilyn. It would have been difficult. I can't think of anything more difficult to fit than a large bust. Perhaps difficult isn't the word. It's just that large breasts and high fashion are not synonymous. The only exception is Sophia Loren. I dressed her in *Black Orchid,* with Anthony Quinn, *Houseboat* and *Heller in Pink Tights.* There's something extraordinary about Sophia. She's a rather voluptuous girl, and yet she can look as high fashion as any model. She has great elegance.

The big bosom, which made girls like Jane Russell and Jayne Mansfield sex symbols, appears to be a thing of the past now that pictures are emphasizing realism. Raquel Welch, who has a fantastic body, is the sole survivor of that particular Hollywood version of glamor.

It's odd, but glamor has gone masculine. In the last couple of years I've done nothing but men's pictures because all the stories are written for men. My last Oscar was for dressing the world's two most beautiful and handsome men, Paul Newman and Robert Redford in *The Sting.*

But that wasn't as creative as, say, designing the fantastic clothes that Ginger Rogers wore in *Lady in the Dark.* I don't call Ginger beautiful, not in the classic sense. Grace Kelly is a classic beauty. Ginger is a pretty woman, a very attractive female. She's a charming girl who looks like a lot of charming girls. But with the proper clothes she becomes someone special.

For the dream sequence in *Lady in the Dark,* when Ginger sang "Jenny Made Her Mind Up," I gave her a mink skirt split up the front and lined in ruby glitter. The outfit was a sensation, probably the most expensive gown ever made in Hollywood. The mink alone cost fifteen thousand dollars. I've done pictures recently where the star's wardrobe ran two to three hundred dollars. How much can you spend on blue jeans and a shirt? That sort of outfit isn't going to make the impact of Dorothy Lamour's sarong. I dressed Dorothy in her first sarong in *The Jungle Princess*. People still remember it, and it did wonders for Dorothy's career. I got a funny letter from somewhere in Polynesia about Dorothy's sarong. She was hidden, of course, from bust to knee, but the letter writer was a purist. "Dear Madam," it said. "Your sarong is incorrect. We do not cover above the waist."

If I could put two of my pictures in a time capsule for future generations I'd choose *All About Eve* and *To Catch a Thief*, with Cary Grant and Grace Kelly. If I had to leave the world something that says Edith Head, it would be those two pictures.

Grace was heavenly to work with because here is a woman who is as well educated as I am. She was conversant with anything I'd want to discuss, something I'd seen in a museum in Rome or Paris, for example. She knew what I was talking about. But the main quality she had was that she was the most objective of all the women stars. Whether it was her frothy, pale negligee and the green raw silk suit I did for her in *Rear Window*, or the golden princess dress I designed for *To Catch a Thief*, or the dreary clothes she had to wear in *Country Girl*, the picture that won her an Academy Award, she didn't object. She knew what was right for her for each part. When she saw the wardrobe I'd designed for *Country Girl*, she said, "These are fine. These are going to help me look the part." Nine out of ten actresses in that pre-blue-jean era would have hated the clothes and would have said so.

The biggest disappointment of my career was not winning an Oscar for my wardrobe in *To Catch a Thief*. It was one of the most fantastic, spectacular jobs I'd done. But I didn't win because *To Catch a Thief* wasn't as popular a picture as the winner, *Love Is a Many Splendored Thing*. It had that great song, and it had Chinese women in little coolie coats and stuff and should not have won, in my opinion. I'm not disparaging the clothes in that picture. They were beautiful, but I

232

thought mine were better. A designer has to think that way. Any creative person has to think that way. It may be ego, but what's wrong with having a healthy ego?

I've never had an instance where a star has rejected my designs because I never show just one design. I always have at least two or three. That's the process. If you show them one design, they may not like it. And what do they do? Either they're polite and say they like it or they go to the director and say, "I don't like Head's designs." But when you give them two or three choices and discuss them, it's more effective. There's no percentage in trying to be a dictator. I don't design *for* stars, I design *with* stars. That's why I've survived and why I've never had a problem surviving.

I've always found that the most professional and intelligent actresses, contrary to the general notion, do not necessarily want their best features accentuated. If the part calls for them to have a small bosom, they'll help me flatten it. If their judgment exceeds their vanity, they'll want to look the part. Doris Day is an excellent illustration. I did her clothes for *Teacher's Pet,* with Clark Gable, and one called *The Man Who Knew Too Much,* an Alfred Hitchcock picture with Jimmy Stewart. Doris was criticized in the press for acting and dressing like a perpetual virgin. I never understood that. When I worked with her, she was a professional actress, period. She did her roles according to what the script called for and wore the right clothes for each picture. I never had any trouble with her.

I think nudity in pictures today is so stupid because there are so few really beautiful bodies. If you are going to do a nude scene where the nudity is suggested in the bathtub or the shower or swimming in a lake, that's perfectly all right. That's interesting because it indicates sex rather than making it blatant. But when nudity is inserted for shock, that's quite another matter. I have nothing against nudity from a prudish point of view. If you want to show a naked body, why, go ahead and show it. I just think it's dull and uninteresting. A body is a body, a hunk of flesh, and that's that.

Look, I want to tell you something. Those beautiful clinging clothes that Jean Harlow wore when she slithered into a room, those lovely skintight satin dresses without a stitch on underneath—*that was sex!* A lot more exciting than if Jean had slithered in stark naked or with her bosoms hanging out.

Until the public demands a different kind of picture, there will never be a return to glamor in films. Don't forget, Hollywood began as a world of fantasy. Audiences don't seem to want fantasy anymore. They want stark ugly realism. Take television, that thing that is at the top of the ratings, *All in the Family*. Well, you couldn't have less of a show for displaying clothes. So when you have that type of public taste, you can understand that my field isn't what it used to be.

How I'd like to get my hands on a script about a girl who isn't poor and doesn't hate clothes and doesn't appear in the raw. Sometimes I think I'd even settle for another elephant.

20

Martin Rackin

A HELL OF A STRUGGLE FOR A YARD

FRESH FROM A DIP in his pool, he's sitting in his wood-splashed den, wearing a robe and sandals. His $300,000 house in Beverly Hills is English Tudor, built by the late producer-director Sir Alexander Korda.

Rackin is a long way from Harlem, where he was born in 1918.

"Growing up, I read every Tom Swift book, every Nick Carter book, every Horatio Alger book. I hoped Horatio Alger was true. You know something? I still do.

"I was Walter Mitty. In every movie I saw as a kid I was Douglas Fairbanks. I was Jack Holt. I was Tarzan. I was all those guys."

He went to school in Hell's Kitchen. "I got shot when I was fourteen and knifed when I was fifteen. I didn't know whether I was going to a school or a blood bank."

He completed his last year of high school at night. Days he worked at the New York Daily Mirror. "It wasn't the greatest newspaper in the world but it had the best newspaper guys, Winchell, Mark Hellinger, Bob Considine, Damon Runyon. I especially admired Runyon. He was a reformed alcoholic, and he scared the shit out of me about liquor. Thanks to him, I never got hung up on booze. Runyon was a giant, a genius. He started a whole new way of literature. He developed a style that everybody copied. He also wrote the book on human nature. He once told me something I've never forgotten, "When you're born, you're about three feet long. When you die, you're about six feet long. It's a hell of a struggle for a yard."

Rackin arrived in Hollywood in 1940 after selling two novels he'd written in his spare time to Paramount and Columbia. He spent the next two decades as a producer and writer. Two of his screenplays, The Enforcer *and* Three Secrets, *were nominated for Academy Awards.*

"They made me head of production at Paramount in 1960. At the time it was a dead-ass studio that was being run by a bunch of old men who knew nothing about the picture business."

Rackin is six feet one, 171 pounds, handsome, rugged, a man of contrasts. Tender and tough. Outrageous and sensitive. Quick to praise, quick to damn. A knowing art collector who paints the air with Anglo-Saxonese. The product of a roiling slum who was entertained by Winston Churchill.

The most intriguing things about him are his wit and candor.

Alan Ladd was responsible for getting me the job at Paramount. Alan had started his own company, Jaguar Productions, and after working for him I'd gradually taken it over, stepping in when he was in trouble. I got his pictures made on budget. He made a lot of money with me. I made, you know, not too much because his wife, Sue, wouldn't let anybody get near anything.

One night Alan called and invited me to dinner at his home. He wanted me to meet somebody.

The somebody was a man by the name of George Weltner, who was the vice-president of Paramount in charge of worldwide sales.

We talked about the picture business and had a marvelous evening. By then I'd written probably forty pictures and produced fifteen or twenty. I had confidence. Nothing got fucked up under me. I knew I could handle stars and directors. Weltner didn't say a thing that evening about my going to Paramount. I learned later he'd told the Paramount brass, "Rackin's the guy we need." I guess he liked what I'd said about picturemaking. And he'd checked me out, what I'd done, the price I was getting things done for. They know whether you're a pro or not. The word gets out whether you're a schmuck.

I forgot about Weltner and I left Alan. I went into business with John Lee Mahin, one of the best writers of all time. We put together the first big picture for the Mirisch brothers, *The Horse Soldiers*, with John Wayne and William Holden, directed by John Ford, written by us. It was the first time that stars had busted into the kind of money we gave them. Wayne and Holden each got seven hundred and fifty thousand dollars. We made the picture in Louisiana, and to attract those stars, a director like Ford, find the book, which John and I bought for twenty-five hundred dollars, write the script and put the whole thing together was a pretty monumental feat for two guys running an independent operation.

About a year after I first met Weltner, he offered me the job at Paramount. I went to New York to sign the contract. I told Weltner, "I want you to know one thing before we start this whole goddamn thing. Babe Ruth has been dead twenty years, and they named a candy bar for him. The bum never hit over four hundred. I won't make a hit every time either. I'm going to do the best I can, and Jesus when I have a flop, and I'll have them, I don't want to hear about it."

When the story broke that I was going to run the studio, everybody said, Who the hell is Marty Rackin? Why him? You know, the usual shit. But it didn't bother me. Anything that I've ever decided to do in my life I can do.

When I walked into my office the first time, it was all brown furniture, brown paneling; everything was Gothic. I called in Hal Pereira, who'd been the art director on the Martin and Lewis pictures I'd written.

I told Hal, "Take down the sign that says 'Mr. Rackin.' Put up 'Marty Rackin.' Take the whole goddamn office and paint it white. Put in a white desk. Paint the breakfront white and put in a white sofa, white rugs, white lampshades, red pillows, blue pillows. Make it bright! We're in show business, and goddamn it, let it look like show business. I want everything bright, *alive!*"

After the office was redecorated, I hung some of my own paintings, and it jumped; it looked like tomorrow, not yesterday. The old thing looked like Scrooge's office at the bank. That's the way their minds were, full of cobwebs.

Most of the guys at the studio were happy about having me there. I'd worked with most of them before. Hal Wallis was happy because he could talk to me. I'd been under contract to Wallis as a writer, and he'd taught me the business. He's the best producer in the world.

I started making myself known around the whole lot. I went to the lumber mill. I went to see Edith Head. I would go to the art department. I'd hang around the different departments and have coffee with them. They'd never seen this. I'd ask everyone, "What's your trouble, your problems? How can we cut overhead? What can I do to make your job easier? What can you do to help me? Do you have any suggestions for me?"

Soon there was a whole different spirit on the lot. I brought people to Paramount that had never been through the gate or had forgotten the studio existed. I brought them Paul Newman, Wayne, John Ford and Henry Hathaway. I attracted people because that's what I am—a born cheerleader. I'm an optimist, and I love this business, but you can love the business too much. Like Jerry Wald, who dropped dead. He was a good producer, but he couldn't spend one evening at home without watching old movies. That's why I never had a projection room built in my house.

I brought Sinatra back to Paramount for *Come Blow Your Horn.* I found Neil Simon. I brought him there. I bought *The Odd Couple* and *Barefoot in the Park.* I signed Neil Simon for everything he did at Paramount.

I was even producing pictures on the side. I was doing everything. I was a one-man band. If you put a broom up my ass, I swept the floor.

Then the studio made a deal with Joe Levine. And I had to produce his pictures for him besides running the studio. Ask Joe, and he'd admit he can't produce a belch after a Hungarian dinner. He'll brag about himself, but he's a supersalesman. I produced *Where Love Has Gone* for Levine. He was in New York, and he never saw the picture until it was finished. I also did a lot of writing on his pictures. I took one Harold Robbins book, and for the same price I got two pictures out of it for Levine: *The Carpetbaggers* with George Peppard and *Nevada Smith* with Steve McQueen. I hired Henry Hathaway, who hadn't been at Paramount in thirty years, to direct McQueen. Jesus Christ, you need a whip and a chair to handle that guy. But I knew Henry could do it, and he did. To this day McQueen calls him "the old man," because he loves him. He's as mean and lovable a son of a bitch as John Ford was. They were and are among my best friends. I adored Ford and he knew it—Hathaway is a screaming madman, but a Teddy bear.

I had a terrible time getting *Hud* made. The studio didn't want to do it because it wasn't truly a "real" Western. It didn't have a conventional beginning, middle and end. The writers, Irving Ravetch and Harriet Frank, had come up with something different. There's no way to pay them enough credit.

I flew to New York and told them that if they wouldn't let me make it, I'd quit. We argued and finally they said I could do it, but only in black and white and if I could bring it in at a certain price.

Paul Newman was set for the lead. I'd made a picture with Paul years before when I was a producer and writer at Warner Brothers. Paul's career in this town got off to a disastrous start because as he said, he wore the wrong frock in *The Silver Chalice*. I told him he looked like a schmuck in the window of a department store. You couldn't take Paul Newman, a German Jew from Cleveland, and have him looking for the Holy Grail. It was stupid, and Paul was fed up with the business.

So before we started shooting *The Helen Morgan Story,* I told Paul, "Look, have faith in me. I won't let Jack Warner fuck you around. I'm not going to let you wear a dress."

In *The Helen Morgan Story* Paul played a bootlegger who pisses on women, and he was tough and he fucked everyone. He was a liar, and he was the kind of guy, you know, the old bullshit, who said, "See that city out there? I'm going to take a bite out of the jungle, and I'm going to chew it up and spit it right in their eye." At least it was Paul Newman with balls. And so Paul trusted me when I told him I'd fight to do *Hud.*

We met in my living room and made the deal. Paul and his partner, Marty Ritt, who was the director, and Jimmy Wong Howe on the camera. I bullshitted them into making it in black and white because that was the only way I could do it. I couldn't afford color.

I told them, "Black and white is the *artistic* way of doing it." You *had* to approach these guys with all this artistic crap. "Garbage looks beautiful in color. But in black and white you'll feel the real dust. You'll feel the heat. We want to get *inside* the people. Everything today is in color, this will be different . . . this will be a work of art."

Jimmy Wong Howe went along with me right away because he was scared shitless of color. He'd made only one picture in color in his whole life, and he had to look on the back of the box the color film came in for the instructions. He'd won his five Academy Awards for black-and-white pictures.

Everybody agreed, and we made the picture.

When the Academy Awards rolled around, we were all there for the ceremony. The first Oscar was for Jimmy Wong Howe for photography. Then Melvyn Douglas for best supporting actor. Then Patricia Neal as best actress. We were just rolling down the goddamn aisle. I said to Paul, "You're going to win. We're going to take everything."

Paul said, "I'm not going to win."

"Bullshit," I said, "you've got it wrapped up."

240

"No," Paul said, "I didn't even vote for myself."

"What do you mean you didn't vote for yourself?"

"I voted for Sidney."

"Sidney who?"

"Poitier. *Lilies of the Field* is maybe the only chance Sidney will ever have."

Poitier beat Paul. Paul had campaigned for him. He was afraid the blacks weren't going to be important in the industry. Little did he know that Sidney and he would end up as partners in a production company and that Sidney would be as big a star as he is.

Things were getting heavier and heavier at the studio. I was slamming around the world so goddamn much. Let me tell you about my experience with Ingmar Bergman. I had a script called *The Stepmother,* and I went to Sweden to talk to Ingmar about directing it.

He lives under an iceberg miles out of town. I tracked him down, and we spent three days together. He finally agreed to do the movie if I'd let him rewrite the script, write the music, and if I stayed off the set.

I told Ingmar, "Go look up the Ford Foundation." While that shit was searching his *auteur* soul, they'd come take my house away and padlock the studio.

I've never been a producer *in absentia.* As an independent and at Paramount I was on the set as often as possible. I like to watch the director so he won't make any mistakes and not change the script. If a movie says, " A Martin Rackin Production," that's what it is. A director can save me time on the schedule in blocking and other routine matters. I allow directors freedom as long as they're right. But if there's one frame in dispute, I always win the argument.

It's very interesting. Everybody in this business is so serious. Nobody has a sense of humor. The moment they start making a thousand dollars a week they become scholars. That's all nonsense. It's ridiculous. They call the business an art form, poetry, or they say it's the same as painting or sculpture. Guys call themselves *auteur* directors or method actors.

If you told the men who started this business, Jack Warner, Harry Warner, Harry Cohn, Louis B. Mayer, Sam Goldwyn, Darryl Zanuck—I call them the six bastards—that it was an art form they'd hit you right in the eye. They only referred to it in two ways: either the motion-picture business or the movie industry. "Movie" or "picture" are the words used by people who do them. It's the movie business; it's an industry. Film is a word used by ego-trip shitheels.

I'd been running the goddamn Paramount machine for five years, and my wife, Helen, thought I was killing myself. She's a coal miner's daughter from a little town in Wisconsin. Her father had a light in his head and a canary on top of his hat till the day he died. Helen wanted me to leave the studio. We had the money we needed. We're not the fucking kooks with the eighty servants, a dozen Rolls-Royces and the country club bullshit. We live a very quiet, unostentatious private life.

I was in the office one day having a disagreement with Howard Hawks and getting nowhere over a picture called *El Dorado* that was in production. In the middle of the brawl, I fainted. I was rushed to the hospital. They thought I'd had a pump attack, that I was a goner. Helen's face turned magenta. Everybody was passing the cup for the mourning. Four guys were already lined up for my job—four very good friends—they say.

What it was, I'd been to Spain and back twice in *one* week, sleeping on the floor of the airplane. It was exhaustion and aggravation. One drop of water doesn't hurt, but after five years of drips, each one feels like a ton of lead. After my doctor read the tests he said, "All you need is a couple of nights' sleep. Take a vacation. Swim twenty laps every day, then go back to work."

Except for the vacation, I took his advice.

By now George Weltner had become the president of Paramount. And he learned something very terrible. He learned how to read. Suddenly this nice film salesman was reading books and making deals in New York without telling me. He was going to 21, and stars were falling all over him kissing his ass and these fucking guys were taking him right and left.

It got to be too much, and I was being torn apart. Joe Levine was saying I couldn't work on anyone else's pictures. "Fuck Paramount," he said. "You've got to work *exclusively* on *my* pictures. I've got a twelve-picture deal for seven million dollars." But even when I was working for Levine, he would tell Weltner, "I don't need Rackin calling me every morning."

Well, what a life. I was like a fucking slave, pulled and pushed in every direction. And then Weltner did the unforgivable. He made a deal with Otto Preminger, who I regard as walking clap, the only man whose picture should be in every post office in the United States. With the lousy pictures he's made he's stolen more money from the movie business than Jesse James stole from the railroads. Jesse James was a fucking philanthropist compared to Preminger. And Weltner, in his hysteria, signed Preminger, who is not a producer, a director, or anything. He's a Viennese fucking lawyer. Like Billy Wilder says, "I always have to be nice to Otto because I still have relatives in Germany."

In the deal Weltner made with Preminger it said that Otto didn't have to talk to me. I had nothing to say about anything he did. That finally tore it. I was just disgusted, really disgusted.

Helen and I weren't having a good life anymore. The fun was out of life. I like fun, and the fun was gone. I was entertaining guys at my house because I needed them at the studio. Stars, producers and directors were eating our food and stamping cigarette butts into the rugs. Helen made all these rugs by hand, and she made all these pillows by hand. All the needlework in the house is by hand, and a fucking actor would just as soon shit in his pants as stop in the middle of a story. Every time they ate they stained things, burned your possessions with cigarettes, and it just wasn't fun anymore.

One day Helen and I were talking about a painting I planned to give her for her birthday. "You know what I really want for my birthday?" she said.

"What?"

"I want you to quit the studio."

"Are you crazy? I've got a contract."

"Quit," she said. "Make that my birthday present."

She was right—the moment had come for me to leave.

I flew to New York and met with Weltner. We had a terrible scene. It was a very heavy number. He wouldn't let me quit. Weltner got hysterical; his eyes started to roll.

"I'm the president," he intoned. "You can't do this to me."

I said, "If you're the president, don't ride in an open car in Dallas. I'm leaving."

"No, you're not leaving. I own you."

"Nobody owns me. I'm no fucking slave picking cotton, and that's it."

The hollering match went on. Weltner became wild-eyed, accusing me of double-crossing him by quitting. But he was letting everybody shit on me. "You can't leave just when I need you the most," he said. Sure, he needed me to protect his job because I was keeping Levine at bay. I was keeping everybody at bay, covering up all their fucking mistakes. I was keeping Duke happy. I made Wayne's deal for him at Paramount on a handshake and Duke wanted it put in the contract that it was only valid as long as I was head of the studio. I said, "Duke, for Christ's sake, Paramount is a public company; you can't put that kind of thing in a contract." He said okay. But when I left, he still had one picture to do for them, and he's never done it. He's never done the picture to this day, and I don't believe he'll do it.

Finally, I said to Weltner, "George, I won't leave you in the lurch. You have my word that I'll go back to the studio and stay for a month because there are scripts in work, there are pictures shooting. I'll break in my replacement, show him what's going on, bring him up to date."

Weltner said, "No, I can't let you quit. Marty, you wouldn't do this to me."

"George, I've got to."

"Think about it, just think about it. We'll work something out."

I went back to the Sherry Netherland, and I called Helen, and I said, "Damn, they don't want to let me quit."

"What plane are you on?" she asked.

"I'm taking a flight out in about three hours."

"If you get off the plane in Los Angeles and you're still at Paramount, I'll be at the Beverly Wilshire Hotel, and you can see a lawyer."

I called Weltner and said, "Look, George, I can't sleep with Paramount. I can't have any children with Paramount. That's it—I'm quitting."

"Marty, you and I are so close," he said. "You're like my own son." All this shit.

"George," I told him, "I'll stay for six weeks, eight weeks, I don't care. I'll break in anybody you want. Not a detail will get lost."

"You'll never know what I think of you, Marty. As long as I live, I'll love you and appreciate what you're doing."

I called Helen back. "Okay, I've quit. It may take a month or two, but what the hell is that in our lives?"

I was in my office the next morning at a quarter till nine. I told my secretary, and she began to cry. "Start bringing everybody up to date," I said. "Call a general meeting. I want to tell all the heads of the departments, all the producers, everybody."

Gene Frank from the legal department came in at twenty to ten. He's a darling man. He said, "Marty, what the hell's happened? I've been with the company for twenty-eight

245

years, and I've never heard anything like this. I'm here to tell you that you have two hours to get off the lot and leave the key to your studio car with me, even if you have to take a cab home."

He read the surprise on my face.

"I've got orders from Weltner to throw you out of the studio and not let you touch anything."

Weltner had thought it over all night, and he was so fucking mad that's how he reacted.

I told my secretary, "Destroy the files. Destroy everything. Fuck 'em all. Let the dailies rot." And that was it. I gave Gene French the key to my car and I went home—in a cab.

I'd kept a diary almost every day I was at Paramount. Sometimes I'd be at meetings all day long, meetings, meetings, meetings. Between meetings I'd go to my office, where I always kept a typewriter, and I'd whack out half a page or so. What was pertinent and funny and sad. Who was pregnant and not married, who got the abortions, who had the clap, who got arrested. I'd write about the dirty double-crossing agents who sold me crummy actors and the actors who'd try to sell me a broad for a part in a picture just so she'd keep humping him. I wrote about all the backstabbing and the infighting among the executives, producers, directors and stars. To think that some people could be that rotten and unethical.

Then I realized the diary was a garbage pail of messy intrigue. And I always felt that somebody would get their hands on it. I wasn't going to publish it. It was for my own amusement. I was keeping it as a newspaperman.

I burned it. I remember who I hate, and I remember the secrets.

Big business is so evil, you have no idea. You see, I'm a picturemaker, and I'm not in that big-business infighting. After I quit, Charlie Bluhdorn, this Viennese madman, came in. He blew Weltner out of the seat. He blew Howard Koch, who'd replaced me, out of the seat. Then they brought in a dressmaker, Bob Evans. Billy Wilder once asked me, "Marty, how can a fellow like Bob Evans do your job at Paramount?"

"Very simple," I said. "If the picture's too long, he'll take up the hem."

The whole business now is in the hands of people who aren't in the movie business. Who's in charge of the studios today? Who are the heads of the studios today? The studios have been gobbled up by conglomerates who also own parking lots, cemeteries, sugar companies, airlines, hotels—all kinds of shit. I can remember in the old days at Warner Brothers, boy, that was a company like the others. Their only business was making pictures, and it was a great gang. Everyone would help each other out, the actors, the writers, the directors. There's nothing like it now.

Where are the Harry Cohns and Jack Warners who used to sit in the projection room until two in the morning, saying, "Take out that close-up . . . drop that reel . . . pull the producer . . . take that fucking writer off the script, I read his scene and it stinks"?

A guy like Hal Wallis, he goes on, he goes on every year. He will come up with an *Anne of the Thousand Days*, a *Mary, Queen of Scots*, or *True Grit*. He's a picturemaker, he doesn't have any other business, and he's richer than all these new guys around today. Hal loves movies, that's what he knows. He's been in it since he came to Hollywood and got off the train to be an assistant publicity man at Warner Brothers. He ended up being the production head of Warner's, and then he finally told Jack Warner to go fuck himself and became the greatest independent producer in the world because he knows motion pictures. I used to tell Hal he's the way he is because he's like Johnny Eager. He never had a dog. When he smiles, I think it hurts him, and his life is playing baccarat with human chips. A guy could come to him while he's shooting and say, "My best friend just died." And Hal would say, "That's great. What's the next camera setup?" But I like Hal,

I like him very, very much, and he and I have been very close over the years.

I don't know, sometimes I have a feeling the sand is running through the glass for me in this business. I still have the same enthusiasm and love for it, but I don't have the patience for it that I used to have. I've lost my hunger. I was always like a fighter with wrinkles in his belly. Always beware of a fighter that has wrinkles in his belly. He'll kick the shit out of you because he needs it. I don't need it anymore. Hal Wallis with his hundred million dollars needs it because he never had a dog. There are certain guys who need it.

What the hell do you really need out of life? I sit here and talk to you. I'm in a nice house, not the best house in Beverly Hills, but it's got everything I need. I want a cold drink, I've got ice water. I want to look at TV, that fucking glass nymphomaniac, I've got one in every room. I want a steam room, I've got a steam room. If I want to take a swim, I've got a pool. So what the hell more do I need? My wife and I lost a grandchild a year ago, a little girl, about eight months old. And you say, for what? What the hell did that kid ever do to anybody? I know pricks in this town that should never live to be three minutes old. You say, "What the hell is it all about?" You see guys who are so fucking hungry, the big agents, the sickies, the producers wearing the love beads because some other schmuck is wearing love beads. They wear plank shoes because someone else is wearing plank shoes. You work in this business with so many sick and untalented people. Directors who can't direct. But they are up stars' asses so far all you can see is shoes. They kiss each other's asses, and they go to the same parties, and you wonder why they don't all have jaws like Pomeranians that keep fucking each other. They are so inbred. The Willy Wylers, the John Fords, they never got involved in that shit.

Sometimes there's no breathing. You watch and see a guy like Peter Bogdanovich who copies Ford or Howard Hawks and ends up with everybody in town saying he's one of the great pricks of the world. When he was starting out, he made love to everybody. Suddenly with success all the shitheel comes out. I think if you can be a nice guy when you're on top, that's better. I don't mind a guy being a prick on the bottom, but when you get there, be nice.

I don't know. Let me say that I've lost my enthusiasm for running in the marathon. Most of these guys I can lick one-handed, but I don't have the appetite for it now. I owned a piece of a hotel in Vegas with a friend of mine. We made a lot of money from the bellytouche, the schmucks stepping up to the crap tables. There was a midget on our payroll for five hundred dollars a week. My friend felt sorry for him, called him a security officer, and when we were selling the hotel, he gave him a contract for seven hundred fifty dollars a week. I said, "That five hundred is pretty good. But seven fifty. . . ." "Don't complain," my friend said. "Just remember one thing. He's a midget twenty-four hours a day."

Some of the people in this town are midgets twenty-four hours a day, and they don't know it. And that's where the problem is. They have to get in and cut and rip and double cross.

It was better when you knew who your enemy was. Everybody at each studio had one enemy, Louis B Mayer, Harry Cohn, Zanuck. Everybody had one fucking enemy who fucked up your picture. He was the prick. But today there are so many of them you can't tell one prick from the other without a scorecard.

And it isn't making pictures anymore. It's making deals. That's what depresses me. You never hear anybody talking about the picture. They talk about the deal. "I got a deal with Bob Redford, but Bob Redford's business manager has to be the associate producer, and then the deal is that his best friend, a lawyer, is going to be the writer, is going to be on the script and we are going to shoot on land Redford owns in Utah." I made pictures with Gary Cooper, Wayne, Gable. We never went through this. They read the script; they said,

"What time do I get there?" They came to the studio and did it, and then they went home. Dustin Hoffman, Jesus, the luckiest Jewish midget that ever lived. Makes a couple of great pictures with great directors, and then he finally goes to an idiot producer that's going to make a picture in New York, and Dustin insists he's going to have complete control. So he hires schmucks, a business manager, a producer, a director whose only credit was a Tampax commercial. The script was him getting his gun off. The picture was *Who Is Harry Kellerman and Why Is He Saying Those Terrible Things About Me?* No one went to see it except Dustin Hoffman and four of his friends in Greenwich Village. I can't take the shit. It's tough to swallow, it's tough.

After Paramount, I went into independent production. I've made six or seven pictures on my own. One was *The Revengers* with Bill Holden. Another was *Two Mules for Sister Sarah* with Clint Eastwood and Shirley MacLaine. Clint's all right; he's a nice guy. Shirley MacLaine is a disaster, a fucking ovary with a propeller who leaves a trail of blood wherever she goes. A half-assed chorus girl, a pseudo-intellectual who thinks she knows politics, thinks she knows the world, thinks she knows everything, wears clothes from the ladies of the Good Christ Church bazaar. She still wears Ruby Keeler bows on her shoes. She'd be better off studying fashion instead of politics. She's a kook. A fine actress, but a pain in the ass. Now she's got to be an authoress, a politician, a philosopher. She's got a project, and the project is to give away to the poor everything *you've* got. Hers, she keeps!

On *Two Mules* I used a director I'd known a long time. To me he was a fifty-seven-year-old failure. Even his teeth, which weren't his, hurt. But he was close to Clint Eastwood. I never heard a director say to the star, "How would you like it if I put the camera here? Would you be happy if I put the camera there?" Then Clint said what do I need this shit for? So Clint is directing himself. He doesn't need him anymore.

We made money with *Two Mules,* but it could have grossed

millions without the director. He kept telling me I'm a Scorpio and that's why I'm a prick. I don't know what sign I am. Guys who worry about their sign and all this bullshit, those are mental cases. I can't live with these people. I'm sure if you asked Henry Hathaway what his sign was he wouldn't know or care. He just goes out and makes pictures.

There is just so much shit that you can take in life. I keep saying to my wife that one of these days I think what we'll do is sell the goddamn house and live a year in France or Italy. I'll write a script if I want to or if I don't want to I'll go into the used Ferrari business. What the hell is the difference? I can make money doing anything. If I decided to sell ladies' shoes, I'd sell more ladies' shoes than anybody who ever lived.

Another thing I can't tolerate is the guy who makes a couple of pictures and becomes an oracle. When it gets oracle time, fuck it. I had James Coburn here. I was going to make a picture with him, and *he* tells *me* what's wrong with the script. Now James Coburn by mistake might be a genius, but I never read a script he wrote. When he left, I told my wife, "He's not going to be in the picture. And he'll never be a star." And Coburn isn't a star. There are guys like him who after a couple of hits start believing their own publicity. If they ever said in the old days to Jack Warner, and that included Cagney or Bogart, "I don't like the script, and I'm not going to do this," he'd say, "Fuck you, you're off the payroll. Go sit in your fucking house, you idiot." That was the way to run studios. Just tell the actors when to show up. Actors act. Writers write. Directors should direct.

With few exceptions, I have very little respect for actors and directors. Most of them have as much integrity as an adder. You have to milk their fangs once a month to keep them in line.

When Bogart was dying of cancer, people said, "Go see him. Go say hello." I said, "Fuck him. Let him go fast. He was a live shitheel, and now he's going to be a dead shitheel." I got into a brawl with Bogart in 1951 when we were making *The Enforcer*. It cost me six weeks' salary. I don't carry beautiful friendships with assholes, even if they are on the way to the grave.

These method people make me sick, too. Doing thirty pushups to get out of breath for realism. If they're in a scene where the temperature is freezing, they've got to climb into a refrigerator to turn blue. What kind of shit is that? Cagney once said to me, "I died in twenty pictures. What do you have to do with these guys? Shoot them?"

They want to know the motivation, the inner character. Some actor once asked Howard Hawks, "What is the reason I go from here to there?" And Hawks said, "Your salary."

These things drive me up the wall. I must tell you I happen to like Marlon Brando as a guy. I think if it wasn't for *The Godfather,* which I thought was a lousy performance anyhow, Marlon would have ended up a ragpicker unless he had his money stashed away. He just fucked himself out of the greatest career in the history of the movie business by being funky, by being the Marilyn Monroe of the men. He wouldn't show up, or he was late on the set. Brando is a brilliant actor with the potential of becoming a fine director, if he ever gets his head on straight. But of course he never will. After *Last Tango,* a great performance, he's so rich he can wear his head sideways.

Jack Warner must piss in his pants every time he thinks about *The Godfather.* He made that picture every week. Instead of Marlon Brando, it was Eduardo Ciannelli.

I remember we made that picture at least fifteen times while I was at Warner Brothers. Cagney used to come out of the cab. He'd come in to the nightclub office and Barton MacLane would be standing there, and Bogart would be behind the desk with the wing collar tuxedo.

Cagney would say, "Well, I'm out of the can, Al."

And Bogey would say, "Great, Rocky. How did you like the blonde, Rocky?"

"Great, Al."

"Things have changed while you were in the can, Rocky. Things are a little different."

"What do ya mean, Al? I still own fifty percent of this joint."

And Bogey would say, "Well, that's what I wanted to tell you. You see, there's been a change downtown. Look, Rocky, why don't you go see Mary? She's waiting for you."

Then Cagney goes into a phone booth and they gun him down.

Well, it's the same shit. Francis Ford Coppola, who directed *Godfather,* they talk about him like he can walk on water. All I know is he fucked up *Finian's Rainbow.* He never had a hit in his life, until *The Godfather* and I used to say if World War III breaks out, I'm going to stand under him. It would be the safest place to be because he hasn't had a hit in so long. If they drop a bomb, stand under Coppola. *You'll* be safe. Coppola wrote *Patton,* but you look at *Patton.* It was also written by Edmund North *and* Coppola. Coppola came in last; he was the second writer. Eddie North broke his ass for five years on that script. But suddenly Coppola turns up, with a knit cap and a muff and Zoetrope Productions of San Francisco, and he's a big hero. *Godfather* had a fellow named Puzo who wrote the book.

I was at Warner Brothers talking to Dick Zanuck. He left there so fast; he was so unhappy. He said it's so weird, so strange, these new guys don't come out of their offices. They eat sandwiches and smoke shit.

Boy, I don't know what they do over there. It's not my way of making pictures.

Hollywood was once the Woolworth of the entertainment business. The poor schmuck who wanted to get away and forget for two hours used to go and be entertained. You can still buy a comb at Woolworth for a dime, but today they make a cheap picture, overcharge for it. Hollywood's mistake is they charge the same for rabbit as they do for mink.

I'm sick of black pictures. Jesus Christ, I'm sick of schwartzers. They feel blacks will go to movies, so Hollywood is ripping them off. I was on the *Irv Kupcinet Show* in Chicago with Jim Brown and a girl by the name of Cash who was in *Melinda* and some lousy actor who was in *Super Fly*, and another colored actor that was in *Come Back Charleston Blue.* I said, "Hey, look at this. I'm a minority. A white Jew." I told the girl, "Jesus, honey, I saw you in *Melinda*. Your acting is ridiculous." She said on the air, "I wanted to make them change the script so it would be like *The New Centurions*. My role didn't have enough depth." I said, "I don't know what the hell you're talking about." And I told the guy in *Super Fly*, "You're lucky you're working anywhere." He said, "I want to play more scientific things and up the black people's standing." I said, "Did Cagney or Wayne ever play a brain surgeon? No. I saw you in *Super Fly*, and you were lousy. The whole picture didn't cost what the wardrobe costs on half the pictures I've made. The picture was made to fuck whitey. Pure hate for the honky."

The trouble is, they charge those poor blacks three and a half dollars to go and see these goddamn pictures. I have a feeling about the movies, that we're overpriced, that we've outpriced ourselves. When the unions say, "Runaway production," I say, "Fuck 'em." Who is an extra to get eighty-five dollars a day to walk by in the background? Who the hell are they? They're the bums of Hollywood. And the makeup men. They're the leeches of the world. I despise them. One can only put makeup on down to the collar bone, and then there's another makeup man for the arms. Typically, one of these guys will say to the star, "Good morning, champ. Gee, you look great." You know why? He wants a watch when it's over or a gold St. Christopher medal, from which he'll remove the engraving and hock. He says, "Who am I working with on this picture? What the hell did he give me last time? Oh, yeah, the gold money clip. I'd rather have cash." They're whores. They work fifteen minutes in the morning, and they always want to be seen in the dailies. Whenever the director says, "Roll 'em," the makeup man steps in and says, "One minute." Then he wipes the star's forehead, or some goddamn thing. That's so he'll be seen in the dailies, and that proves he was working hard. Well, bullshit.

That's why I like guys like Bill Holden. He has no permanent makeup man. He doesn't wear makeup and has no stand-in. No secretary. He has nobody. You say to Holden, "Hey, we're going to make a picture in India." And he says, "Fine." And he shows up with a little suitcase with two pair of slacks and a shirt and says, "Okay, let's go." If you suggest sending a car to meet him at the airport, he says, "I'll grab a cab." He's a star! He's a man! That's the difference.

When I was running Paramount, we'd send stars out on publicity tours. You wouldn't believe the things they did. They'd go into jewelry stores and charge wristwatches, buy twelve pair of silk pajamas, robes, shoes—like they had no clothes. They'd put hookers on the expense account. Terrible things. Order New York steaks for breakfast just to leave them on the plate to get even with the studio. Recently there was a broad that a studio sent out on tour. I don't even know her name; she's an unknown, and she'll always be unknown. She fell apart on the tour because she'd left her lid of marijuana under the mattress and the maid stole it. This was the star of a new picture who had posed for *Playboy* and all this shit.

Christ, you say to yourself, "Forget it." There's such fun working with great picturemakers, and it's such a pain in the ass working with bums because it's just as hard to make a bad picture as it is to make a good one. It takes the same number of hours in the sun, the same number of hours of standing on your feet, the same number of hours in the cutting room. You need the same size orchestra to put in the music. The film costs the same.

I admire professionalism. That's all I admire. I want to tell you something. At the end of a picture—you know, everything in this town is so phony—everybody gives everybody a gift or a party. I did a picture with Mike Curtiz at Warners and he said, "Marty, the party. When the picture is over, we give a party, huh?"

"What for?" I said.

"For the crew, the cast."

"Fuck 'em," I said. "If I hadn't broken my ass writing it, they wouldn't be working." I told him that when I send for a plumber because my toilet is clogged, the guy comes, he does this and that, runs a snake down, he cleans the shit out, he flushes it four times. Then he says, "It's all finished, Mr. Rackin." What do I do? Applaud him and give him a party?

I told Curtiz, "No party. Everybody was overpaid anyway."

Jerry Lewis, the sickness of his life was that he had his own standby jeweler. A guy used to come on the set with a thing on wheels. He had wristwatches, money clips, God Bless You St. Christopher medals, St. Genesis medals that said "God Bless My Career." It was nothing for Jerry to give out twenty thousand dollars' worth of cufflinks and all that other fucking stuff. I've got boxes of that gold shit here from him and others. I don't even carry insurance on it. I wish I could melt it down. I wish I needed a bridge. But I have my own teeth. Jesus, I wish I needed gold in my teeth.

I wrote pictures for Jerry and Dean Martin at Paramount and we were all great friends. Years later, when I became head of the studio Jerry and I ended up in a lawsuit, because Jerry decided he was Charlie Chaplin and I decided he wasn't. We didn't talk for years, until Jane Murray brought us together.

It gets pretty dull in this town when you're in a room with people who all think the same way. There's no excitement. I like a good argument—"Say that one more time and we'll step outside." I like that kind of evening. I don't like what I call the Carl Reiner-type evening. You go to one of these things, and somebody says, "We're all here to raise money for retarded children. Half the money is going to the black

retarded, and the other half to the Chinese retarded." Fuck
'em. You're expected to buy some tired lithographs for the
cause. I've spent enough money in this town to buy my own
retarded child. I just don't enjoy that kind of thing. I'm not a
joiner. I don't belong to any clubs. I don't even belong to the
Book-of-the-Month Club. I don't play golf because I don't
want to play with agents. I don't want to listen to all that bullshit. Most of these guys don't play golf because they like it.
They play because the course is a place to make a deal.

Another thing that burns the shit out of me is when a guy
will say to me, "Jesus Christ, I tried to get in touch with you
Sunday. I really wanted to talk to you."

"Well, why didn't you call me? I was home all day."

"How the hell was I going to get your number on Sunday?"

"Look in the fucking telephone book."

"You're in the book?"

"I've always been in the book."

It becomes a status symbol not to be in the book. Let me
tell you about Gable. One night we came back here after dinner at Chasen's. Gable and his wife Kay, John Lee Mahin and
his wife Nicka, Helen and myself. Gable was smashed. So was
Kay. So were John and Nicka. My wife doesn't drink. Out of
friendship I'd had a couple of glasses of wine. We closed
Chasen's that night. By the time we got to the house Kay Gable was setting my wife's hair with creme de menthe. That's
the kind of evening it was. And Gable was, you know, getting
more Gable by the minute. We were going to give Kay a big
thrill. John and I had gotten a sixteen-millimeter print of
Clark Gable, Aerial Gunner, made for the Eighth Air Force,
directed by Willy Wyler and written by John. It was a record
of Gable's actual missions which he flew over Schweinfurt,
and no bullshit. Gable hadn't seen the picture in twenty
years. None of us had seen it. We had gotten the only print.
We ran the picture twice, and it was around three thirty or
four in the morning. In those days I smoked. The roof of my
mouth felt like I needed a chimney sweeper inside it. The

257

room was blue with smoke, fucking booze all over the joint. Gable finished a bottle of brandy and was really gassed. Now, finally, he's going to leave. And I loved him, and I said, "Christ, Clark, do me a favor. Don't drive home."

He said, "Why? I can drive."

"I know you can drive, but you don't have to prove anything. Some drunk is liable to hit you."

I gave him that shit. He had a Mercedes 300SL with the gull wing, and he drove like he was playing *Test Pilot.* He was a hell of a guy.

Then Kay Gable said, "Poppa can drive."

"Do me a favor, Clark," I said. "Fall down here. Go home in the morning."

Gable said, "What are you talking about, Marty? I'm okay. I can drive, and I'm going to drive."

I was really upset. Jesus, I thought, I wouldn't want this man to get killed on his way home from my house.

"It doesn't pay for you to go home anyway," I said. "We have an appointment in a couple of hours, at nine o'clock."

So Gable said, "I want to sleep in my own bed. Got to take a shower and shave."

I knew he was never going to come back. I knew he wouldn't make it. I tried to insist he stay, but he wouldn't listen. So I said, "Do me a favor, pal. If you won't sleep here, give me a call the minute you get home. How long do you figure it will take?"

He said, "From here? I live on Tippet Avenue. Over Coldwater and out Ventura. I'll hit Encino in forty-five minutes. That son-of a-bitchin' car, you can grind it up to one hundred and eighty."

Jesus, I'm picturing him off the road, off a cliff, and Helen is really worried, too.

"Call me the minute you get home," I said. "I'm not going to sleep till you call."

"Hey, I'll be okay. Get *your* sleep, and I'll be back here at nine in the morning."

I said, "Then I'll wait forty-five minutes, and I'll call your house. Just to say hello, so I'll know you're okay. Otherwise, I won't sleep."

"All right," he said.

"By the way," I said. "I don't have your number here. It's in the office."

And Gable said, "Well, shit, I'm in the phone book. I've been in the Encino phone book for thirty years."

So I said, "You must get some wild calls."

"No," he said, "never had one."

They probably looked in the book and saw "Clark Gable" and figured it couldn't be *him!* Hell, even Gable didn't have an unlisted number, so who are all these shits that aren't in the book?

He went home, and I called him, and he answered. He'd made it. I went to bed and said to my wife that he'll never make it back by nine. He's so gassed he won't even remember.

At ten to nine I was really sawing wood. The maid came up. "Mr. Rackin, Mr. Gable is downstairs."

I went down in a robe. I needed a shave. My mouth tasted like somebody shit in it. All I could taste was cigarettes, and here's Gable in a light-gray flannel suit, blue shirt, black tie, carnation, dark glasses—in immaculate shape, looking like he just fell out of the fucking window of Saks Fifth Avenue.

I mumbled, "Hi."

And he said, "What's the matter, kid, can't take it?"

I said, "What do you drink, rubber bands?" I never saw a guy bounce back like that. "You want some coffee while I shower and shave?" He said, "No, but I'll have a light bloody Mary."

You know what he was in town for? So we could go to Saks. They were having a sale on socks. It was the first morning of the sale, and Gable wanted to buy a dozen pair. We walked around Beverly Hills. God, he was an iron man, a giant. We talked about everything except pictures—airplanes, broads,

259

baseball. We didn't talk deals or movies, all that petty shit. Gable was a man!

Wayne's the same way. I spent three weeks on Duke's boat, the *Wild Goose* and we never talked about movies, never.

I'll never forget one time I was flying into Paris with Holden. On your landing card you fill in your name, birthplace, age, occupation. And when we got to customs, the guy said, "Ha, Monsieur Holden, ho, ho, ho. You've put down 'businessman' and you're an actor." Bill said, "Don't you *ever* call me an actor." See, that's what I love. Holden thinks of himself as a businessman, not an actor.

I don't have too many friends that are actors. I have a lot of acquaintances who are actors. Duke is a friend. Bill Holden is my friend. If you said to me, "Marty, you're in real trouble. You need a friend. Who should I call?" "Call Duke or call Bill," I'd say. Those are friends. I don't even think of them as actors.

It's very difficult to have actors as friends. I admire great actors. I liked Gable, I really liked him very, very much, and I was very fond of Cooper. I like Paul Newman, but I'm no longer in the swim with Newman because I'm not interested in getting publicly involved in politics.

I love the movie business, but I don't like the peripheral bullshit that you go through.

I enjoy making a picture. I enjoy selling a picture. When I i nish a picture, I go out on the road, to Cincinnati, Cleveland, Detroit, Chicago. I talk to the critics and the newspaper guys. I talk to the exhibitors. I watch the ads and look at the theaters that are playing my picture. I enjoy that. I like people. I love being with the newspaper guys. I love going out and having lunch with the critics and talking with the people that are seeing the movie. Hollywood people don't see movies. They're too busy making a deal for their next one. Or they'll say, "Let's all go to so-and-so's house tonight and see a picture." How can you see a picture at somebody's house with eight guys and eight wives, and in the middle of it a guy gets up and says, " I know that broad. My agent used to fuck her." And he walks in front of the screen. How the hell can you enjoy a movie in that atmosphere? It wasn't made to be watched in the living room with a guy saying who is humping the star or, "Do you remember when her fucking nose was over here?" I don't enjoy watching movies that way.

Sometimes my wife and I will run up to Westwood at six or six thirty in the evening and see a double feature. We'll go across the street and have a hamburger during intermission. Then we go back and see the second picture. That's our evening, a big night, a film festival. But we see the audiences. I see where they laugh. I see where they hate the picture. I say, "Hey, the picture is doing good." Or you hear somebody say in the lobby, "Oh, why did we get screwed three dollars for that?" See, that's what the guys never hear who only watch pictures in somebody's home or in a projection room. Even though I touch the audience, it doesn't mean that I don't make flops. I've made more flops than hits. But it's like I told you about Babe Ruth never hitting four hundred.

A flop or a hit depends on the return for money invested. Paramount also tried to stop me from making *Alfie* with Michael Caine. The goddamn picture cost six hundred thousand. I would rather own *Alfie* than *Lawrence of Arabia*. *Alfie* grossed about sixteen million for six hundred thousand. *Lawrence of Arabia* cost between nine and thirteen million, so it went out and did fifty million. But what the hell does that mean? *Carpetbaggers* cost three million and did about twenty-six million. Those are hits, super superhits because it's not what you gross, it's what you keep. It's how many times the return on your investment. That's how you tell how successful a picture is.

I can thank Paramount for *the* moment in my life, the weekends I spent with Winston Churchill at Chartwell as his guest. Just to sit down with Churchill, Lady Churchill, Anthony Montague Brown, who was Churchill's right arm, and Field Marshal Montgomery was the greatest thing in my life.

261

Imagine me, playing croquet with these people—picture me playing croquet at Chartwell. And the sitting and boozing with Churchill. I drank a little of his brandy and smoked his cigars and talked painting with him in his library, and I looked at the black swans in his lake. He told me how he'd built the brick walls at Chartwell and that he was an honorary member of the stonemasons' guild.

I was there to buy Churchill's book about his youth. It was my idea to make *Young Winston.* I negotiated the whole deal. I bought it for Paramount, but they wouldn't let me make it, and after I left, they sold it to Carl Foreman, who took it to Columbia.

I discussed the casting with Churchill, everything down to the last detail. And I kept going back, spending one weekend after another with him. While I was there, he fell and broke his hip. He got over a hundred thousand telegrams. Bob Musel, head of the United Press in London, printed mine on the front page of the London *Express.* My wire said: DEAR SIR WINSTON. I WAS SHOCKED TO HEAR THAT YOU FELL AND BROKE YOUR HIP. IF I'M CORRECT, THE AMERICAN HALF OF YOU WILL GET UP FIRST. And he loved that.

I had fights with Montgomery over the war. I was always against Montgomery. I thought he was a phony. At dinner one night, he said the English had won the war. I said, "*We* won the war. Fuck *you.* The American Air Force won the war. *We* did it. You assholes, *we* saved you." And Churchill whispered loudly, "Give it to Monty! Give it to him!"

Then we started talking about painting, and Churchill and I got into an argument over Monet and Manet, over which one was the greatest painter. Churchill pointed his big cigar at me and said, "You're wrong, wrong, absolutely wrong!"

And I said, "You're wrong. You can tell them how to build floating docks for D-Day and all that stuff, but I want to tell you something. The painting you have in your sitting room of the water lilies by Manet isn't as good as the one Edward

G. Robinson has in his home. There's a lot you don't know about painting." And we got into a whole thing.

My last night there I told Churchill, "You and I have a lot in common. You have a dog named Rufus and I have a dog named Rufus (an Airedale that I lost). You were a lousy student in school. I was a lousy student. We both like paintings, even though you don't know shit about paintings."

He started to laugh like hell. And I started to roar. He was beginning to turn purple and getting a little gassed. We talked into the night, and I had a couple of brandies because he insisted. Suddenly I laughed out loud, and Churchill said, "Now, what's struck you so funny?"

I said, "Can you imagine when I get back to America and stop over in New York and visit my mother on Seventy-third Street and tell her, 'I just spent the weekend with Winston Churchill, and we argued about paintings.' She lives in an apartment-hotel with a lot of old Jewish ladies, and I can see her telling those broads, 'My son just came from seeing Winston Churchill.'"

Churchill broke up, laughing like hell again.

Sure, there's a terribly, terribly rotten side to Hollywood, and Runyon was right when he said life is "a hell of a struggle for a yard." But the picture business has given me the chance to meet Churchill and a lot of other people I've admired and loved. The picture business has been my passport to the world.

21

Ward Kimball

THE WONDERFUL WORLD OF WALT DISNEY

"WALT WAS A hard guy to get close to. He was a workoholic. His career was his whole life. I think I was as good a friend as he ever had."

Kimball, a pixie-featured man of sixty, five feet nine and a half, 160 pounds, has spent his entire career at the Disney studio. As a producer and director he's won two Academy Awards and an Emmy. His 1954 Oscar was for Toot, Whistle, Plunk and Boom, *the first CinemaScope cartoon. It's* Tough to Be a Bird *was judged the best short of 1969. The 1961 Emmy was for a segment of the* Man in Space *series.*

He lives in the wealthy suburb of San Gabriel. In the backyard of his rambling ranch home he's created the "Grizzly Flats Railroad." A train buff of impressive dimension, he began his collection in 1938. Through the years it has grown until it now consists of more than 1,000 feet of track, an engine house, a water tank, a windmill, three restored steam locomotives, six antique railroad cars and a waiting room-station filled with memorabilia.

I went to a college-level art school in Santa Barbara, California, and quit after one semester because the teachers were stupid.

When I quit, I was disowned by my folks. They kicked me out of the house, but two weeks later my mother softened and took me back.

Somebody said, "Jesus, Ward, with your ability and your

sort of whimsical way of drawing, why don't you go to Holly-wood and get a job in one of the cartoon studios?" My ambi-tion was to be a painter, and cartooning didn't much appeal to me. But money was important—this was in Depression 1934.

If I had to be a cartoonist, I thought I may as well work for the best. My mother had just enough gas to drive me down to the Disney studio. I walked in with my thick portfolio, oil paintings, watercolors and charcoal sketches. The studio was a casual and informal operation then, and the receptionist sent me to see Walt. I showed him my stuff, and he was im-pressed enough to hire me as an animator. No one had ever brought a portfolio before. After I did it, every applying art-ist was asked to show a portfolio.

I started on April Fool's Day. A year later, believe it or not, I was doing animation on my own, miscellaneous scenes for *The Tortoise and the Hare* and *Elmer Elephant.* At the age of twenty-one I was already considered a half-assed prodigy at the studio.

If you were a top animator at Disney, you would work on the *Silly Symphonies* because they were the artistic cartoons. *Mickey Mouse* was the potboiler. That sounds funny because *Mickey* is such a camp hero now. But the *Silly Symphonies* were in color and the *Mickeys* were in black and white. That was status symbol number one. Status symbol number two was that the *Symphonies* had a little more money spent on them. Also, we didn't grind them out like the *Mickeys*.

In 1936 I was assigned to *Snow White.* That was our first feature-length cartoon, and it took two years. Later on we learned to do them faster.

Snow White came close to never being made. Walt couldn't get any financial backing for it. He went all over town trying to get loans, and they thought he was crazy. He was told, "Stick to shorts. Why do a feature? You'll bore people to death."

Walt finally nabbed Giannini at the Bank of America and

talked him into putting up the money. Walt was a supersales-man. He was the world's best salesman because he believed in his product. You know, it wasn't just a con routine with him. I used to sit in awe watching this guy when he'd sell a banker or a group of private backers on an idea. He'd get up and act out all the parts. He could see the whole thing. After he finished, so could everyone he was talking to.

As work progressed on *Snow White,* Walt would imitate all the dwarfs whenever he wanted me or one of the other ani-mators to make them behave in a certain way. I always thought he was as good a pantomimist as Chaplin.

Snow White was a real tearjerker. I remember the pre-miere. The whole goddamn audience was crying—which was really something for a cartoon—when these funny, gross, blubber-legged dwarfs gathered around Snow White's bier. They cried even though they knew there would be a happy ending. Very few cartoons have that impact.

Everybody had said no one is going to sit for an hour and a half and watch a cartoon feature, but Walt proved them wrong. I can look at it five times a year and still laugh and cry. *Snow White* is the *Gone with the Wind* of the cartoon. It's an ageless picture, and it's revived every year. So is *Pinocchio, Bambi* and *Peter Pan.* The only one that isn't revived is *Alice in Wonderland* because it sort of bombed. When Walt was alive, *Alice in Wonderland* was the only one of our cartoon features that he allowed on the Sunday television show. The others were strong enough to keep playing in the theaters.

You know, there's been so much unfair criticism about the Disney product. The critics say we created an unreal world, that the fairy tales we adapted were emasculated and changed and sugarcoated. We didn't put a cock and balls on our male characters. The females had tits that were nonexis-tent or overly decorous. Well, hell, if the Nixon administra-tion could sugarcoat and twist and lie, if the Westerns could distort the West like they have, why couldn't we distort, too?

266

See, Walt realized a lot of these fairy tales were pretty grim. He realized you had to have a balance, you had to have gags and laughs to offset the pathos, the heavy stuff. He took the same license everybody takes with a story. What movie hasn't done that?

The reason for the incredible success of the whole Disney operation was Walt's demand for high quality. No half efforts were permitted. He would do things over and over until he was satisfied. *Pinocchio* is a good example. After we'd worked six months on it, Walt thought the story wasn't just right. So he threw out all the animation we'd done, and we started over. When he made *20,000 Leagues Under the Sea,* he spent fifty thousand dollars reshooting one scene with this giant squid that was in the picture. Walt wasn't satisfied with the way the squid worked its tentacles. He made them do the whole damn thing over again with money no object.

Walt was a perfectionist. Everybody else in town didn't give a damn. They'd knock out a *Tom and Jerry* at Metro or a *Bugs Bunny* at Warners. The idea was to make a fast buck. Walter Lantz, who made *Woody Woodpecker,* never gave a damn about quality a day in his life. He always wanted the quick buck.

If you want to know the real secret of Walt's success, it's that he never tried to make money. He was always trying to make something that he could have fun with or be proud of. He told me once, "I plow back everything I make into the company. I look at it this way: If I can't use the money now, if I can't have fun with it, I'm not going to be able to take it with me." That's the way he talked. That's the way he felt. The guy even hocked his life insurance to open Disneyland. That may not be the right philosophy for everyone, but in Walt's case it usually worked. We always said at the studio that Walt was constantly falling into a pile of shit and coming up smelling like perfume.

You can call it an ego trip or anything else, but Walt really was more concerned with the end result than money. If it made money, fine. He felt that if you put your heart into a project and if you were a perfectionist, people would automatically like it. They would appreciate the quality. That's what made *Mickey Mouse* catch on at the very beginning. Walt put that little extra something into *Mickey*. He would take a little more time, spend a little more money. And he made sure there was a good story blocked out from the beginning. The others who produced cartoons just made up the story as they went along.

Walt invented the storyboard. He invented cartoon continuity at the source. Every sketch was pinned to the storyboard so he could tell by just looking at it where we were and where we were going. This is the technique that everybody uses now. It was invented because Walt wanted to see the whole plot on a couple of boards. He wanted to see it visually. Reading meant nothing to him. Words meant nothing to him. Pictures were his whole bag. He'd come in and look at the story. He'd criticize. He'd say, "We need something else here, and this stuff over here is monotonous." And he'd rip the drawings off the boards just like tearing pages out of a script.

Walt could be very cruel about certain things. He was completely insensitive to the way a person might feel in some situations. In all honesty I think he was so wrapped up in his work he didn't realize he was pissing people off and embarrassing them. He had this way of bawling you out in front of other people. When I feel someone's committed a no-no on a picture I'm producing or directing, I take the offender off to one side. I don't chew him out in front of others. Artists are pretty touchy individuals; they aren't bricklayers. It takes very little to hurt their feelings. Walt was never quite aware of that.

Walt was a rugged individualist. He admired Henry Ford. He thought Ford was the cat's ass. Maybe Ford and Walt were the last of the great ones, the last of great rugged individualists. Maybe that was why they were impatient with people of lesser talent and impatient with themselves when they made mistakes.

Animation is a complex thing. Sometimes it can get very dull. There are twenty-four frames a second in a cartoon. One frame can take fifteen minutes to draw, and it appears on the screen for only a fraction of a second. There's no other way to do it—it just takes time. So to relieve the monotony, we'd do things like, well, on *Snow White* we'd draw porno things. That happened all the time. Here was this beautiful, saccharine-sweet girl in the story, and after making so many drawings of her during the day, our impulse was to draw her naked with one of the dwarfs standing there with a giant erection. A lot of those drawings found their way out of the studio. During the war I think every guy on the assembly line at Lockheed had a copy of a booklet somebody put together. It was called *Snow White and the Seven Truckdrivers.* Snow White is sitting on a little chair with her dress up, and the dwarfs are all standing in line with their cocks out. The cocks of the dwarfs varied in size. Old Grumpy had one that looked about three feet long.

There were also a lot of cartoonists and artists who didn't work at the studio who'd draw porno versions of Disney characters. I've seen drawings of Dumbo flying through the air dropping elephant turds on everybody with Mickey Mouse in the foreground with a week's stubble of beard giving himself a fix or jerking off. There was one of Goofy boffing Minnie Mouse.

Perhaps the reason for this sort of thing is that everything seemed so perfect and dreamlike in Disney's world. That led to the urge, I know it did with us, to make these drawings. It was something we had to relieve ourselves of.

So far as I know, Walt never saw any of those drawings. He

269

was a funny guy. His humor was quite different than that of the man in the street. You could never tell Walt a dirty joke. The word got around quickly to new employees not to try and ingratiate yourself with Walt by telling him an off-color story. He thought dirty jokes were terrible, and he was embarrassed by them. But he could turn around himself and go into a lengthy discourse on defecation . . . and think nothing of it.

One time he was late for a screening. He apologized by saying, "I was taking a shit." He'd often talk about turds. He'd talk about the outhouse on the farm where he was raised in Marceline, Missouri. He'd talk about how big and juicy and light brown turds were when you're a baby and how, as you got older, they get blacker and harder, and all that stuff. He'd go on and on, and you kind of looked at him and wondered, when is he going to get to the punch line? There wasn't any punch line. He would just dissect something like that. He had a hang-up about taking a crap. It was something in his moral background. He came from a very religious family. People like that are apt to have sex hang-ups. And maybe Walt's preoccupation with excrement was a reaction to his strict upbringing. Instead of considering defecation a normal biological function and a private matter better left undiscussed, he saw nothing wrong with talking about it for half an hour.

At the same time he was never on to slang expressions, like, for instance, getting off your gun. I was animating *Pecos Bill,* and when Slufoot Sue kissed him on the mountaintop just for a gag in the first pencil version, I had Pecos' two pistols going boom, boom, boom, boom, boom! This got to be a big gag among the guys. When Walt saw the pictures, he fell down laughing. I told him I was going to take out the booms, but Walt said, "No, no, that's great. Leave them in." To this day that is in there, and people ask me, "How did you ever

270

get that in the picture?" Walt was very naïve about things like that.

Guys like L. B. Mayer, Jack Warner and Sam Goldwyn were despots. They were untouchables. You would have to speak to a guy who would speak to a guy who would speak to their secretaries in order to see them. Walt wasn't like that. He mixed with everybody. You didn't say Mr. Disney like you said Mr. Mayer or Mr. Warner. Christ, if you called Jack Warner by his first name, he'd fire you. Walt didn't want anybody to call him anything but Walt.

He'd walk down the halls in his shirt sleeves, come into your office and say, "Ward, I've got an idea that might improve this sequence." In other words, it wasn't beneath him to fraternize with his workers. That was unheard of with the other big guys who sat in their offices, their throne rooms. You came to see them on your knees. Walt came to see you without giving a second thought to protocol and pecking order.

Walt never mixed much with the other tycoons. He'd see them at an Academy banquet or some industry function, but he never liked any of them except Darryl Zanuck, who was a friend of his. The closest he ever got to the other moguls was when he took up polo in 1934. He formed a Disney polo team, and he played with the other biggies once in a while. Other than that, he didn't socialize with them at all.

Of course, when I came to the studio, there were only a hundred and ninety people there, including the janitors. When we got up to around three thousand, it got to be a big tremendous thing, and it got to be impossible for Walt to know everyone. Still, with his key people, there was always the personal touch that made everything go. I believe in that. I don't believe in rule by committees. I don't think anything can be done well through group action. This is another thing

271

that made Walt great, because all the decisions on a picture were checked by him, down to the last detail. If you came up with a new idea, you just didn't go ahead and do it without checking with him.

He walked over every inch of Disneyland, telling them to move a fence a little more to the left because you couldn't see the boat as it came 'round the corner. I'd be with him out there, and he'd say, "The lake is too small. Maybe we should make it larger. Let's find out if we can move the train wreck over another fifty feet." He thought of everything. He was sloshing out there every day in his boots—"Put some water lilies here, and over here we'll have the alligator compound, and that's the wrong design for that building." Every damn thing that you see at Disneyland, Walt checked on. That was the difference between Walt and your usual president of a company. Thoroughness. He said, "My fun is working on a project and solving the problems. If I just sit in the office and okay drawings and what we're doing in Anaheim, what fun is that? Why let other people have all the fun doing all the work?"

Walt was in on everything at Disneyland from the time it was excavated. He'd even spend Saturdays and Sundays there. Finally the doctor told him to slow down, that it was nonsense, that it was dangerous for him to work that hard. It was bad for his heart. The doctor told him to relax and get away from it all.

"Goddamn it," he said to me one day after that physical checkup, "you have more fun than anybody I know. How would you like to go back to the Chicago Railroad Fair with me?"

That was 1948. I couldn't believe it at first, Walt taking a vacation and doing nothing except trying to enjoy himself. He never took a vacation. Every time he went to Europe it was to figure out some deal. Now he was going to take a week off, and he was inviting me to go with him to the Railroad

Fair. It was his first and only vacation. Going to that fair was great for me because I'd have Walt's company and because railroading was my hobby.

We had adjoining Pullmans on the Super Chief. On the ride to Chicago, Walt relaxed a little and dropped his guard somewhat. We sat and talked, and Walt reminisced.

He told me his whole history. How he was conned out of his first cartoon creation: Oswald Rabbit. How a couple of guys took all his artists away and left him with nothing. And how he'd had to invent Mickey Mouse. The endless hours he worked on Mickey and how he used his own voice for Mickey so that he could save money.

Once as he looked out the window at the thousands of miles of desert and country going by, he said, "I can't figure out why in the hell everybody lives in the city where they don't have any room and can't do anything. Why don't they come out here where they have this great empty land, filled with opportunity and silence?" He worried about things like that.

We had a ball in Chicago. The fair was the history of America through railroading. They had all these famous locomotives, the DeWitt Clinton, the Tom Thumb, the old 99. When they heard Disney was there, it was carte blanche. We could do anything we wanted. So we'd go down in the morning, and they let us run the steam locomotives around the three or four miles of track they had there. Running the De-Witt Clinton was one of the greatest thrills of my life. It was like shaking hands with George Washington.

One day it was too goddamn hot to go back to the hotel. This was before air conditioning. Walt said, "Let's take a ride on the el. I think I know where all the trains go." Well, he grabbed me, and we take a taxi to some station. I didn't know where the hell we were. Walt said, "Yeah, this is the one we take." We got on this thing, and it was unbelievable. Here we were roaring through the tenement districts, and you are

273

three feet away from guys sitting on the bed reading the paper in their shorts. Walt said, "I remember this whole thing." We got off at some isolated station, which was noisy and dirty, and he said, "I know where we are now. This is where I used to catch the train that made the connection downtown." He was reliving his youth. He knew Chicago well. As a kid he was a butcher boy, hawking newspapers and candy on the train that ran from Kansas City to Chicago.

It was a great nostalgic week for Walt, and he was a man who loved nostalgia before it became fashionable. That's why so many of his pictures were set in the harmless period of American history, the Gay Nineties or the early 1900's—because that was when he was a kid.

He came from a pretty goddamn poor family. He had four brothers and a sister. There wasn't any extra money to spend. Walt had this craving for ice-cream sodas and candy bars because as a kid he couldn't afford them. When he built his big home in Holmby Hills, he had this huge clubroom down by the pool, about the size of this house. It was stocked with a complete soda fountain. He had all the attachments, all the ice creams and syrups. There was chocolate syrup, strawberry syrup, every one you could think of. He'd get behind the fountain like a soda jerk and fix these huge goopy things for his guests, ice-cream sodas and the biggest banana splits you ever saw. He loved doing that. He loved having that soda fountain because as a kid he couldn't spend money for ice cream. His youth was scratching for pennies and nickels and tossing whatever he earned into the kitty at home.

Walt was also a nut about music. All of his early *Mickeys* and the *Silly Symphonies* were based on music. And they had a plot, too, superficial as it might be—the opening with the hero or heroine in jeopardy, the chase, the villain, the climactic confrontation between good and evil and the happy ending. But he did things through experimentation that no one else had done. So there was a warmth and charm to his

274

work which was unlike any other cartoons. Everything in his cartoons had to have a personality. He insisted that if a tree was bashful, it had to act like it was bashful. If it was a villainous tree, it had to behave like a villain. He always demanded complete character delineation from his animators.

You've got to realize that by 1930 Mickey Mouse had been in existence just two years and by '32 you can safely say that Mickey was a worldwide character, just like Chaplin. The great things that Mickey and Chaplin both had was pantomine and music. Mickey didn't talk for two or three years. It was all done with music and pantomime, which means you could run them in India, South America, anyplace. Four years after he was invented Mickey was a household word whether the house was in China, Moscow or Beverly Hills.

We would get one Mickey out every two weeks, but the shows in the theaters then changed twice a week, and we just couldn't make enough of them to satisfy the demand. I produced the Mickey Mouse anniversary show on television in 1968, and I found an old letter in the files from Mary Pickford to Walt saying how much she and Doug enjoyed Mickey and how they would run them in their private projection room. "Please, Mr. Disney," Mary wrote in that letter, "can't you make more of them and make the world happier?"

Mickey was a great character in the early days when the plots were very, very simple. Most of Mickey's antics were based on playing musical instruments or tap dancing or doing something like the Charleston with Minnie.

The turning point in Mickey's career was a cartoon I worked on called *The Orphan's Benefit*. Mickey, Minnie and a bunch of other little mice go into a theater to see a vaudeville show, the proceeds for charity. Donald Duck was introduced in that cartoon, the feisty, quick-tempered duck. Donald was trying to recite "Mary Had a Little Lamb." He got as far as the first line, but he couldn't remember the rest of it. Well, the reaction that came pouring into the studio from the country was tremendous. The kids in the theater loved or hated or booed Donald Duck.

We were on to something, and what we were on to apparently was the real beginning of giving cartoon heroes a personality. Donald Duck was inserted into more *Mickeys,* which was great planning for the still crude medium of the cartoon. Donald always stayed in character—he was always getting the hook. People fell off their chairs laughing at Donald, and so more and more of our cartoons went toward personalities. About that time Pluto hit it big, too. He was always a dog, and he would just bark and react like a dog. And he was the size of a real dog as Donald was about the size of a real duck. Somehow that helped make Pluto and Donald more plausible and acceptable. It occurred to us then: Whoever heard of a three-and-a-half-foot-high mouse?

Our dilemma became one of trying to find new, logical material for Mickey, more sophisticated material, if you will. As we got more personality and character into the other cartoons, it became more and more difficult to cope with Mickey. He became less of a factor in the studio's product. Mickey was really an abstraction. He wasn't based on anything that was remotely real. That's what killed him. Writing for Mickey became very difficult. Mickey began to be relegated to roles that were Boy Scoutish in nature. And then we just couldn't fit him into anything—so we finally discarded him. Mickey just faded away.

Besides doing occasional porno drawings, we used to fight monotony with practical jokes. I guess the funniest involved Karl Karpe. Walt was given bulletins on the gag as it progressed, and he enjoyed it as much as the rest of us.

Karl had an ulcer or something, and every day on his way to work he'd buy a can of succotash for his lunch. It was one of the few things he could eat. We came up with this rather elaborate gag of switching labels and cans on Karl when he'd step away from his desk.

One day Karl opens his cans of succotash, and lo and behold it was cabbage juice. Somebody said, "Karl, you ought to take it back." So he goes to the grocer and raises hell. The grocer apologizes and gives him another can, scratches his head, looks at the can that says succotash but has cabbage juice in it and says, "This has never happened before in all the years I've been in business."

We let Karl go another week, and then powie! He opens his succotash and it's got beets in it. "It's happened again," Karl said. So he takes it back and raises more hell with the grocer. And the grocer starts raising hell with the distributor.

We let it go for another week or so. When he opened the can this time, there are sweet potatoes in it. This is the end for Karl and the grocer. Neither of them has an answer.

We suggested to Karl that he send the story in to Robert Ripley, whose *Believe It or Not* panel was very popular at the time. Karl said, "Goddamn it, I think I will send it to Ripley." So he sits down and types the whole story out. About two weeks later Karl's opening his can of succotash and this time it's sauerkraut. And floating on top of the sauerkraut is a note that says, "Dear Sir. I don't believe a word of your story. Sincerely, Robert Ripley."

You could never be sure about Walt's sense of humor, which is a little strange because he was in the business of making people laugh. Walt should have appreciated the gag we cooked up with Nelson Eddy.

We were doing a picture called *Make Mine Music,* a story about a whale named Willie who wants to sing at the Met. I was animating the thing, and Ham Luske was the director. Nelson Eddy was doing Willie's voice. Nelson was a great guy and when he came to the recording studio we told him what we had in mind . . . and he went along.

Walt knew that Nelson was on the lot, and he came into the studio to listen to Nelson record.

"Okay, Nelson, you're on," Ham Luske said as soon as Walt walked in.

277

Nelson starts singing and gets through four or five bars. Then Ham pushes the button and says, "Cut! Cut! Cut! Nelson, I'm sorry, but you're a little flat. On bar three your B flat was a little sharp, and you also got a little flat on that next phrase."

Nelson said, "I'm terribly sorry. Let's try it again."

Walt couldn't believe it. He knew Ham had a tin ear and didn't know a damn thing about music. Raging mad, Walt screamed at Ham, "You can't carry a tune in a paper sack. What the hell are you doing criticizing this great star? How dare *you* tell *him* he's flat?" Then Walt turned to Nelson. "Let me apologize. I thought you did it perfectly. It was beautiful."

Well, we all broke out laughing. Walt still doesn't know what's happening. We tried to tell him it was a joke, but he wouldn't listen. Walt's still yelling at Ham. "Goddamn it, I told you to apologize to Mr. Eddy." And Walt went on and on like that. Walt finally realized we'd been putting him on— but he didn't think it was funny. And he always held it against Ham.

Walt was a chain smoker. He had a heavy cough for years. I used to say to him, "Walt, why don't you give up smoking?" He'd always answer, "A guy has to have one vice, doesn't he?"

I was in Paris when I heard about Walt's death. One of the men in our office there called and told me. "It's in all the papers," he said.

I couldn't believe it. Walt was too tough to die. He didn't have the time to die; there was too much that he still had to do. But now, suddenly, he was gone. . . .

I couldn't go to sleep. I spent the whole night in that bed wide awake, thinking about Walt and everything that had happened since the day I walked into his office the first time and he hired me. Then I thought about the changes that would be made at the studio. What the hell are we going to do now? I didn't think anyone could replace Walt. And no one has. Walt was the godfather. He was always there. He protected you, and he always knew what to do.

By the time I got back the myth surrounding Walt's death had begun. In a way, it was understandable. There was no funeral. And the family didn't waste any time getting rid of him. Everything was hush-hush.* There were a lot of us who would have liked to say goodbye to Walt, but we never got the chance.

Walt died of something they called a rampant cancer. His lungs were just wiped out. But I think some of the reason for his death was severe emotional stress. I thought I worked hard. But if you sat down and made a list of what he did every day, it was incredible. He was always improving Disneyland, keeping track of everything that went on. He read scripts every night from the different units. He was still okaying every damn detail about every damn thing on every damn picture. Lunch was always business with someone. He was also working on the development of Disney World in Florida.

The guy had been doing too much. A company can reach a point where it gets so big that there aren't enough hours in a day, there isn't enough physical stamina in the human body

---

*Disney died on December 16, 1966, ten days after his sixty-fifth birthday. The services were held within twenty-four hours of his passing. The Los Angeles *Times* reported: "Secret rites were conducted at the Little Church of the Flowers at Forest Lawn. The services were a closely-guarded secret. Family services were announced only after they had been concluded. Studio and cemetery officials refused to reveal details, including disposition of the body." Cynics in Hollywood suggested, and many still believe, that the haste was a concession to business. There would be more profit for the studio's product if Disney's death was played down as much as possible and if the impression was fostered, particularly among children, that Disney was still alive.

279

for one man to take care of everything. But Walt never gave in, never let up. The smoking may have set the stage for his death. It probably weakened his physical condition. But I'm convinced it was the emotional stress he was under that killed him.

People still constantly ask me if it's true that Walt's body is frozen and if he believed he could come back someday.Well, it's such a dull world. So when I'm asked that, I say Walt was very curious and infatuated with science. And I say that if any of the star names in Hollywood would go for that, Walt would. Just to stir things up I tell everybody he's frozen. Actually, he was cremated.

One of the great disappointments of Walt's life was that he never had a son. A son to take over the business. Every man wants that, especially a man like Walt. When one of his two daughters had a boy and she named him after Walt, he was very proud of that. He passed out cigars with special bands on them and with the boy's name printed on them, just like the child was his son and he was the father.

I'd directed a picture for Walt called *Mars and Beyond*. We had a screening and a cocktail party for the press. Walt got a little loaded that night. He put his arm around me and he was calling me "son." It was like if he ever wanted a son, I'd be it.

I don't give one good shit about working for the studio anymore. I'm going to retire soon.

The studio now isn't the studio I knew. These new guys running it never think of saying, "Hey, Ward, why don't you come up and talk about this?" And, of course, it would be beneath them to come to my office to talk to me the way Walt did.

Now the Disney operation is a corporation with many, many bosses and committees. The people who run the place don't have any personal relationships with the creative peo-

280

ple. The thing that made Walt great was that he was creative himself and he recognized creativity in others. The guys running it today are administrators. Some of them make ninety thousand dollars a year, but to me they're Chevrolet salesmen, high-priced messenger boys. There's no longer any innovation or excitement. The new regime just sits around trying to second guess how Walt might have done it. That's quicksand. Not that the place is suffering. It's like a giant machine. It's self-perpetuating. There's this tremendous backlog of film. They could close the studio down and just reissue the old films, and they'd still make a fortune every year.

The artistic people are slowly being forced out. And they're being replaced with guys in white shirts who operate computers. They figure out everything for the whole corporation—the studio, Disneyland and Disney World. It's kind of frightening.

So it's boring. It's a corporation where they play it safe. You copy yourself copying yourself. Walt would never stand for that. He never repeated himself. He would say, "We've done that. Let's do something new." He'd frighten everybody half to death by challenging them that way. But then you'd get with it, and new ideas would come. Walt kept everyone on pins and needles. Everybody getting pissed off at him was very healthy. See, you had a guy steering you all the time, and that made you work to capacity. It pulled the best out of you.

Walt's private life was a gray area. It was gray, I guess, because there wasn't much to his private life. I remember meeting Walt's wife at the opening of Disneyland. I asked her, "What do you think of all this?" She said, "Well, it keeps Walt from playing around with other women." I thought that was a funny remark. One thing I'm sure of about Walt—he had no extramarital affairs. He didn't play around like all the other studio heads. He had a wife, and that was it. And she certainly didn't waste any time getting remarried after Walt died. I'd swear that Walt didn't have broads on the side because it would have taken too much of his time. He once said to me, "I love Mickey Mouse more than any woman I've ever known."

There was a book written under the name of one of Walt's daughters.* In it she gave credit to all the people who helped Walt up the ladder. About five minutes after Walt died, the guys running the studio ordered the book rewritten. All the people who'd done their share in making the studio successful were scrubbed out of it. I think that was a dirty trick. Walt was a giant, but he didn't do it all by himself. That's the unmistakable impression the new book conveyed. The book, which is still around and is still selling, is life rearranging history.

Walt's virtue is all they want to perpetuate. The great doer of good, the manufacturer of children's entertainment. Sure, he was that. But he said "shit" and the rest of the words, and as I've said, he'd talk about turds for thirty minutes without pausing for breath.

At the bottom line Walt was a down-to-earth farmer's son who just happened to be a genius.

*My Father, Walt Disney by Diane Disney, published in 1958.

22

Stanley Kramer

SO YOU CAN HEAR SPENCER TRACY SAY, "THIS THEN IS WHAT WE STAND FOR. . . ."

THERE ARE MANY (and this writer is one of them) who believe that Kramer's body of work adds up to perhaps the finest, most distinguished one-man achievement in the history of Hollywood.

His benchmark in thirty films has been to attack the screen as a producer and director with intelligent, daring, controversial, thought-provoking entertainment.

Yet he has been strangely neglected and underappreciated by the film establishment—critics, commentators and the Academy of Motion Picture Arts and Sciences. Though Academy Awards are an uncertain measure of accomplishment, Kramer has yet to win one, his talents superseded by men who've made lesser or flashier contributions to the art of filmmaking. He's been nominated for an Oscar three times, for The Defiant Ones, Judgment at Nuremberg *and* Guess Who's Coming to Dinner. *Four stars who've worked for him have won Oscars—Jose Ferrer in* Cyrano de Bergerac; *Gary Cooper,* High Noon; *Maximilian Schell,* Nuremberg; *and Katharine Hepburn in* Dinner.

Nothing so diminishes the insight and taste of the members of the Academy as its long failure to honor Kramer. Not that he appears concerned. "The Academy thing would be nice. But it's a complex process of selection. Boiled down, it's a roll of the dice. And the dice haven't come up seven for me . . . yet."

Burned out of his office in the 1974 fire on the Goldwyn lot, he is ensconced in the Wolper Productions Building near Beverly Hills.

His office is not large; the furnishings are quietly utilitarian, non-mogul.

Dressed in a cream sports shirt and black slacks, the twice-married Kramer is, at sixty-one, a thoughtful, zestful, engaging man. He doesn't come on as the expected firebrand crusader or a card-carrying intellectual. His brilliance and concern for the human condition are leavened by honesty, wit and pragmatism.

My filmgoing as a child was pretty well controlled by my mother. My father was long gone, and my mother, who worked as a secretary for Paramount, used to get passes to their theaters.

My first contact with the movies was on Saturday afternoons. As a very small boy, Tom Mix was my hero, that's for sure. I mean, Tom Mix with the gloves and Tony made quite an impression on me. I didn't get in on the spicy stuff for quite a while. That happened when I fell in love with Viola Dana, a silent screen star who was considered pretty daring for her time. She played light comedy and what was then called fashionable drama in pictures like *Rosie O'Grady, A Chorus Girl's Romance* and *Merton of the Movies.*

I had dreams of becoming a criminal lawyer, of becoming another Clarence Darrow. That fit perfectly with my mother's wishes. "My son, the lawyer" was then a popular thing among the Jewish population of New York. I guess it still is.

I thought I was going to go to law school, but in my senior year at New York University, Twentieth Century-Fox was bringing what they called junior writers to Hollywood. I'd done a little writing for the college magazine, *The Medley,* just some interviews and jazz. For some reason I've never quite fathomed, Fox chose me along with four or five other fellows from some of the universities on the East Coast. They brought us out with three-month contracts, supposedly to teach us how to write for the movies. But I think it was only a public relations ploy because at the end of the three months nobody had taught us anything and they kicked us out on the street.

The only reason I stayed in Hollywood was that I didn't have the fare to return to New York. I obtained a series of back lot jobs. The first one was at Fox, the same studio where I'd been working as a writer, theoretically. I worked on the swing gang, which was the group that moved the furniture on and off the sets at night. I wasn't very good at that sort of thing, but I needed the eighteen dollars a week. Eventually I worked my way up to assistant film cutter at thirty-six dollars a week. Then I became an associate producer—that was just a title—on a couple of pictures for Albert Lewin. I was then drafted into the Army for four years, three months and eleven days. I was in the Signal Corps, and I made training and orientation films and came out as a first lieutenant.

Hollywood was the only future I could see, but when I hit town again, I had no job, no company, nothing. I was thirty at the time, and I thought that was very old. My prospects, to say the least, were dim.

I formed a small independent company just out of thin air. I didn't know anything about organizing a film production company, but I did it anyway. There were five of us, myself, a couple of writers, Herbert Baker and Carl Foreman, a public relations man George Glass and an attorney, Sam Zagon. Nobody was being paid. We used my uncle's office. He was in the agency business.

One day Willie Schenker, whom I'd met when I first came to Hollywood, came in to see me. And, you know, this is the kind of story when you are telling it, you have to say, "Cross my heart, it's true."

Willie was a man with two ambitions. The first was to open a Chinese restaurant. The second was to get into the film business. His father, who was a successful dress manufacturer in New York, had told him, "Willie, you're a bum. You'll always be a bum. But here's seventy-five hundred dollars. Go to California and open your Chinese restaurant. If you're smart, you'll be back in a year after you've failed and you'll get into something substantial, like my dress business."

Willie told me he'd rented a location for his restaurant in the Valley. He'd hired a Chinese chef on option. He had a bartender, and *he* needed seventy-five hundred dollars from *me* to close the deal. He remembered that my mother had had a little money before the war, but Willie didn't know she'd been wiped out. To make a long story short, and I always say this softly, I promoted Willie out of his seventy-five hundred dollars.

With Willie's money, I took an option on two Ring Lardner stories and I gave Willie eighteen percent of the company. Why eighteen percent? I've wondered for many years how come I gave him eighteen percent. Why not fifteen or twenty or ten? I don't know. Everybody in the company had percentages. If they had all added up their percentages, they could have voted me out because my share was forty-five percent. As a matter of fact, they did vote me out later, but that's another story.

At any rate, I had Willie's money, and I was very naïve. I didn't know much except that I wanted to make pictures.

The Lardner stories I'd bought were called "The Big Town" and "Champion." Because I had the Lardner properties, I was able to scrape together enough additional financing to make one picture. I chose, unfortunately, to make "The Big Town." I changed the title to *So This Is New York*. The picture was a satire, and George S. Kaufman said satire is what closes on Saturday night. We didn't even make it to Saturday night. *So This Is New York* closed on Thursday night. It closed all over the country before it opened. Nobody thought the picture was satirical or amusing. It was, and I'm hesitant to say this because it sounds like a lame excuse, a little bit ahead of its time. It did have funny things in it.

The picture failed miserably, and Willie's seventy-five hundred went down the drain. My sense of guilt about Willie was horrible. I mean, the Chinese restaurant had gone up in smoke. Willie was threatened with a fate he thought was worse than death, going back to New York to his father's clothing business. So to pep him up, I said to him one night, "Willie, they'll never let me make another picture. But if they ever do, you've got the same eighteen percent in the next two."

Well, lo and behold, through a stroke of good fortune I'll tell you about it in a minute, I got two pictures on the boards almost simultaneously. Those were *Champion* and *Home of the Brave*. Both were made very cheaply, and both were smash hits. Willie's eighteen percent added up to more than three hundred thousand dollars, which was a pretty good return on the original seventy-five hundred I'd borrowed from him. He opened his restaurant, The China Trader, and it became very successful. Willie was in his glory. Unhappily, Willie drank up all the profits and drank himself to death.

In my attempt to finance *Champion,* I went to Bernard Giannini, who was a vice-president at the Bank of America. I was in Mr. Giannini's office, seated at this desk, but it soon became apparent that he wasn't really aware of my presence.

"I have a great story," I said, "and Kirk Douglas is going to star in it."

"You mean Melvyn Douglas," Mr. Giannini said.

"No, Kirk Douglas. He's a new fellow and a wonderful actor." That morsel of information was met with screaming silence. I went on. "I've also got a wonderful new director by the name of Mark Robson. And the script is by an excellent writer, Carl Foreman. I have a budget, and I have everything broken down, and I have a great cast."

"You seem to have a great many things, Mr. Kramer," Mr. Giannini said, "except money and a reputation." Then he asked me a question in italics that I'll never forget. *"Who are you, Mr. Kramer?"*

That kind of broke the straw that broke the camel's back. I

did some business later on with Bernard Giannini, and it worked out all right. But the banks at that time wouldn't give you direct financing, even if you were important in the industry. Times were tough, and money was tight. The banks would put up money, but it had to be one hundred percent guaranteed. If you borrowed five hundred thousand dollars, you had to put up five hundred thousand in security. In other words, they weren't giving you anything. They would only advance money against collateral, and I had no collateral. Worse, here was Mr. Giannini asking who I was. I guess it was a fair question. I wasn't anybody except a guy who'd produced one of the biggest bombs ever to hit the screen.

I was bloody but unbowed. I got a lucky tip from a studio manager I knew by the name of Charlie Glett, who told me that if I'd be willing to take the son of a very wealthy, retired mercantile man as the associate producer of *Champion,* his father, who lived in Florida, might finance it. That seemed all right, providing I got the money.

I borrowed the fare to fly down to Miami Beach to see this man. His name was Stillman. He was an elderly gentleman, and he was married to a lady much younger than himself. There was quite a substantial difference in their ages. Mr. Stillman was sixty something, and she was twenty. They'd just been married. The bride had been graduated from the University of Florida no more than five minutes ago.

We had dinner on a kind of a little boat dock which jutted out of their house and overlooked a lagoon. It was a beautiful setting, trim boats rocking gently on placid water. It was the lap of luxury, fine food and good wine. Ordinarily I'm not a drinker, but after a few glasses of Mr. Stillman's vintage wine, I was ready to go.

After dinner, Mr. Stillman leaned back in his chair and lighted a cigar that was four feet long.

"All right, my boy," Mr. Stillman said, "tell me the story. But before you start, I want you to know that I like a lot of fighting and action in a film."

For the next two hours I told Mr. Stillman the story of *Champion*. Despite my assurances to Bernard Giannini, Carl Foreman had not yet written the script because I had no money to pay him for the job. So I ad-libbed a very liberal interpretation of Lardner's short story. I intruded into it a great many colorful characters and bloody, carnage-laden, action-packed fight scenes. All the fights, of course, were fixed by gangsters who made Dillinger and Clyde Barrow seem like choirboys. There was killing and shooting and mayhem in every frame. Not one bit of what I told Mr. Stillman ever appeared on the screen except the death scene, which was part of my improvisation. That was the scene in the picture when Kirk Douglas smashes his fist against the locker and then collapses and dies. That one piece of business was no great accomplishment on my part. Out of two hours of improvising, I should have come up with *something* I could use in the film.

The story, as I told it, was short on character development and long on action and gore. Mr. Stillman was getting what Mr. Stillman wanted. He went for it hook, line and sinker. He financed the picture for five hundred thousand dollars. *Champion* made Kirk a star and launched me, thanks to Mr. Stillman.

I then produced *Cyrano*, *High Noon* and *The Caine Mutiny*. After those, I directed the rest of them myself, feeling I wanted total control. The first picture I directed was *Not as a Stranger*. It was a medical film, not too good but very successful. It was an exposé about fee splitting in the medical profession. It starred Robert Mitchum, Sinatra and Broderick Crawford. I have already given you half the alcoholics list in Hollywood right there.

A couple of years later (1960) I produced and directed *Inherit the Wind*, which was labor of love. *Inherit the Wind* became more and more topical as it spun around inside my head. It was marvelous material, and it was based on one of the landmark cases of Clarence Darrow, who, as I've told

289

you, I'd admired when I was a younger man. The picture also had to do with the fundamentalist Bible Belt, which had given me a great deal of aggravation in my time, particularly with *Home of the Brave,* which was a story about prejudice against blacks.

I feel that everyone has the right to believe as he likes, but because of that fundamentalist hard hewing to the line, the Darwin theory of evolution was completely sidetracked. Tennessee didn't want to teach Darwin. That sort of thing is still going on in the South. In 1974 a lot of people in Charleston, West Virginia, wanted to outlaw certain books. They wanted to outlaw them so much that a school was dynamited and one minister, presumably speaking in the name of Jesus, asked God to strike dead all the members of the school board who favored the books. *Inherit the Wind,* which dramatized the Scopes trial, is as fresh an issue now as it was when I made it.

The picture had so many basic things in it in which I believe. Darrow telling Mencken that the trouble with William Jennings Bryan was that he looked for God too high up and too far away, that there is more power in a single child's imagination than in all the shouted amens and hosannas in church.

These were things that hit some with me and excited my imagination. I thought I could reach a mass audience with the ideas embodied in that picture. But I never did. It was a very unsuccessful picture, commercially speaking. *Inherit the Wind* had tremendous receptivity on a high level but it absolutely never broke the crust into the mass audience.

Its greatest success came when it was released for television. I began to get swarms of mail about the film. I'd never had any reaction at all when it was in the theaters, even though we had a good advertising and publicity campaign on it and probably the two finest actors in the world, Spencer Tracy as Darrow and Fredric March as Bryan.

Since its release on television, *Inherit the Wind* has become a minor classic. It's replayed all the time. As a result, I've had tremendous demand for prints. I finally put the picture on cassettes, and I send them to universities and other institutions that request it.

Actors, I have to tell you, are not my favorite form of human life. But Spencer Tracy was an exception. Tracy, to my way of thinking, was the motion-picture actor incarnate.

He reacted better than most actors act. He understood the medium. He came from the theater, but nobody ever captured the movie medium as well as Tracy because he moved his eyes less, did less with his face, did less with his body than anybody else. He knew the screen multiplied whatever an actor did many times, and so he achieved twinkle and humor and pathos and power and all the emotions from one end of the spectrum to the other beyond anyone else by doing less.

Tracy was completely honest, really completely honest. He never wore makeup. He always came to the set understanding what he was doing and understanding what everybody else was supposed to be doing. He always responded within the character he was portraying. He could snap right back out of it and snap right back into it because he was so immersed in it when he was doing the part.

Beyond that, I had a true emotional feeling for him.

Most of my aggravation in this business has come from actors, yet they are so necessary to me. I am one of those people who recognized and am willing to take a great deal of aggravation and stand still for a great deal of devious conduct and childlike perturbation from actors because I need them so badly for what I want to do and what I like to do. Actors are my strongest weapon for communication.

Now, the so-called modern filmmaker says, "I don't need the actor. I'll do it with the camera, with the lighting, with mood, with effects." Not so with me. I'm very well aware of those techniques. But for me the spoken word has always been the weapon which I've used. It's the most dangerous weapon because you can overuse it. You can overspeak. You can overtalk. Yet, for me, the spoken word spoken by the most talented actors I can find remains my primary source of translating ideas onto film.

In that sense, Spencer Tracy was the strongest weapon I ever had. The way he delivered his summation speech in *Nuremberg* was incomparable. No one else could have said it the way he did.

Tracy worked for me in the last four pictures he did, *Inherit the Wind, Nuremberg, It's a Mad, Mad, Mad, Mad World* and *Guess Who's Coming to Dinner. Guess Who's Coming to Dinner* was a much-maligned film, but it was the most successful commercial film I ever made, which has no meaning other than the fact that it is pleasant to have a commercially successful film.

In that picture, I had to take a mass audience, not a bunch of bogus intellectuals, but a mass audience and turn them on to intermarriage, turn them from their natural prejudices which were channeled through Tracy, who was objecting to the marriage. Tracy had to take them and turn them around, and I think he did when he said, "Look, there are going to be a lot of people who won't like this marriage. But if you're in love, really that's all that counts. So go and get married and the hell with those people."

I want to tell you that I couldn't risk that kind of thing with any other actor except Tracy. Some other actor could say it, but nobody could say it so that the entire audience came with him when he said it. I subscribe to the idea that the mass audience all over the world wanted the black man and the white girl to be married because they were in love. They were rooting for them at the end. Tracy made that happen.

Guess Who's Coming to Dinner was Tracy's last picture. I was aware that he'd been dying for five years. I'd known him for about ten years, and he'd never been well. Columbia didn't want to make the picture because Tracy couldn't get insurance. He couldn't pass a medical examination; his bladder and kidneys were shot.

So Katharine Hepburn and I put up our salaries in lieu of

the insurance. That satisfied Columbia, and they let us do it.

Tracy came to me three days before we finished and he said, "You know, kiddo, if I die on the way home tonight, you are all right. You can release the picture because my scenes are finished and you don't need me for these last three days."

He died twelve days later.

I've been saddled with the message-man business from the beginning of my career. That great cliché from the exhibitors—if we want a message, we'll go to the to Western Union. That's baloney. If there is a category called message pictures, and I'm not sure that there is, the exhibitors really don't mind messages. They don't like messages that don't make money. The ones that make money make them very happy.

Home of the Brave and *The Defiant Ones* were smash hits. They made a lot of money for exhibitors, and they were both what *they* would call message pictures.

I've never started out to make a film thinking, Now here's a message. Here's something I want to get across. This is going to be wonderful for people to think about. It will engage their minds. From their darkness, I will bring them light. That's nonsense and much too patronizing.

I've thought a good deal about this message thing. All through that period when I was the darling of the critics and then the revolution came and I had to take some beatings for what was supposed to be my decadent liberalism and all the things that hang with that as it applies to the making of films.

Early in the game I became imbued with the idea that it was necessary to say on film not just the things that were happening but to anticipate some of the things that were going to happen. That, I thought, would be the most exciting way to entertain people and titillate their imagination. That idea was really responsible for *On the Beach*. It said what might or could happen if the atomic bomb were allowed to get out of hand. *Home of the Brave* looked forward to the relationship of black and white in this society. Those two films were really casting a searchlight out ahead, which intrigued me and apparently intrigued a great many other people.

I try not to define. As soon as you start making definitions, I think you're in trouble. Everybody said I as a dramatic message guy. So in 1963 I made a comedy called *Mad World*. Then they said, "Ah, it's a comedy but it's about greed. That's why he made it, as a message against greed."

Well, all comedy is about greed. I mean, just think back to all the classic comedies. They were all chases for money. They always have been. I didn't make *Mad World* as a message about greed. I made it because I wanted a different kind of film experience.

I regret the passing of the star system. I thought at the start of its demise I'd be glad to see the end of it, that the play's the thing and that the play would prevail. But suddenly I began missing the Tracys, the Garbos, the Gables. They had mystique, and with their passing something very significant has been lost in this business. Which is not to say that seven-tenths of the time these stars were doing anything worthwhile. But the other three-tenths of the time they did great things, fantastic things.

I always used important stars because obviously that was the only way I could get the pictures made and that was the only way the people who had to sell the pictures could sell them.

I used Gary Cooper in *High Noon,* although he was not my favorite actor, my kind of actor. But Cooper belonged in *High Noon.* That part was made for him, the pebble-kicking, nonreacting, all underneath kind of man who is tight-jawed and restrained. Cooper was interesting to me, but I don't think that what he did was necessarily acting. I think there are a certain number of actors in the world who are not actors. They are merely people who can be believed and we call them actors. Some people come on, and they can be believed from the beginning. That's their whole virtue. But they are not really actors.

Judy Garland, who I thought was extremely effective in *Nuremberg*, was a classic actress, beautiful, one of the most talented people in the history of the world. Mr. Mayer, which is what everybody at Metro called him, signed Judy Garland when she was a very young girl. If you put a ten-year-old girl under contract, then you have to take some responsibility for her. You are responsible for most of the hours in her life. She hasn't that much family connection. I think then that you have to be responsible for how you raise her and what supervision she has. Judy Garland was crowded too hard at Metro. Mr. Mayer was partly responsible for that and what happened to her. You can't have a girl making four pictures a year, going on personal appearance tours, rehearsing and the rest of it and having her take diet pills, pills to go to sleep, pills to wake up. The girl has to end up disastrously. In the last analysis what happened to Judy Garland wasn't anybody's fault but Judy's. She was helped along to her untimely death, but we all finally have to assume responsibility for ourselves, don't we?

I brought Marlon Brando to Hollywood from New York. He wasn't a star then, but I think he was probably the most exciting young actor I'd ever met. He was fire! He was desire! He was reaching for the stars every moment! After he achieved total stardom in *A Streetcar Named Desire* and *On the Waterfront*, he seemed to go through so many years of not caring. He just seemed to lose interest. It's wonderful to see his talent reemerge in *The Godfather* and *Last Tango in Paris*. As a director I could zero in on Marlon's dynamics much more easily than Cooper's method of play. Both had their virtues, though I preferred Marlon to Cooper. Yet *High Noon* was a great success, and the two I made with Marlon, *The Wild One* and *The Men,* are perhaps the least successful films in which he's appeared.

It takes me a few years to look back at a film and see it in perspective. My last one, *Oklahoma Crude,* was not a success. It wasn't done as well as it might have been done. I can't tell you exactly why. People have written me from all over the world saying they enjoyed *Oklahoma Crude.* Well, there wasn't anything really to particularly dislike about the film. But it missed. It should have been a smash. It had a great American actor, George C. Scott, and a great American actress, Faye Dunaway. I think the problem with that film was that the basic situation was not sufficiently believable. The basic situation of the men below the oil well sitting in that camp. They could have taken that place any time they wanted. In terms of suspense, that may be what hurt it.

I've been fortunate in maintaining my stars as an independent filmmaker. That has advantages and disadvantages. When you have an umbrella in the form of a contract with a studio, you know that next year you won't have to scramble. That's a comforting feeling. But the scrambling keeps me on my toes. As my hair gets a little whiter, my days of scrambling get a little more frantic. There are still a great many things I want to do on film. I want to write a book about my career. And I want to write it myself.

It's a fair question to ask which is my favorite film. My answer is that I don't have a favorite. That isn't a cop-out. Without exhibiting any mock humility, I think there's something wrong with all my films. I think back to each, and there isn't one about which I can't say, "I wish I had cut that sequence or I wish I hadn't used that actor or I wish it had been paced better." That feeling of incompleteness about every film I make is going to go on foreever.

Why do I keep directing? That's an easy question to answer. Because you once heard Spencer Tracy say in that extraordinary speech he gave in *Nuremberg* when he sentenced the four Nazi judges to life imprisonment: "Before the whole world let it be known that this then is what we stand for— truth, justice and the value of the individual human being."

23

Jack Lemmon

A LONG, SLOW WALK UP THE VELVET CARPET

NO ONE QUITE like him has ever appeared before a motion-picture camera. Both the range and quality of his performances have been astonishing. He is Charlie Chaplin and Laurence Olivier, the only actor deservedly to win Academy Awards for comedy and tragedy. For the bounce and dash he gave the bubble-headed Ensign Pulver in Mister Roberts, *he won an Oscar in 1955. In 1974, he turned his talent 180 degrees away from Pulver to snag another Oscar for his portrayal of doomed, disillusioned Harry Stoner in* Save the Tiger.*

Boston-born John Uhler Lemmon III, sipping white wine and puffing a lean, unlit cigar, sits at the edge of the blue couch in his Jalem Productions office in Beverly Hills. Just in from his Malibu beach house, he's wearing a light-green sports shirt, white slacks and brown loafers. The hair is salt and pepper, and from the hazel eyes the view of his past, present and future is benign but not uncritical.

As far back as I can remember I wanted to be an actor. I don't know what psychological reasons caused that. Maybe the need for attention just a little bit beyond the normal. All kids say, "Look at me, Mommy, look at me, Daddy. " Everybody wants applause.

I adjusted to my needs very early. There's a bromide that says talent will out if you give it time. I don't necessarily agree with that, but I understand it. In other words, I must have had some kind of natural leaning or an indication of talent that somehow or other showed itself when I was young.

I'm a renegade Ivy Leaguer. A might-have-been H. M. Pulham, Esquire. I was an only child of eminently respectable people. My father, who was an executive with the Doughnut Corporation of America, assumed I'd follow him into that business after I graduated from Andover and Harvard.

But from the time I was four, when I played, sterlingly I might add, the lead in an amateur production of *Gold in Them Thar Hills,* I was hooked on acting. I'd never forgotten the applause.

When I told my father after college that I wanted to borrow three hundred dollars to go to New York and try to crash show business, there was a long silence. Finally, he asked, "Is that what you really want to be—an actor?"

I told him that's what I *had* to be.

Perhaps unconsciously, I'd learned a great truth at an early age. A guy can have five million dollars and then commit suicide, and the press and public still call him a successful man who just happened to die. I don't consider a guy like that successful. With all his money and prestige he killed himself because he never made it with himself. That's no success story to me. Success comes first from your own opinion of yourself, not from a bankbook. Trite perhaps but true.

In New York my father's three hundred dollars went pretty quickly. I lived all over Manhattan and took whatever kind of job I could find. I was a food checker in a restaurant. I did anything to keep myself alive while I was keeping my dreams alive.

I can't say it was tough. Nothing is tough when you're in your late teens and early twenties. You are absorbed with yourself. You're filled with yourself, and you don't need material things. You don't need comfort. You don't need anything because you're absorbed with achieving the goal that you want to achieve.

I never suffered. It would be swell to say, "Oh, what I went through," but it wouldn't be true.

There were times when I didn't have any money and I'd sleep in free places like buildings that were condemned and had X's on the windows.

I was living in one of those places with six other young, ambitious people, a couple of gals and four guys. We were trying to put a show together for the Catskills. It was an old, old condemned building near the East River. One morning we were all konked out with the cockroaches on these sheetless mattresses when all of a sudden—whack! A big enormous steel ball came through the window. It hit like an earthquake. Unbeknownst to us, a wrecking crew was at work, demolishing the building. They were very efficient. Stone bricks were flying around the room like bees. The whole six floors were coming down on us. The scene was the end of the world. Incredibly, while that steel ball was swinging in and out, none of us were hurt. Nobody was even cut. I never saw a bunch of young people move so fast, with the lithe grace of jungle cats. I knocked out a window that had crossboards over it, I knocked it out and we went right through it. Thank God, we were on the ground floor. When we all piled out of there, the workmen stopped and stared. People started screaming. We just ran, since we weren't supposed to be in the building in the first place.

The first real job I had in show business, the first really paying job, that is, was as a master of ceremonies for a comedy revue at the Old Knick Music Hall, which was a converted movie house. It wasn't much of a job, I had little to do, but it led to television. God, I did an enormous amount of television. First I had running parts in two soap operas, *The Brighter Day* and *Road of Life* on radio. Eventually I did a *Studio One*, a *Robert Montgomery Presents*, a *Suspense*, a *Playhouse 90* and a *Kraft Theater*, plus tour series.

A fellow named Max Arnow, who was the head of talent at Columbia, a post which no longer exists, saw a *Kraft* show on an old kine. Columbia, I subsequently learned, was looking for someone to play opposite Judy Holliday in a new picture they were doing. So Max asked his people in New York to track me down. For some reason, Max thought I might be ideal for the part.

By the time they found me—this was in '53—I'd hit Broadway in a revival of *Room Service*, which only lasted for eighteen performances. Fortunately, I got good reviews. But the play didn't hold up anymore, marvelous as it once had been.

When I was approached by Columbia, I said I had no desire to come to Hollywood to work in films. I thought Hollywood was for curly-haired, pretty boys. My friends and I would sit in Walgreen's drugstore on Broadway and talk lovingly about theater and complain and bitch about movies. I adored Tracy and Hepburn, a few directors and certain writers. But in general my idea of film at that point was distinctly negative. I wanted no part of Babylon. I just wanted to be as good an actor as I could be. I wanted to be a star, sure, but in the theater. The TV I was doing was to make a living. But the theater, for me, was the alpha and omega and the omega and the alpha.

I was with the William Morris agency, which was a very big agency. I was a pimple on their mountain, but I was with them. Mainly because of Charlie Baker, who'd been representing me for several years, I changed my mind about Hollywood.

Columbia had sent over a script. "At least read it and consider it," Charlie said.

I read the script, and I certainly couldn't knock it. And I couldn't find fault playing opposite Judy Holliday. They weren't asking me to work in Siberia, but giving me a chance to costar with one of the greatest comediennes ever to walk on a sound stage. I'd particularly admired the job Judy had done in Gar Kanin's *Born Yesterday*.

They still had the old seven-year contracts in those days, which I signed with the proviso that I could do plays and live in New York. You see, that way I thought I wouldn't be selling out one hundred percent.

The picture with Judy was called *It Should Happen to You,* which was an unfortunate title because it should happen to nobody. Nobody could remember the title. The picture was good, but the title hurt the box office.

Halfway through the picture I fell in love with the film business. Suddenly a whole new vista opened up. I loved the people, the smell of the whole thing. Hollywood wasn't the ogre I'd assumed it would be.

I met Harry Cohn for the first time after the picture was finished. Max Arnow called me and said, "The boss wants to meet you."

So I did the long, slow walk up the velvet carpet to old Harry sitting in his office with the sun beaming down on his bald head. He was holding a riding crop in his hands. I reached out to shake hands, but instead of shaking, he smacked the crop down on the desk. I was standing there with egg on my face, and without further preliminary he said, "The name's got to go."

"Why?" I said.

"Because the critics will use it like a baseball bat. They'll kill you. They'll say Lemmon is a lemon. The picture is a lemon, everything connected with Lemmon is a lemon. There's no way you can keep your name. You've got to change it."

"I don't want to change it. But if I did, what would you call me?"

He said, "We'll call you Lennon."

"That's worse than Lemmon," I said. "Do you want to name me after a Russian revolutionary?"

He was ready for me, or so he thought. "I looked that up. He pronounced it *Leneen!*"

It was useless to argue. "Go home and think about it," he said. I turned to leave, and when I reached the door, he slammed the crop down on the desk again. "Take your time," he shouted, "but let me know your decision by eight o'clock tomorrow morning."

And that was my introduction to Harry Cohn.

I flew back East and went off on a fishing trip through Maine and New Hampshire. Somehow Harry tracked me down. He was chasing me up and down the New England coast. Every time I'd pull into a town there was the same telegram waiting for me: WHY CAN'T YOU ANSWER. WHY DON'T YOU CALL?

I didn't realize I was being presumptuous. I didn't think of Cohn in terms of the monster he was supposed to be. I just thought here's a guy who wants to change my name, and I don't want it changed. So I ignored his telegrams. Finally, after he'd sent at least a dozen wires, I sent him one in which I said I'd thought it over and my answer was still no. I won't change my name.

Harry ended up giving me bigger billing than my contract called for after the first preview of *It Should Happen.* He brought the name thing up only once more. He said he thought he was still right and I was wrong. He never quite reconciled himself to my name. He used to call me "My Harvard man."

After that first wild brush with Harry, I got along with him great. I think he liked the fact that somebody had stood up to him. He was tough, but I loved him. He could be crude, but he was a very bright man, and above all, he was a giant. He could really run a company, and despite all the rough edges, he had artistic taste. Possibly one of the biggest problems we have today is that there are people running the studios who may be great businessmen but they don't really know how the hell to make a movie. I don't think that could be said about Cohn or Mayer or Warner or Goldwyn.

The next three pictures, *Three for the Show, Phffft* and *My Sister Eileen,* didn't hurt me but they didn't do all that much for me. The turning point was when John Ford gave me the part of Ensign Pulver in *Mister Roberts.* I won the Oscar as best supporting actor for that in '55, but it wasn't until four years later that the big breakthrough came in *Some Like It Hot.* There's no question that *Mister Roberts* was very important in my career, but *Some Like It Hot* pushed me onto a whole different plateau, where fortunately I have stayed, more or less, ever since.

Some Like It Hot opened the whole vista of working with Billy Wilder through the years in *The Apartment, Irma La Douce, The Fortune Cookie, Avanti!* and *The Front Page.*

When I signed for *Some Like It Hot,* I'd never met Marilyn Monroe. And I was anxious to meet her. There was a certain fascination about her and this incredible thing she had become because of the publicity, the husbands and pictures like *Gentlemen Prefer Blondes, The Seven-Year Itch* and *Bus Stop.*

Primarily I was wondering what Marilyn would be like to work with and what kind of person she was. I'd heard all the rumors and stories about her problems, such as her lateness on the set and other idiosyncrasies.

We met at a big party in Beverly Hills given by Harold Mirisch, a lovely man who was head of the whole Mirisch Brothers production company and who is no longer with us. There must have been at least a hundred and fifty people at the party. You know, with the tents in back, champagne and hot and cold running butlers all over the place.

True to form, Marilyn arrived about two hours after everybody else. She was with her then husband Arthur Miller. She came over to me and grabbed me and kissed me, and she couldn't have made me feel more wonderful. She was so sweet and charming, and she started reeling off different parts that I'd played and what she liked and didn't like about each. I was stunned. She had me right in the palm of her hand.

So all through the picture we got along beautifully, and I really loved Marilyn very much. (I am using that term loosely. You can say, "I love somebody," without meaning it literally.) I got as close to her as you could get as a friend. It's hard to explain. You could get just so close, and you didn't get any closer, or I didn't anyway. I'm sure she had a small coterie of friends that were very close. But I didn't get to the point with her where she could confide her problems or deepest secrets. Judging by all the people who've written about her since her death, I may be the only person from Hollywood to New York who'll make that statement.

I think the reason she wouldn't let many people get close to her is that when you do that you become more vulnerable and maybe you're going to get hurt again. I think Marilyn spent a lifetime being hurt. This is just armchair analysis, but I'll bet you ten to one that I'm right. She didn't want to give too much or open up too much and get too involved because she knew she'd probably get hurt again. We didn't get involved as man-woman, and we didn't get involved as intimate friends. You just got so far with her, and then you could feel a curtain drop—and you didn't go beyond that. I suspect nobody in the world really understood Marilyn.

You can ask why a Marilyn Monroe didn't survive this town and why a Jack Lemmon did. I think a lot of things may account for it. I was very, very fortunate. I don't consider myself lucky. Maybe the difference between luck and good fortune is just a question of terminology or semantics. But to me luck is when you win at poker. Good fortune is an entirely different thing.

First of all, there was the good fortune of being born at the time I was born. And that I happened to arrive at a moment when there was something called television beginning to emerge. It was just starting and growing like a mushroom that had gone crazy.

The networks were expanding faster than producers could put doors on their offices. Television became instant stock. I got experience in one year that you can't get today by doing stock for eight years with a good company. I got parts written by Paddy Chayefsky and Rod Serling. I was working with young punks called Arther Penn, Sidney Lumet and Johnnie Frankenheimer that nobody had yet heard of.

In a period of four to five years I did about four or five hundred television shows, and nobody again will ever get that kind of experience. I was in the right place at the right time. You see, that's good fortune. That's not the luck of opening the right door—the lady or the tiger.

I didn't realize it at the time, of course, but television gave me what a professional actor needs—security, confidence, the joy of learning your craft.

I also had the good fortune, from the first picture I did, to work with enormously gifted people. I learned a great deal from them. And I've had unusually great parts at times and always good parts. Even in my flops the parts were good. I've never knowingly done a lousy part.

I give myself credit for learning to appreciate first-rate material and hold out. I can make mistakes. But I've never been pushed into something that I didn't really want to do. Of the rotten ones I've made I blame absolutely nobody but myself. I thought they'd be good. And I was right in holding out, at times, not even working for a year, until something came along that I felt was right for me and excited me.

I never worked because I thought a picture would be a commercial hit or because of the money. If I'd done that, I don't think I'd be here talking to you. You wouldn't have been interested in talking to me. I simply would not be here. I might have a TV series or be doing something I hated somewhere in Europe, but I would not be here.

Above and beyond everything else, there's one great stroke of good fortune that I've had, that's kept me going. The other types of good fortune I've mentioned are nothing compared to that of ending up as a success working in a job I love. I love what I do, and I don't think the majority of people love their work. I'm not sure that Marilyn did. If she had, she wouldn't have been as tentative as she was, as unsure; she wouldn't have been late. Arriving late on the set is fear, and fear comes from lack of confidence in what you're doing and lack of love for what you're doing.

It is behooving that a man work, let alone a woman, if she wishes. But a man has to make a living if he leads a normal life. He has obligations unto himself and his family. He has to go to work unless he's a debauch or something and he lives off his old man and drops dead at forty from alcohol. You have to go out and do something, and if you're fortunate, you do something you really love.

It's odd, but some films never turn out the way you think they will. *Luv*, which I did with Peter Falk and Elaine May, is a supreme example. I knocked my ass off for a year trying to get that made, and it was awful. I don't blame anybody. It just didn't work.

On the other hand, I've had successful films that helped establish me and helped make me number one at the box office for several years which I didn't think were all that very good. But the public did. *Good Neighbor Sam* and *Under the Yum Yum Tree* were tremendous hits. Go figure it. I was stupefied when they became so successful.

There are some pictures that you love more than others. I did a picture that no one's heard of that I think is one of the best things I've ever been in, including *Roberts* and *Some Like It Hot* and *Save the Tiger*. It was called *Operation Mad Ball*. Nobody knows that film, but to me it was one of my best.

As a matter of fact, if it hadn't been for *Operation Mad Ball*, I probably never would have done anything with Billy Wilder. Billy saw that film, and he dug it too. He saw it at the time he was casting *Some Like It Hot*. They wanted Frank Sinatra for that picture, and Frank might have been marvelous in the film. I'm glad I didn't have to find out. But Billy Wilder felt I was right for it. They had Marilyn and Tony Curtis, and they wanted a third major star. I wasn't a major star then. Sinatra was. Everybody said, "Oh, I think the kid's all right, but he's not for this." But Billy held out for me because he liked what I'd done in *Mad Ball*. Billy won, thank God. And, as I've said, everything changed after that—the plateau became higher.

I've been asked if I'd do what Marlon Brando did in *Last*

Tango. I have to go back to what I said about a film exciting me. You have to do what grabs you.

Marlon's a friend of mine. Quite obviously he didn't have to do *Tango.* He didn't have to do anything again, and he would still have been a legend, and rightly so. He did that picture because he saw values in it that were important to him.

I'm quoting Marlon directly—he was sitting where you are when we talked at length about *Tango.* He took hold of that picture and put one hundred percent into it. He wrote most of it. It was his childhood that he was writing about. No Italian wrote that. How could an Italian write that dialogue? It was Marlon writing those words, making them meaningful. He turned in a great performance, so much so that he had the whole world talking about the film.

Marlon would hardly do a film because it was sensational or about sex. *Tango* isn't a pornographic picture. It's about a man leaning on sex because there's nothing left for him at that terrible point in his life, that male menopause. In a way what Marlon was saying was like Marilyn cutting you off and saying don't get too close. The character played by Marlon was saying, "This is the one way I can exist, not to have any kind of relationship in which I'm going to get murdered emotionally." *Tango* was hardly a piece of crap like *Deep Throat.* So, yes, I'd do a *Tango* if I believed in it totally and honestly. I'd say, "Screw everybody. This is for me, and I want to do it."

It's interesting that there are certain similarities between the man Marlon played in *Tango* and Harry Stoner in *Save the Tiger.* Harry Stoner was also middle-aged and disillusioned. His life is a failure, and it's bothering the bejesus out of him. He reacts to this fix he finds himself in. He has to confront the awful reality of what he thought his life was going to be and what his life turned out to be.

More than any part I've played, I was totally alien to Harry

Stoner. I couldn't relate personally to anything about Harry, but I could see aspects of him in society in general and in people like him that I know. It's a matter of degree, but I feel that Harry Stoner exists in all of us. At least he does to some extent in everybody I know, except a saint, and I don't know any saints.

Personally I've never faced any of the terrible choices that Harry had to make. But I realize that you can reach a point in life when all of a sudden a decent man can do very indecent things because the ends seem to justify the means. Harry Stoner reached that point. It's like Watergate. Are all of them terrible, terrible people that shouldn't be let loose on society? Or are they people that were slowly corrupted? I can't believe that all those guys, the Ehrlichmans, the Haldemans, the Nixons, were that terrible, although about Nixon I'm not that sure.

I did *Save the Tiger* for nothing, for scale, a hundred and sixty-five dollars a week or whatever it is. That's how important it was to me.

I didn't do the picture to get an Oscar. The thought never crossed my mind. But when the Oscar happened, I was grateful. I was grateful because it said to me that what Harry Stoner was and wasn't is a very crucial matter in our society. I was grateful, too, because the film was a labor of love on the part of all the wonderfully talented people who made it work. They know they are part of any and all recognition it received.

One of the first people to reach me after the Academy ceremony was Marlon. He was very pleased about what I'd said and my reaction to winning. The minute I got off the stage, I was zinged by the press. The reporters kept asking, "What about George C. Scott and Brando? They refused their Oscars; they have no use for them. Why have you accepted yours?"

I told them that for me the Oscar was a hell of an honor. I

didn't look at the award the way George and Marlon did, but to each his own. I understand the faults of any kind of an awards system. I'm on the board of governors, and I know all the faults. But that's not the point. I happened to appreciate receiving it, and I won't degrade it or refuse it. Also I'm not going to knock George or Marlon for their point of view since I have immense respect for both of them.

I'm fifty now. I'm getting old enough to move into the meaty character parts, and I love the thought of that. That's another thing that keeps me going, that makes me say the next ten years will be even better. They'll be richer.

Ten years from now, if I'm not run over by a truck or a producer in the meantime, I hope I can look back and say most of this good fortune I've been talking about took place between fifty and sixty, that those were my best years.

I don't buy the "Hollywood is dead or dying" point of view. With just a couple of the right elements, I swear we could come into a remarkable age of film. The talent in this business is incredible, abundant. It's screaming to be let out. If we reach the point where we allow more individuals to make personal statements on film and do away with "formulas," we could have some remarkable pictures.

The public is getting more wary. The audience is learning more and demanding more, searching for and willing to accept something that isn't formula.

I'm an eternal optimist. My instinct about the future of film is positive. There are people all over this town who'll give you dozens of reasons why film may be going into a dark period. I disagree. I know what can happen if the catalysts are there and the right circumstances evolve, and I think the best is yet to come for this business.

I'd like to say a little more about good fortune. My success was no "overnight" bull. My walk up the velvet carpet was long and slow. I've never been one of these popular figures

309

where people go ape over you or the kids run up and grab at you and rip off your clothes. That's happened a few times but not often enough to really matter.

I've gradually gotten accustomed to being what is called a celebrity. I think it's very flattering, but at times it's a pain in the ass—in the sense that you lose your freedom. When I was anonymous in my New York days, I'd ride the subway for a nickel. I would sit and look at people. That fascinated me because I've always been curious. I can't do that now. If I go to a town and just want to browse around, it's difficult. Being recognized is flattering, on the one hand, but on the other hand, it's difficult to relax or feel unselfconscious.

If I were Marlon, I probably would have led my life as secretly as he has. When he hit, it was such an enormous thing. He was an atomic bomb that went off. He just was the biggest thing that ever was. He couldn't move; the man couldn't move. He had to have the maid drive to and from the house while he hid in the trunk of the car. So I can understand him. I'd go fruit cake if that ever happened to me, I really would.

My career, thank God, went up in slow stages. I cringe when I read things about Marlon and Marilyn and a lot of other people in this business, including myself. Despicable, lousy, untrue things that are written in the press.

I've never been subjected to it on the scale of Marlon and Marilyn or Burton and Liz Taylor, but I've had my share of viciousness and lies printed about me.

I think it's a risk any time you talk to a writer, even to the extent where we are talking now, except that you have a better reference with your tape recorder.

There are times when I can't blame a writer entirely when things come out wrong. Let's say you do an interview with a pencil and paper, and you jot down this and that. Now you go back and shape it, but it still comes out different. You may not even realize it, or you misunderstood what I said. Then when it's edited on top of what you've written, it can really come out different.

But there have been hundreds and hundreds of times where they just write anything. I have read things about me such as how I've supposedly taken a girl and held her arm over an open flame and she's in the hospital with third-degree burns. I'm not kidding. I've read that stuff in those cheap weekly national newspapers.

Then there's the fan magazine lies. I picked up a thing written by, you should pardon the expression, a supposed friend of mine. He was talking about not only my wife throwing wine in my face but that "rumor has it that she'd also thrown a hamburger in his face in a restaurant in front of a good-sized crowd." A totally willful, unadulterated lie.

I would love to be able to dismiss it all and say it doesn't bother me, but I can't. It does bother me. It's just like reviews. I don't believe actors who say they don't read or care about reviews. Sure you care about them. You care when anybody prints something about you. Somebody is going to read it, and they may be dumb enough to believe that my hobby is holding a girl's arm over an open flame or fighting with my wife in public. I don't want people to believe things about me that aren't true.

I resent literary parasites and literary whores. They suck your blood. They make their living using my name or names that are comparable. They know goddamn well that what they are printing is a bunch of lies. It's armchair analysis time again, but I've thought about it. Maybe they hate what they're doing so much, and they resent the fact that they have to use you or else they aren't going to sell what they write. They aren't going to sell it on their own name. They have to use Jack Lemmon or Richard Burton or whoever. They write these lies or semilies or exaggerations, and they hate you even though you've helped them, given them your time, given them permission to use your name. They resent the fact that they have to use you. So they nail you to the cross.

It's like when people borrow money from you. They resent, they hate having to ask you, but they're stuck. Fortunately you are in a good enough position where you can help them. Now I know this because it's happened to me personally. From the time I've loaned money to them, they won't even speak to me. They hate that indebtedness; they resent me. All of a sudden they are no longer my friends.

That has a parallel to what happens in the press. Prior to the time these people write about me I think of them as friends. Then they write those things, and they turn away. They are no longer close to you. They won't call me anymore. The friendships are gone. They used me, and they resent me, and they hate the fact that they did it. But they'll find a reason to justify it and a reason to be mad at me more than themselves.

The one time it really got to me was with a guy named Slavitt. He changed his name and wrote a piece of crap that was a big seller.* This was when the New York *Herald Tribune* was still around. He wrote a Sunday piece about me that was absolutely vicious. He took things totally out of context and made me the horse's ass of the world. He was clever. He was really clever. But it was just the meanest goddamn thing, because I was very open and was speaking with him the way we are talking now. But he managed to twist everything. His story even started out by describing my eyes as "green and hungry." And then a lot of real trash I'd prefer not to repeat. Why? I felt so humiliated that I could be that wrong about somebody, that I could be that taken in. I felt like I'd been raped. In the final analysis I guess I shouldn't care that much what anybody writes about me. What I do isn't going to be judged by that. I don't believe there is anyone alive that can destroy me except myself with lousy performances. And I don't think that is going to happen.

The Exhibitionist, published in 1967, written by Henry Sutton, a pseudonym for David Slavitt.

24

Mike Medavoy

NEW MOGUL, INVISIBLE MOGUL

INTERIOR MARY PICKFORD'S OFFICE DAY FULL SHOT
TIME: THE PRESENT

MARY PICKFORD WONDERED who was occupying her old office at United Artists, this storied, ghost-haunted place where she, Chaplin, Douglas Fairbanks, Sr., and D. W. Griffith once gathered to sip brandy, to do battle and to feed themselves from the cornucopia of Hollywood money and prestige. Here the plans were made for a flurry of pictures, among them Pollyanna, City Lights, Modern Times, Robin Hood *and* The Three Musketeers. *Those five films alone grossed some $150,000,000 on an investment of less than $5,000,000.*

The last time Miss Pickford saw the office was in 1956, when she bid hail and farewell to UA after negotiating the sale of her founder's interest in the company. At that time the present occupant of the office was an undergraduate of UCLA. Distant from each other in Zeitgeist as well as age, Miss Pickford and Medavoy have never met. The parade moves swiftly, and there has not been a moment or an occasion for Old Hollywood to shake hands with New Hollywood.

CLOSE-UP MEDAVOY

Sure, I'd like to meet Mary Pickford. I'd like to hear about her experiences in this town. How she started the studio. What she thinks of the picture business today. But more than anything else, meeting her would be a matter of curiosity on my part. Other than the few films of hers that I've seen, I don't really have much of an image of Mary Pickford. I know Chaplin, Fairbanks and Griffith were eager to sell, but she

313

wasn't. She wanted to stay in the mainstream as long as possible. And she did. Of the four founders of UA, she was the last to sell her shares. I assume she was very smart and a pretty tough lady.

CAMERA CUTS TO VARIOUS ANGLES

The office is much the same as Miss Pickford left it. Elegant. Antique bric-a-brac. Flowered easy chairs. Three tawny-hued couches. A conference table. A small desk on which is piled a sheaf of scripts and best sellers, the dreams and hopes and prayers of scores of writers.

MEDIUM SHOT MEDAVOY

Miss Pickford's undesignated heir is a chunky, 170-pounder who wears his red hair fashionably long. His climb to the summit is pure Horatio Alger, swift and astonishing. As recently as 1965, he was a mail boy at Universal.

Medavoy has headed UA since April, 1974. His formal title is Vice-President, West Coast Operations. He is the key voice in determining how, if and where a $100,000,000 yearly budget will be committed for the making or the financing of UA's product. The rustle of big money still rends the air of the storied office.

There is—as yet—no mogulmania in Medavoy. Unlike his titan predecessors, anecdotes about him are sparse. He has no publicity man. There is no official handout studio biography about him. His name never appears in the gossip columns and seldom in Variety *and the* Reporter. *He and his wife, Marcia, live quietly in Brentwood with their three children. "My wife has two and I have one, both from previous marriages."*

Medavoy's profile is so low that it borders on invisibility. Though no one outside the industry knows his name, inside the industry he's very well known indeed.

The following conversation was incessantly interrupted as his telephone console lit up like a swarm of fireflies. Richard Burton from London. Paul Newman from Connecticut. Hong Kong, Honolulu, Paris and Rome are also heard from. Stars, directors and producers reporting progress and problems on the twenty projects Medavoy is masterminding around the world.

Most important is the daily call from New York, with reports of grosses. On this particular day a film about a sea disaster, Juggernaut *starring Richard Harris and Omar Sharif, had racked up $1,650,000 in the first ten days of its release. "Good," Medavoy says tersely. The UA version of a novel about a subway hijacking,* The Taking of Pelham One Two Three, *has earned back $110,000 in its first five days in the theaters. He makes no comment. He isn't as yet sure whether or not the Walter Matthau-Robert Shaw-Martin Balsam film will be a hit.*

Seemingly, invisible mogul Mike Medavoy wears his mantle of power as casually as he dresses. His outfit is a nondescript khaki shirt and brown corduroy trousers. He is thirty-two years old.

Close-Up Medavoy

My parents were Russian Jews. They emigrated to China when Stalin intensified his persecution of the Jews. I was born in Shanghai. I lived there for eight years, and then we moved to Chile, where I lived for ten years. I speak Spanish but no Chinese. My parents came to California when I was eighteen. At UCLA I majored in history and minored in political science.

I considered other careers, but the reason I went into the film business was the movies of the thirties and forties I'd seen while I was growing up. As a kid living in a foreign country, those films had a tremendous impact on me. The only contact I had with America was the movies. I knew I'd land in America—to emigrate here was the goal of my parents from the time they were forced to leave Russia.

Going from the mailroom at Universal to where I am now in a relatively short time actually involved a lot of luck. And the timing was right. I came along as the business was undergoing enormous changes.

The vehicle that propelled me upward was the agency business.* I spent eight years as an agent. I started with Bill Robinson, a small agency, and then went to GAC [General Artists Corporation], which merged with CMA [Creative Management Associates]. I left there after three years for IFA [International Famous Agency], where I became a vice-president and spent two years building their motion-picture department.

My best-known client was Jane Fonda. Representing her, since she was established, was not a great challenge. The challenge came from starting a lot of young, more or less unknown people on their careers. As a matter of fact I would say the major changes in this business today in terms of people who've emerged as new and outstanding filmmakers began with me.

Some of the people I handled, encouraged and helped to start are Steve Spielberg, John Milius, Terry Malick, Hal Ashby and Carol Eastman.

Spielberg moved from directing movies of the week on television to features. He did a picture called *Sugerland Express,* with Goldie Hawn as the star. He's now directing a very important property, *Jaws,* with Robert Shaw. Milius is a writer-director. He wrote *Judge Roy Bean,* with Paul Newman. John Huston directed it. Milius wrote and directed *Dillinger,* and he's in Spain now as writer-director of *The Wind and the Lion,* a mid-nineteenth-century period piece, with Candice Bergen and Sean Connery. Malick wrote *Badlands,* and Ashby directed it. Carol Eastman was the writer of *Five Easy Pieces,* which

---

*"The agency business has become a training ground for top-echelon motion-picture executives," Medavoy adds. Former agent Lew Wasserman runs Universal. Ted Ashley was an agent for more than thirty years prior to his appointment as chairman and chief executive officer of Warner Brothers. He ran that studio for five years before he resigned in August, 1974. The trend of agents at the apex of the industry is not generally popular in Hollywood. The traditional flesh-peddler, noncreative, ruthless, anything-for-a-buck image of the agent lingers. For the most part, the image is still accurate.

was an artistic and critical success. She's since written a picture for Faye Dunaway, *Puzzle of a Downfall Child.*

More than handling individual stars, directors and writers, I became a packager, which is the essence and ultimate of the agency business. The packaging of film properties by agents rather than studios is perhaps the most significant of the enormous changes in Hollywood that I mentioned a moment ago.

Packaging is trying to fit together as many of the elements as possible that go into the making of a film. Creatively finding the story, the director, the stars. Creatively arranging financing, salaries and percentages for all concerned. You must also come up with the right producers, studio and distributor. For an agent operating in that manner, the question boils down to: Beyond the fact that you represent people, are you able to put a picture together? I think an affirmative answer in my case is probably what garnered the attention that led to this job.

I packaged *The Getaway,* with Steve McQueen and Ali McGraw. Jimmy Caan in *The Gambler. Young Frankenstein* with Gene Wilder as one of the stars. Wilder cowrote it with Mel Brooks.

The most successful, of course, was *The Sting.* That was a film that began with Tony Bill, an actor turned producer, talking to another client of mine, a writer named David Ward. Ward had dictated the idea for *The Sting* on a piece of tape. Tony Bill liked it, but he needed half the money to finance the option of the script. So he went to producers Michael and Julia Phillips. The three of them put up twenty-five hundred dollars for the option. When the script came in, I sent it to Bob Redford, who committed to the picture. I then went to Dick Zanuck at Universal, who agreed to back it. We brought in George Roy Hill, who'd made *Toys in the Attic, Hawaii* and *Butch Cassidy and the Sundance Kid,* as the director. Eventually Paul Newman was also brought in, and the deal was complete.

The Sting was pure entertainment, which is still the name of this business. It was made for six million two hundred thousand. Redford and Newman each received four hundred thousand plus a percentage of the gross. So far the picture has earned more than fifty million dollars. It probably will do close to a hundred million. The seven Academy Awards helped.*

The Sting was a good example of the product emanating from the New Hollywood. It was made for comparatively little money, considering that we had Redford and Newman. George Roy Hill is a director who doesn't come cheap.

How much I'll spend on a film here at UA depends on the property and how badly we want it. There's no hard-and-fast rule, but there are limits. I can't imagine, for example, spending twenty million on a *Cleopatra* because the more you spend, the less chance you have of making back a significant profit. You must cut the financial risk as much as possible because it's such a fickle business. The studio that's doing well today may not be doing well tomorrow. So you spread the risk. You do more pictures, generally speaking, for less money. That way you have more times at bat, so to speak.

You must remember that the moguls who made this business couldn't lose. They made the pictures and they owned the theaters. Now, of course, we don't enjoy those advantages. Also, there are about twenty million people a week who go to the movies as opposed to the sixty to ninety million a week that you had before telelvison. So there is a big difference between then and now. For my generation of filmmakers, there's more pressure. Today a film has to have something very special to attract a large audience. You must give the public a film that is really entertaining, one that they will

*For best picture, best director, best script. Edith Head won for best cu tume design, Marvin Hamlisch for best scoring and original song, Henry Bumstead for best achievement in art direction and James Payne for best set direction. The Academy hasn't as yet created an award for best packager, but in the New Hollywood anything is possible.

enjoy for each minute it's on the screen. An adventure, an experience, something that either makes you laugh or cry.

A lot of people call me a mogul or a tycoon, I think face-tiously. I don't dislike it or particularly like it. Anyway, it's too early for me to assume the title of mogul or tycoon. What I am is a representative of the New Hollywood.

Because of my age, I've also been called another Irving Thalberg.* But I don't think I can be compared to him, at least not yet. It's too early for comparison. Hopefully some-day somebody will compare someone to Mike Medavoy.

The founding of United Artists, in a way, was the begin-ning of the New Hollywood. The people who started this company believed that they didn't need real estate. That has proved to be the best aspect of the New Hollywood because it is very expensive to own that real estate. We are able to turn the savings that one nets from now owning real estate into the making of films. That's a big plus for the UA operation. In that sense, we are not a studio. What we do is rent space at other studios for the films we initiate or finance. We have the world's largest distribution system. We put a picture in thirty to forty thousand play dates around the globe.

One thing I've learned to avoid in this job is yes-men. Sam Goldwyn, from what I've been told, apparently had a lot of sycophants and yes-men around him, though he obviously did quite well despite them. I like people around me who don't agree with me. That way I feel I get another view. My single mogul-type luxury, if you want to call it that, is my one gofer. He does a lot of research for me or whatever I need to have done.

I don't find it difficult dealing with stars or anybody else in this business so long as they're honest. Right now I do a great many things for the sake of expedience and because of a par-ticular need at a particular moment with people who are

---

*He too started in the Universal mail room. At twenty-four Thalberg was production chief of MGM under Louis B. Mayer. He was ousted when he was thirty-four. Three years later, burned out, he was dead.

something less than honest. But I will deal with them in time.

In spite of my comparative youth, I'm not intimidated by anybody. Part of the reason I was able to succeed in the agency business was that I was never intimidated by anyone. There were times when I was cautious and in awe of certain people. I was in awe of Lew Wasserman when I was at Universal. I was awed by Freddie Fields [the president of CMA] when I worked there. but I soon learned they were human beings, too. They made mistakes as well as anyone else.

My heroes? Actually I'm quite hero-oriented. But I can't think of anyone I could mention offhand.

No, I'm not concerned about the high attrition rate among people who run studios. I'm perfectly well aware of that problem, and it holds no terror for me. I plan to hang around as long as I want to hang around, as long as I'm challenged. I left the agency business because it no longer presented the kind of challenge I wanted. This is a new challenge. Maybe I'll be successful. Maybe I won't. Listen, we are all one day or another going to be gone and life will go on. Nobody's indispensable. There will be another Paul Newman. Another John Wayne. And another Mike Medavoy.

Where will I be ten years from now? I have no idea. I'm not certain where I'll be a year from now.

CAMERA PULLS BACK AS MEDAVOY AGAIN ANSWERS THE TELEPHONE

CUE MUSIC: "HOORAY FOR HOLLYWOOD" AS WE SLOWLY FADE OUT